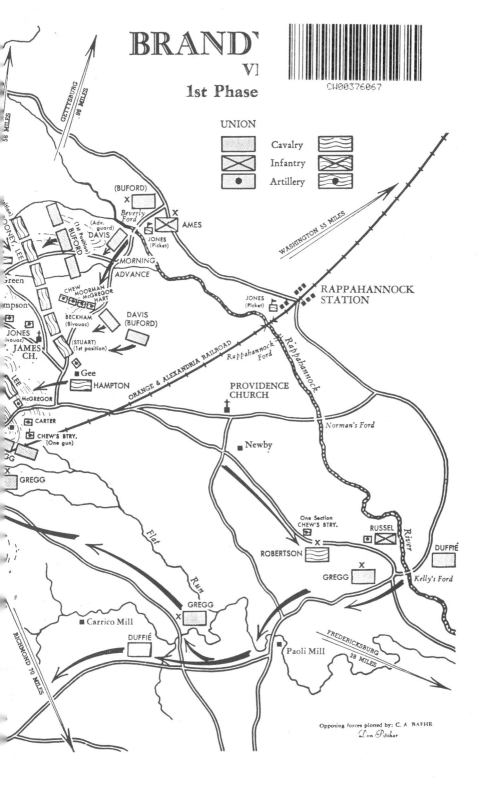

BRAND`
VI
1st Phase

CW00376067

UNION

	Cavalry		
	Infantry		
	Artillery		

GETTYSBURG .96 MILES

56 MILES

WASHINGTON 55 MILES

(BUFORD)
X

Beverly Ford

X AMES

JONES (Picket)

(Adv. guard) DAVIS

(1st Position) BUFORD

MORNING ADVANCE

CHEW MOORMAN McGREGOR HART

BECKHAM (Bivouac)

DAVIS (BUFORD)

JONES (Picket)

RAPPAHANNOCK STATION

(STUART) (1st position)

ORANGE & ALEXANDRIA RAILROAD

Rappahannock Ford

Rappahannock

■ Gee

HAMPTON

PROVIDENCE CHURCH

Norman's Ford

CARTER

CHEW'S BTRY. (One gun)

■ Newby

GREGG

Flat

Run

One Section CHEW'S BTRY.

RUSSEL

River

DUFFIÉ

ROBERTSON X

Kelly's Ford

GREGG X

GREGG X

■ Carrico Mill

DUFFIÉ

■ Paoli Mill

RICHMOND 70 MILES

FREDERICKSBURG 28 MILES

(Division) ONEY LEE

Green

ampson

JONES (bivouac)

JAMES CH.

LEE

McGREGOR

GG

X GREGG

Opposing forces plotted by: C. A. BAEHR

Don Pitcher

CLASH OF CAVALRY

Other Books by FAIRFAX DOWNEY

History

THE GUNS AT GETTYSBURG
SOUND OF THE GUNS
INDIAN-FIGHTING ARMY
DISASTER FIGHTERS
OUR LUSTY FOREFATHERS
HISTORY OF DOGS FOR DEFENSE
HORSES OF DESTINY
DOGS OF DESTINY
CATS OF DESTINY
MASCOTS
GENERAL CROOK, INDIAN FIGHTER
FAMOUS HORSES OF THE CIVIL WAR

Biography

THE GRANDE TURKE; SULEYMAN THE MAGNIFICENT
BURTON, ARABIAN NIGHTS ADVENTURER
RICHARD HARDING DAVIS: HIS DAY
PORTRAIT OF AN ERA, AS DRAWN BY C. D. GIBSON

Historical Novels, Juveniles

WAR HORSE
DOG OF WAR
JEZEBEL THE JEEP
CAVALRY MOUNT
THE SEVENTH'S STAGHOUND
ARMY MULE
TRAIL OF THE IRON HORSE
A HORSE FOR GENERAL LEE
THE SHINING FILLY

Humor and Light Verse

A COMIC HISTORY OF YALE
FATHER'S FIRST TWO YEARS
WHEN WE WERE RATHER OLDER
YOUNG ENOUGH TO KNOW BETTER
LAUGHING VERSE (edited)

CLASH OF CAVALRY

The Battle of Brandy Station, June 9, 1863

By
FAIRFAX DOWNEY

DAVID McKAY COMPANY, INC.
New York

Library of Congress Catalogue Card Number: 59-12258

Grateful acknowledgments are made to the following for permission to quote from their publications: Houghton Mifflin Company, *A Cycle of Adams Letters,* by Charles Francis Adams, Jr.; Peter Smith, *Memoirs of the Confederate War for Independence,* by Heros von Borcke; from *John Brown's Body,* Rinehart & Company, Inc., Copyright 1927, 1928 by Stephen Vincent Benet, Copyright renewed 1955, 1956 by Rosemary Carr Benet.

Also to the *Journal* of the Company of Military Collectors & Historians and to Colonel Frederick P. Todd (1st Virginia Cavalry and Hampton Legion drawings), Charles McBarron (2nd U.S. Cavalry drawing), and Colonel Harry C. Larter, Jr. (6th Pennsylvania Cavalry drawing).

Reprinted 1987 by
OLDE SOLDIER BOOKS INC.
18779B NORTH FREDERICK RD.
GAITHERSBURG, MARYLAND 20879
301-963-2929

International Standard Book Number 0-942211-18-9

*With deep gratitude to a true
friend and invaluable critic*

COLONEL HARRY C. LARTER, JR.
U.S. Army, Retired

This and previous books have drawn heavily
on his profound knowledge of American military history, including detailed minutiae of arms
and equipment. Combat veteran, student, and
artist, he has given unsparingly of his aid and
advice to the work of many.

Foreword and Acknowledgments

THE Civil War has aptly been described as a war of "firsts," of initial appearances or the earliest effective employment of various weapons and methods of warfare. "It was the first war in which the railroad was used on a large scale for the strategic transportation of troops and supplies. It marked the first use of the telegraph for transmission of military dispatches. It was in the Civil War that the metallic cartridge was developed, and the machine gun first rained its 'mortal sleet' upon the battlefield. The rifled cannon first came into use on an appreciable scale. Railway artillery was another innovation, as were barbed wire entanglements, long-range rifles, and flame projectors." *

To that remarkably modern list were added: pioneer military aviation—an early use of observation balloons—and the cannon fire against them which was the debut of antiaircraft artillery. Aerial psychological warfare—the dropping by kites of Lincoln's amnesty proclamations behind Confederate lines. Ironclad ships, revolving turrets, and electrically-exploded torpedoes. A submarine † that sank a ship of the Union Navy.

Cavalry, although almost as old as warfare itself, also established Civil War "firsts," or at least developments in the use of the mounted arm so advanced as to be novel. The science of outposts, of screening operations, was brought to a high point. Foreshadowed only by our mounted riflemen at King's Mountain in the Revolution were the dismounted tactics increasingly and tellingly practiced. The conflict

---

* Secretary of the Army Wilber M. Brucker to the Civil War Round Table of the District of Columbia, May 13, 1958.

† A preceding submarine, Bushnell's in the Revolution, failed in its mission against a British vessel in New York harbor.

between the states of the Union and the Confederacy marked the zenith of American cavalry and of cavalry everywhere.

Brandy Station as the greatest cavalry engagement of the war may therefore be considered to deserve the full treatment, given in the following pages, because of its historical significance, as well as for its immediate consequences and its drama. The Civil War's magnitude has begun to prompt more studies of single battles in addition to those of Gettysburg, which never lacked them.

This book strives to describe Brandy Station in the detail that must be forgone in a general history and to place it in its perspective. As prologue to the Virginia combat of June 9, 1863, chapters of the text, along with appendices, are devoted to the officers and troopers who fought it; to their horses and to their arms and equipment; to their training and earlier campaigning; to their traditions and other background. Such are the components of a battle that give it character and sway its outcome.

As with two previous works, *Sound of the Guns* and *The Guns at Gettysburg*, I greatly depended upon the advice and criticism of Colonel Harry C. Larter, Jr., in the writing of this book. Its dedication strives to express my appreciation.

Maps were produced under the guidance of General C. A. Baehr, who performed the same expert service for my book on the artillery at Gettysburg. To follow the cavalry movements and attacks at Brandy Station the maps he so carefully supervised are as indispensable an adjunct to this text as they were for that of the greater battle.

My sincere thanks for all their help are offered the following: Harold L. Peterson, authority on the American sword and firearms; James W. Green, editor of *The Orange Review*, Orange, Virginia, for the origin of Brandy Station's name and other aid; Bruce Lancaster, historian and historical novelist, whose *Night March* opens at Brandy Station; Colonel Leo A. Codd, editor of *Ordnance* magazine; my son-in-law, Lieutenant Colonel William A. Knowlton, Armor, whose original enlistment was in the cavalry; John Hathaway, maker of miniature cannon and keen student of military history; Professors Jay Luvaas and Robert L. Crispin of Allegheny College for making available the latter's translation from the German of von Borcke's book on the battle; my able editors, Kennett L. Rawson, President, and Mrs. Douglas Ryan, of the David McKay Company; my wife, Mildred Adams Downey, whose author's first aid—criticism, typing, proof-reading, and indexing—has carried through loyally from my first book in 1925 to this one; my invaluable literary agent, Oliver G. Swan, of Paul R. Reynolds & Son.

Gratitude for research facilities is due the following: Dartmouth College Library, where the bulk of my reference was done in its own excellent collection and through interlibrary loans; the Library of the U.S. Military Academy, which supplied a useful bibliography; the New York Public Library with its excellently catalogued regimental histories; the Library of Congress and that of Yale University; that of the University Club of New York and its invariably helpful librarian, Mark Kiley.

I am also grateful for permission to reprint chapters that appeared in *Ordnance* and *Civil War Times*.

FAIRFAX DOWNEY

West Springfield, New Hampshire

Contents

Illustrations

xiii

Illustrations in the Text

CLASH OF CAVALRY

CHAPTER 1

A Battlefield Is Named

•••

> ### BRANDY

THE keeper of the little country store in Culpeper County, Virginia, finished the last letter of the sign and let the paint dry. Then he hung it where it would catch the eyes of passengers on the stagecoach line that ran past his door. Like as not, the driver would pull up and give travelers a chance to take advantage of the announcement that there was a stock of apple brandy in the rear of the store, brandy freshly distilled at one of the orchards that dotted the countryside. What if there was no age on it? It would warm a man on a frosty morn.

That sign was still in place when the Orange and Alexandria Railroad was built in 1856, closely paralleling the original stage line. People had begun calling the small town that grew up around the store Brandy. Now it became Brandy Station.

A few years later the pounding of the hoofs of stagecoach horses would be a thousandfold revived by the galloping thunder of many regiments of cavalry in gray and blue. Clash of sabers would echo the clanking of car wheels on rails, and shells the hissing of locomotives steaming into Brandy Station. In and around the little town would be fought the greatest cavalry battle of the Civil War, the greatest ever fought on the American continent.

The storekeeper, lettering his crude sign, had written a name that rings like a trumpet in history.[1]

By the 1860's most of the land in the vicinity of Brandy Station had long been cleared and cultivated. There as elsewhere the woodman's ax had opened an arena for cavalry, previously cramped and circumscribed by the forests and finding opportunity for development only on the treeless plains of the West. The ground was largely level or gently sloped, ideal for charge and countercharge. Although at the outset of the war the fields were well fenced, rails and gates and draw bars soon disappeared before armies quick to pull down obstructions, or in search of handy firewood. Ditches, some of them broad and deep enough to be treacherous, remained, but none to match such a pitfall as the sunken road at Waterloo. Here and there patches of woods, some threaded by roads, afforded concealment for horsemen and cannon or a rallying point for a shattered squadron. North of Brandy Station rose the grassy knoll called Fleetwood Heights, crowned by a farmhouse, site for a command post and observation point. In that terrain nature and the hand of man "had created as fair a field as knights could have asked for a tournament." [2]

From 1862 through 1864 it served as lists for a dozen conflicts as savage as the *combats à l'outrance* of the medieval tourneys, notably the day-long battle of June 9, 1863,[3] with its far-reaching consequences. Trumpets sounding to horse, the gallop, and the charge repeated the brassy summons of the fanfares of yore. Sabers hewed and thrust like broadsword or leveled lance. Bullets of carbine and revolver dealt as deadly blows as had mace and battle-ax. Smoke wreathed the guns of the horse artillery as it had the bombards at Crécy five centuries before. Here in Virginia, as on countless earlier fields, mounted men met in mêlée and single encounters to fight some of the last fierce battles in a vanishing era of cavalry warfare.

Natural features of the field, splendidly adapted though they were, could not determine alone its selection as a battleground. Its choice became inevitable when Virginia seceded from the Union, and her capital, designated also as that of the Confederacy, confronted Washington, with the two cities chief pawns of the war in the East.

Brandy Station [wrote a cavalryman who fought there] [4] was directly across the line of advance or retreat of the armies, between Washington and Richmond, a station of the Southern railway (then the Orange and Alexandria), which either army, occupying Culpeper, used for the purpose of supply. It was a point from which the road south diverged eastward to Fredericksburg, to the Wilderness and the lower Rapidan, and westward to Madison and Orange; going north they diverged towards Kellyville and the lower Potomac. So it was an objective point to the movements of either army, in either direction.

A more direct approach from one capital to the other, the present U.S. Route 1, was too frequently cut by waterways and impeded by forests to be favored. Open to the armies of the North was an alternative: invasion by river and sea, commanded by the Union Navy. That would save long miles of marching, but strength would be sapped by the necessity of leaving troops to cover Washington. General McClellan attempted it, with transports carrying his army down the Potomac and along the coast to land at Fort Monroe and advance up the Peninsula, the neck of land between the James and the York rivers. His defeat in the Seven Days Battles and repulse from Richmond shifted the seat of warfare back to northern Virginia.

So it became the destiny of Brandy Station and Culpeper County often to hear the clatter of cavalry, the rumble of artillery, and the tramp of infantry. How well they fulfilled their fate as a magnetic avenue of access or a strategic blocking position was proved by the great battlefields that encircled that ground like a diadem—Bull Run or Manassas, Fredericksburg, Chancellorsville, Spotsylvania. The railway that ran through Brandy Station, an invaluable supply line, was a prize in itself. From the picturesque town of Culpeper Courthouse branched two systems of roads: one to the northeast, leading to Manassas, Fairfax, Alexandria, and Washington; the other to the north and northwest for an advance into the Shenandoah Valley. Confederate armies could threaten attack by either path or both, as could their opponents. At Brandy Station cavalry of the adversaries, leading and screening an offensive or warding it off, like a modern armored column, must force or defend the fords of the Rappa-

hannock River and clash in battle at a halfway point between the
Culpeper base and those crossings: the fields whose orchards furnished the storekeeper's distillation.

The horsemen in blue and in gray or butternut brown entered
the arena bounded on the west by the long ramparts of the Blue
Ridge. To the southeast the land rolled away toward thick, tangled
forests. Distant hills to the northeast masked the Manassas plateau.
Where the squadrons converged, June clover, ripe for cutting, spread
its fragrance, and tasseled cornstalks thrust up from new-plowed
earth, richly red or brown. Acres of wheat, glowing yellow in the
sun, formed a background of the cavalry color, and the arm's insignia, crossed sabers, were magnified to the flashing blades of
troopers who fought around the little town with the mellow name.

Some combats are fortuitous, the contending armies blundering
into them without design. Others, equally unplanned, are fought
on spur-of-the-moment decisions by field commanders. Still others
seem almost foreordained, waged like some of those in Asia and
Africa during the World Wars on ancient battlegrounds, perhaps
with the same tactics that prevailed centuries before. Many, of
course, are deliberate—culminations of campaigns or maneuvering.

The June, 1863, engagement at Brandy Station partook to some
degree of the character of the last. It was the result of a reconnaissance in force by the Union cavalry of the Army of the Potomac
to discover the intentions of General Lee, who had concentrated the
Army of Northern Virginia for an invasion of the North that would
end at Gettysburg. Prior to the Civil War the fields around Fleetwood Heights had seen no bloodshed unless it was in forgotten
fights between early settlers and Indians or skirmishes with the
British or Tories in the Revolution. Yet the conflicts around Brandy
Station were predestined, as has been noted, by its geographical
situation, and the large-scale encounter in June, 1863, was pre-
eminently the fateful meeting, long deferred but inevitable, of a
champion and a challenger—the Gray cavalry and the Blue.

Heralds of yore vaunted the prowess of knights, voicing their
deeds and lineage proclaimed by the emblems and quaterings on

shields. For these Civil War cavalrymen their regimental markings and their standards and guidons, shot torn perhaps and decorated with battle honors, similarly served. Such were tokens of their fighting quality.

Behind that hard-won attribute lies the story of their mustering and their training; of their horses, "the cavalryman's second self"; of the weapons they wielded; of the officers who led division and brigade, squadron, and troop.[5] All are prelude and prologue, martial genesis, for a mighty passage at arms.

CHAPTER 2

Death Rides a Black Horse

••-•••

THE Black Horse Troop of Fauquier County, Virginia, rode toward the battlefield of First Manassas or Bull Run with more of the heft of history in its saddlebags than a single unit is usually privileged to carry. By its action in the approaching combat it would exert an inordinate amount of influence on the course of the war. And on that twenty-first day of July, 1861, it forged the first link in the chain of events that led two years later to Brandy Station.

Part of Colonel J. E. B. Stuart's small cavalry command, 334 officers and enlisted men, the Fauquier troopers sat their black mounts proudly, riding boot to boot. Having been organized two years previously, they considered themselves no raw levy. Shortly they would become Company H, 4th Virginia Cavalry, one of the forty regiments of horse which that state ultimately put in the field. Chief source of pride was their horses, mostly animals of fine bloodlines. Their comparatively uncommon color set them apart and made them memorable, for bays were predominant among American breeds, with browns a close second and chestnuts third. Blacks ranked fourth, exceeding only the grays, roans, and conjugates.[6]

Matching a unit's horses in color was a custom derived from European cavalry whose smart dress was enhanced when the hides of mounts were of one shade. "The horses in the ranks can't be chose too much alike," observed a British officer in 1726.[7] Such cavalcades were immensely impressive, not only in parades and other ceremonies but in war. The sight of "the terrible grey horses" of the Scots Greys, charging at Waterloo with running infantrymen clinging to stirrups, is declared to have made Napoleon wince.[8] In the Russian army the horses of each cavalry regiment and those of each artillery battery were matched, as admiringly noted in 1855 by Captain George B. McClellan, U.S. Cavalry, observing the Crimean War.[9] The reason for uniformity was ease of recognition and efficiency more than handsome appearance. Horses, grouped by color, worked better together and actually developed a clannish spirit; they resented intrusion by an animal of an unfamiliar hue.[10] While the "magnificent chestnut chargers" of the Philadelphia Light Horse may have originally been purchased to afford a "fine spectical," their military advantage proved more important. The matching color of the mounts of that gallant little troop, along with its exploits in the Revolution, distinguished it.

Thus from Revolutionary times a number of American units had followed the color pattern. In the Civil War such establishments, chiefly state troops both in the South and North, enlisted as a body, and various newly-recruited regiments took pains to conform. The mounted services esteemed the similarity as highly as the owner of a beautifully matched pair of bays, hitched to his carriage, or as a farmer did his work team of twin roans.

The 6th Michigan sorted its mounts by color. So did the 1st Maine and, unlike most regiments, managed on the whole to maintain the arrangement throughout the war; three companies rode bays, two brown, two sorrel, two black, and one each grays, roans, and chestnuts. The 1st Massachusetts allotted bays to its first battalion, chestnuts and roans to its second, and blacks to its third, with grays for the band. Gray was the traditional hue for the mounts of musicians, for the bands and trumpeters. A trumpeter's gray, making him more easily spotted by his commander, reinforced the device of earlier wars whereby the colors and facings of his uniform were reversed from those of other troops.[11] Gray was a favored shade for troop horses as well as for the music. Phil Kearny's company of dragoons in the War with Mexico rode iron grays. So did one of Lieutenant Colonel Robert E. Lee's battalions of the 2nd U.S. Cavalry, serving in Texas before the Civil War; the three others were assigned sorrels, bays, and roans. During the Mormon campaign in Utah shortly before the Civil War, Battery B, 4th U.S.

Artillery, matched the colors of its section teams: bays for the right, blacks for the center, and sorrels for the left; the battery wagon and forge were drawn by grays.

By the second year of the war battle and disease had begun to take such heavy toll that it became impossible to restore color combinations from remounts supplied. Sufficient serviceable animals to keep cavalry in the saddle and the artillery rolling was the primary consideration; hue of hide and quality of breeding had to be almost entirely disregarded.

But the mounts of the Fauquier Black Horse Troop were in fine fettle when they marched to Manassas with Jeb Stuart's column to make their indelible mark in the annals of the war.

On that sweltering hot July day, picnicking Congressmen, their ladies, and other spectators from Washington watched the tide of battle between untried troops rise in favor of the Union. Then Confederate reinforcements arrived. Up on the brow of Henry House Hill General Thomas Jonathan Jackson and his brigade stood firm, winning him his nickname of "Stonewall." But they were hard pressed, and a courier from General Pierre Gustave Toutant Beauregard galloped to the leader of the Gray cavalry with an order to charge.

It was one of many Jeb Stuart would deliver, on until his last one on the fatal day at Yellow Tavern. He marshaled the Black Horse Troop and the rest of his command. Sabers flashed from scabbards, and the charge swept down on an advancing Union Zouave regiment.

The men in fezzes, yellow-braided blue jackets, and baggy red trousers fired a volley. Saddles emptied, Captain Welby Carter of Fauquier reeled and slid to the ground beneath the pounding hoofs, but the charge did not falter. Frantically the Zouaves plied ramrods. One of Stuart's officers [12] believed that if the infantrymen instead of attempting to reload had grounded slanted rifles with fixed bayonets and formed a hedge of steel like medieval pikemen, they could have repulsed the oncoming horsemen. There was no time to deliver a second volley. Only stanch infantry—and these were green troops—could have stood off this sudden onslaught. The

Zouaves recoiled before a surging wave that seemed composed of jet-hued steeds with flaring red nostrils, gleaming sabers brandished above their tossing manes. The charge smashed into them, broke, and scattered them.

A long-remembered yell burst from the throats of the fleeing Zouaves, "The Black Horse!" [13] The cry caught up and echoed across the field was "destined to endure terribly through the war." [14] The charge, no more than a local success, did not win the day. It

SECESSION CAVALRY
(From a wartime envelope)

was Confederate flank attacks that finally folded up the Blue lines and drove them back in retreat. When a Rebel shell crushed a wagon, blocking the stone bridge over Bull Run, and a panic ensued, cavalry did not harry the jetsam of defeat streaming back to Washington. By then most of Stuart's command had been detailed to escort prisoners to the rear. But in the imagination of every fugitive the dreadful apparition of black-mounted horsemen galloped at his heels.

That day at Bull Run Death rode, not the pale horse of the Apocalypse, but a black. Then and for at least two years thereafter rumor mounted virtually the entire Cavalry Corps of the Confederate Army on formidable sable charges. Few units have swayed the course of a conflict more definitely than that one Black Horse Troop of Fauquier County, Virginia,[15] by its brief action in the first great battle of the Civil War.

Seven troops of Union cavalry, Regulars, had guarded the right flank of the army at First Bull Run and helped cover its confused retreat.[16] They, like their adversaries in gray, were heirs to the traditions of the dragoon regiments of the Revolution; to those of the mounted riflemen who rode to Kings Mountain, tied their horses to trees, and blasted back British assaults with deadly fire—novel cavalry tactics which the Civil War would see fully developed. Lineal descendants of two dashing cavalry leaders of the Revolution, Light Horse Harry Lee and Wade Hampton, commanded Southern brigades at Brandy Station. The company which was the nucleus of the 9th Virginia Cavalry was named Lee's Light Horse in honor of the former, and in the early, equipment-scant days of the war it was armed with Revolutionary sabers, Starrs of the 1818 issue, and other heirloom weapons.

That "the past is prologue" is never more evident than in military history. The hoofbeats of 1861 echo those of the horsemen of Anthony Wayne's Legion at Fallen Timbers, of continuing Indian fights in the West, and of the War with Mexico. Back in the saddle again were troopers who had faced the Mexican lancers, and riders whose uniforms still carried the plains dust of campaigns against the Comanches, Kiowas, Sioux, and Apaches. Except upon those treeless expanses, American cavalry hitherto had been afforded only limited scope. Now with trails widened into roads, and cultivated fields opening such arenas for combat as the ground around Brandy Station, the mounted arm was about to come into its own.

At the outbreak of the Civil War the United States mustered five regiments of regular cavalry, shortly adding a sixth. They stemmed, as has been noted, from the dragoons of the Revolution, the Seminole and Mexican wars, and from those mounted riflemen whom a member of Congress had once quaintly termed "mounted gunmen." While they were now designated as cavalry and had discarded

dragoon orange piping, except for the 2nd Cavalry which refused
to give it up for cavalry yellow, they still retained the aspect of

> ... the dragoon bold he knows no care,
> And he rides along with his uncropped hair.
> He spends no thought on the evil star
> That sends him away to the border war.

For a time they continued to wear the plumed, black Hardee hat,
brim bound up on one side by a brass eagle and escutcheon; that
ornate headgear, disdained by soldiers of the line, was dubbed a
"Fra Diavolo" after the opera bandit. Beneath light blue overcoats
with capes were blue jackets, trimmed with yellow braid. Brass scales
were fastened to their shoulders as armor against saber blows.
Trousers of pale blue were strapped under their boots. Until their
fancy plumed hats were replaced by forage caps, the shoulder scales
dropped, and breeches stuffed in boots, they seemed relics of the
past in a modern war—much like some of the Southern horsemen
who first mustered in gay-colored militia uniforms until they could
be provided with Confederate gray.

Most of the blue-clad Regulars were, nevertheless, hard-bitten
troopers, behind them years of service in the West against the
Indian tribes, as formidable barbaric cavalry as the world has ever
seen, notably the Comanches. On their record stood extraordinary
marches and tough little combats where they were ably led by
officers the majority of whom would transfer their allegiance to the
South, among them Albert Sydney Johnston, Robert E. Lee, engineer
turned cavalryman, Hardee, Jeb Stuart, Fitzhugh Lee. Also unfortunately for the Union the regiments of Blue horse, converging
on Washington from their distant stations, would prove to be far
too few and they would dwindle, since no bounty was offered for
enlistments in the Regulars. Four of them, maintaining sufficient
strength and their proud esprit, would fight at Brandy Station.

Except for a few militia units, the North possessed no cadre for
volunteer cavalry. The services of established troops, along with
offers to recruit new regiments, were declined by the War Department on the advice of General Winfield Scott, commanding the

United States Army.[17] That old artilleryman, veteran of 1812 and Mexico, predicted that the war would be decided by cannon.[18] Certain battles would be markedly swayed by artillery—Malvern Hill, Fredericksburg, and, to a considerable extent, Gettysburg,[19] but no war is finally won by a supporting arm. Scott argued fatuously that the Southern theater would be impossible for cavalry. In November, 1861, the once-great old soldier, ill and too corpulent to mount a horse, had the wit, somewhat rare in superannuated officers, to resign and the wisdom to offer succession to his command to Robert E. Lee, who would demonstrate on the other side that cavalry could operate efficiently in the South.

FEDERAL CAVALRY
(From a wartime envelope)

So in the Union's first call for volunteers cavalry was either refused or its acceptance authorized only if the states provided horses and equipment. A still frugal government shied away from the heavy expense. The equipment alone for a regiment of 1,200 horsemen cost $300,000. Under ideal conditions forage for each animal would amount to 50 cents a day, and where it was not readily accessible and must be transported, to three or four times that figure.[20] The arm required long training; in some European armies a cavalryman's enlistment ran seven years.

Until First Bull Run the assumption was allowed to stand that six regular regiments of horse were ample. It was on a par with the delusion that ninety-day enlistments were long enough for winning the war.

Naturally the existence, let alone the efficiency, of cavalry presupposed the ability to ride a horse.

It was amazing how swiftly that skill had vanished in the more heavily populated sectors of the North until by the mid-nineteenth century it was comparatively rare. Now the Iron Horse was king. Railways linked the cities and towns. Where they did not run, stagecoaches, carriages, and wagons served, traveling over a growing network of reasonably good roads. The telegraph had rendered the post rider obsolete. Horses did the farm work and logging, but most of them were too heavy and slow to be used as cavalry mounts. Men who drove them were seldom on their backs except perhaps to ride them home to the barn after plow or stoneboat had been unhitched. On the speedways wealthy sportsmen raced their blooded trotters, light animals as unsuitable for military service as the ponderous farm horses. Save for the more isolated communities in the North and the pioneer settlements of the Midwest and West, horseback riding had become nearly a lost art. Railroads, wire communication, and all the appurtenances of the industrial revolution would play a major part in winning the war for the Union. Yet the horseman they had superseded must be summoned back from limbo, if cavalry were to fulfill its vital functions on the battlefield. He must acquire a forgotten skill, must not only ride well but drill and maneuver in formations, must be able to endure many weary miles in the saddle and give his horse the care that made those miles possible, must manage his mount, wield saber, and fire revolver in the press of combat.

For many Federal cavalrymen, untutored in all those difficult essentials, humiliation and bitter defeat were in store. It would take them two long years in the hard school of experience to learn.

In glaring contrast was the situation in the Southern states. Horsemanship survived as a daily necessity, as a favorite pastime, as a cult with thousands of ardent devotees. Forerunners of the Western cowboys were the Southern planters of colonial days who rode at headlong gallops through the woods to round up herds of wild horses whenever their stables needed restocking. A number of Virginia families treasured as mementos miniature golden horseshoes, awarded by Royal Governor Spotswood to members of the expedition he led across the Blue Ridge to explore the Shenandoah Valley. Because of the rough trails their usually shoeless mounts had been shod. The little emblems bore the motto: *Sic juvat transcendere montes*—such as these aided the crossing of the mountains. Descendants of the Knights of the Golden Horseshoe would fight as Confederate cavalrymen through that valley their grandfathers had ranged.

Knighthood seemed still to flower in the sport of tilting at rings when horsemen, lances couched, rode at full speed to catch the small suspended circles on their weapons' points. In fact the medieval aura that still surrounded horsemanship in the South would draw frequent, bitter references by worsted Federal cavalrymen to "the Southern chivalry." It engendered a legend: arrays of plumed knights, bearing the escutcheon of Dixie as they rode down helpless, clumsy masses of Yankee peasantry. It spanned decades to revive the glory and glamor of the Napoleonic horse. Each Confederate trooper seemed to carry in his saddlebags the baton of a Murat, a Ney; every man a Marbot.

Saddle racing, formal or informal, was widely practiced. The hunting horn and the view-haloo still resounded. "Every great plantation had its pack of hounds, and foxhunting, an heirloom from the English colonists, still flourished. His stud was the pride of every Southern gentleman, and the love of horseflesh was inherent in the whole population. No man walked if he could ride, and hundreds of fine horsemen, mounted on steeds of famous lineage, recruited the Confederate squadrons." [21] In 1861 again echoed from hunting to battlefield the exultant cry of a Virginia planter turned Revolutionary general, George Washington, when the Redcoats were routed at the Battle of Princeton: "It's a fine fox chase, boys!"

Those elements which had all but banished horsemanship from population centers of the North were inconsequential in the South. Railway lines were far fewer, roads scantier and rougher. Carriage travel over the rutted turnpikes usually was confined to the elderly or invalids. Belles, bound for a ball at a manor house, rode pillions behind their beaux, or donned habits and were lifted onto their sidesaddles, changing to a party gown on arrival. Even for short distances men vaulted onto a horse's back. It was said that if the war of which everyone was talking broke out, no Southerner would walk—even to a battle.

Such was the background of the Confederate cavalryman. Upon it rested the proud affirmation that the Virginia cavalry was "born, not made"—a claim that could also be advanced for troopers from other seceded states. Horsemanship learned in boyhood and constant riding long lent an overwhelming superiority over less practiced Northern adversaries. Lord Wolseley, the celebrated British soldier, made a caustic comparison following his tour as an observer in 1862. Of the Southern horsemen he wrote that

all the men rode well, in which particular they present a striking contrast to the Northern cavalry, who can scarcely sit their horses, even when trotting. Indeed, I have no doubt but that all who have seen Northern troopers on duty in Washington, will agree with me in thinking them the greatest scarecrows under the name of cavalry that they ever saw. Apropos of them, a Southern lady told me that on one occasion, when jesting with a Northern officer about the inability of his troops to contend with the Southern "chivalry," although the latter were not half so numerous, he said, "What can we do? We can never catch them; for whilst we are opening the gates they are all over the fences." Every man in the South rides from childhood, and consequently is at home in the saddle; whereas to be on horseback is a most disagreeable position for a Yankee, and one in which he rarely trusts himself. In the North thousands keep horses, but only to drive them. "What is the use of having good roads if you don't drive on them?" they say. To have a horse that can trot a mile in two minutes forty seconds is the pride of a New Englander; but a good fencer would be as useless to him as an elephant.[22]

It was all too true that for long the Federal cavalry was virtually roadbound. Rail fences and stone walls, even ditches, were insuperable objects. Creeks and fordable rivers were barriers before which they hesitated. The breakneck, cross-country gallop of the fox-hunter was left to Rebel horsemen. Worse still was a dash through woods which would shred and tangle a Blue regiment until it became a helpless, disorganized mob. Natural hazards and lack of horsemanship to overcome them left such primary cavalry missions as reconnaissance and raids largely to the men in gray.

Once in the saddle a Southerner, though he might be ungainly on foot, became a figure of grace and harmony, one with his horse. Horsemastership and the ability to handle arms mounted were as widespread south of the Mason-Dixon Line as they were negligible north of it. Feats of the Texans—bending down at a full gallop to pick up hats and stones from the ground—were matched by skilled riding exhibitions by horsemen from other seceded states. Exceptions to good horsemanship were notable by their rarity. Stonewall Jackson, despite the fact that in his boyhood he had won races as a jockey, had been trained in the West Point riding hall, and served in the artillery in the Mexican War, rode like a sack of meal. Yet it did not matter how the General, who was usually at the right place at the right time, sat his saddle while he was getting there.

Small wonder that the Confederate cavalrymen contemptuously branded their opponents "Yankee tailors and shoemakers on horses." In those first years of the war it not infrequently happened that a Southern horseman, pursuing some hapless rider in blue, did not bother to shoot or cut him down. He simply jerked the fugitive from his saddle, caught his horse, and rode back to prod his fallen enemy to his feet and march him to the rear.

Both paean and epitome of the dashing spirit of the Confederate cavalry was Jeb Stuart's rollicking battle song, sung to the twang of Sam Sweeney's banjo:

> If you want to smell hell—
> If you want to have fun—
> If you want to catch the devil—
> Jine the cavalry.

In Virginia, the Deep South, and the Border States the troops mustered on their splendid mounts. Some few boasted traditions of long standing; others had been raised in the late 1850's at the gathering of the war clouds. All were essentially volunteer cavalry, which the North had refused to call to arms. Among them were no Regulars, whose regiments remained loyal to the Union, with the already noted exception of some of their officers and a few—a very few—of the rank and file.

Booted and spurred, they rode to join the armies, some in smart, more in nondescript, uniforms—no less jauntily worn. Plumes nodded from other hats than that of the debonair Jeb Stuart, soon prompting cavalry regulations to chide: "Fancy hats, with plumes of ostrich or other feathers are only suitable on parades and reviews, but, on campaign, they are a useless encumbrance." [23] Some troops were followed by wagon trains, laden with trunks, shortly to be discarded. In a number of units nearly every cavalryman from captain to private was accompanied by a Negro body-servant, functioning as valet, groom, and cook and riding his master's spare mount or a mule. What harm if warfare's inevitable hardships were mitigated by a few comforts so long as the latter did not interfere with the business in hand? The Negroes made themselves scarce when the shooting started, but most of them bobbed up afterward when they were needed. No Gray cavalryman would have traded his servant for a Federal officer's enlisted striker.

For the two bodies of contrasting cavalry approaching conflict one highly important characteristic can be listed on the credit side of the ledger for the Union. And that, slowly but inevitably, would exert an overwhelming effect.

The average Confederate trooper was an individualist. He lived in a land where the rule of aristocracy was as deeply ingrained as that of democracy in the North, and the two ways of life strongly affected discipline. The custom whereby a unit elected its officers originally prevailed in both South and North, but in the former it was more inflexible and endured longer, extended sometimes to include enforced resignation of officers on petition of troopers they had failed to please. It was, in the modern phrase, "a hell of way to run an army." The effect on leadership was often ruinous. In troops of Virginia cavalry for a time even corporals had to be elected; and only they, one of them confessed, cared sufficiently little for rank to risk it by enforcing discipline. One stubborn non-com deliberately marched a guard detail through the middle of a mud puddle, declaring that corporals were given so plagued little authority that he meant to make the most of it.[24]

"The man of good family felt himself superior, as in most cases he unquestionably was, to his fellow-soldiers of less excellent birth; and this distinction was sufficient, during the early years of the war, to override everything like military rank." [25] A company commander, who subjected a private to double duty for absence from roll call, was forced to apologize for the "insult." Camp cleaning fatigue was passed on to servants; their masters sat on fences and supervised. Substitutes for guard duty were hired at twenty-five cents an hour.

The typical Southern cavalryman was a resourceful scout, a daring, dashing raider. Sudden forays, swift, isolated actions, were his fortes. He would, like his opponents, gradually learn cavalry tactics, though never as thoroughly. Because he was predominantly a horseman, he was disinclined toward dismounted combat; and the mounted rifleman, fighting on foot, would carry the day on more and more fields as the war progressed. Confederate troopers delivered as valiant, headlong charges as any recorded in cavalry annals. Less frequently theirs was the ability to drive home the crushing mass onslaught of a disciplined, readily-wielded striking force. That would become a telling talent of the Blue horse. It would come close to winning victory at Brandy Station, and when Sheridan took command of the Union cavalry, it would contribute heavily to final triumph.

Tardy word that the U.S. War Department would accept volunteer cavalry and horse and equip it came in the summer of 1861. From Maine to Maryland, from New York through the Midwest, the regiments began to organize.

Trouble and turmoil could have been plainly predicted from interviews at scores of recruiting stations. Would-be troopers thronging to them, when asked why they wanted to join the cavalry, did not mention the lure of glamorous charges with flashing sabers, although such inducements were in the back of many minds. Answers were prosaic and practical. In the infantry a soldier had to walk. In the cavalry a horse carried him comfortably through marches. At the end of them the animal, recruits happily anticipated, would be put up "in some peripatetic livery stable." Next morning steeds, watered, fed, groomed, saddled, and bridled, would be led forth by hostlers to be mounted by well-rested cavalrymen and ridden on to war. The name of such innocents was legion, and their approaching disillusionment was more than melancholy—it was shocking and painful.

No observer summed up recruit motives as graphically as the historian of the 1st Maine Cavalry.[26] Many applicants, he discovered, had heard that in the infantry there was too much idleness, relieved only by dull guard duty. They believed they would be kept busier in the cavalry with scouting and so on, thus mitigating boredom, homesickness, and chances of sickness.

Then the idea of long and forced marches on foot led many who feared they would not be able to endure this portion of the service [there was a proportion of seafaring men on the 1st Maine's roster] to prefer a service in which they could ride. Then there hung about the cavalry service a dash and excitement which attracted those men who had read and remembered

the glorious achievements of "Light Horse Harry" and his brigade, and of "Morgan's Men" in the revolutionary war, or who
had devoured the story of "Charles O'Malley," [27] and similar
works. In short, men who had read much in history or fiction
preferred the cavalry service . . . It may be, as intimated by the
Professor in the *Atlantic,* that it makes common men look
dignified and imperious to sit on a horse. This is probably so,
and may furnish the explanation why the cavalry service—certainly much harder than the infantry—has been sought after by
so many men of means. Men—and sometimes women—like to
rule, and if it is only a horse, it yields some satisfaction. The
conquerors of the world are always represented on horseback,
and from Marcus Aurelius in Roman bronze down to the
"man on horseback" in Gen. Cushing's prophetic speech the
saddle has been the true seat of empire.

Recruiting officers of the 1st Maine followed selection instruc-
tions more closely than they were observed for numbers of other
regiments, directions to enlist "none but sound, able-bodied men
in all respects, between the ages of eighteen and thirty-five years,
of correct morals and temperate habits, active, intelligent, vigorous
and hardy, weighing not less than one hundred and twenty-five or
more than one hundred and sixty pounds." Even the sailors and
fishermen, more used to the bounding main than a bounding mount,
were often familiar with horses as part-time loggers and farmers.
Elsewhere recruits were frequently signed up without any regard to
their ability to ride or the slightest knowledge of horses. Big men,
too heavy for the average cavalry mount, were taken without question. Classification for arm of service according to skills and apti-
tudes was still years ahead for the U.S. Army, and for the Union
cavalry of 1861 it would have been virtually inoperable. Good
horsemen—horsemen of any sort—simply were not available in the
numbers required.

Regiments filled to strength, assembled, and encamped. They
drilled dismounted. They were issued horses, not infrequently unbroken, and many a trooper made for the first time the unpleasant
acquaintance of an animal he quickly came to consider a rampaging

wild beast. He had scarcely fathomed the misery in store for him when he and his regiment were shipped off to Washington.

A captain of New York cavalry sympathetically recalled his regiment's first ride into Virginia on escort duty: [28]

Such a rattling, jingling, jerking, scrambling, cursing I have never heard before. Green horses—some of them had never been ridden—turned round and round, backed against each other, jumped up or stood like trained circus horses. Some of the boys had a pile in front of them on the saddle, and one to the rear, so high and heavy it took two men to saddle one horse and two men to help the fellow into his place. The horses sheered out, going sidewise, pushing the well-disposed animals out of position, etc. Some of the boys had never ridden anything since they galloped on a hobby horse and they clasped their legs close together, unconsciously sticking their spurs into their horses' sides. Blankets slipped from under saddles and hung from one corner; saddles slipped back until they were on the rumps of horses; others turned and were on the other side of the animals; horses running and kicking; tin pans, mess kettles, patent sheet iron stoves the boys had seen advertised in the illustrated papers and sold by sutlers of Alexandria—about as useful as a piano or a folding bed—flying through the air; and all I could do was give a hasty glance to the rear and sing out at the top of my voice, "C-l-o-s-e u-p!" but they couldn't "close." Poor boys! Their eyes stuck out like maniacs'. We went only a few miles, but the boys didn't all get up till noon.

It was such precursory scenes—and this was by no means an isolated case—that made the performance of the Union cavalry at Brandy Station seem all but incredible.

CHAPTER 3

The Cavalryman's Second Self

For the want of a horse the rider was lost,
For the want of a rider the battle was lost.
                Benjamin Franklin: *Poor Richard's Almanack*

SUCCESS or failure of the cavalry arm of the 1860's, along with its supporting horse artillery, hinged finally upon maintenance of the supply of saddle and draft animals. Brandy Station saw the Union's rising, while the Confederacy's was past its peak and sinking alarmingly.

Competing with the cavalry and horse artillery for available horses were the many batteries of light artillery and the transport wagons, although the invaluable mule hauled the bulk of the latter. Generals and other high-ranking officers, requiring to be well mounted, skimmed the cream of the plantations' stock and of breeding farms, and splendid chargers entered the horses' hall of fame: Lee's Traveller, Grant's Cincinnati, Sheridan's Winchester, Hampton's Butler, Jeb Stuart's string of big hunters, and many others.[29] The Civil War was not our last conflict in which the horse was of high importance. Cavalry would help infantry [30] win the campaigns against the Indians in the West. In the First World War the still vast horse reservoir of North America was tapped, first for the Allies, then for our own forces, to the extent of some 380,000 animals, chiefly for field artillery, since trench warfare and the machine gun had tolled the knell for cavalry.[31] But on this continent the War between the States was the heyday of the cavalry mount.

A cavalryman's companion and friend upon whom his life may depend—his second self. So one who wore the gray fondly spoke of his horse,[32] and thousands of his comrades could echo his words. Both in quality and quantity immediately available the Confederacy's horse supply was initially superior to the Union's, as indicated in the previous chapter. Virginia in particular and scarcely less so some of the more southerly states were "full of horses of noble blood." [33] Selective breeding preserved the strains of imported English thoroughbreds, such celebrated racers as Eclipse, Sir Archy, Boston, Timoleon, Diomede, Exchequer, and Red-Eye. Rich sources also were the great horse-breeding regions to the west. For more than a year the Confederate armies drew upon them heavily. Not until the summer of 1862 were they largely cut off by the loss of Kentucky, Missouri, middle and western Tennessee, and trans-Allegheny Virginia through Union victories.

Georgia, Alabama, and Mississippi provided horses and nearly as many mules; Louisiana more of the latter. Greater use in wagon trains of the long-eared animals, excelling in draft, released many horses for the mounted arms. There was a vast surplus of horses in Texas,[34] as well as in neighboring Mexico, but they were mostly small mustangs, degenerate descendants of the steeds of the Spanish conquistadores. It is a curious commentary that territory which had seen the introduction of the war horse, a primary instrument of conquest, into North America could now furnish few suitable for cavalry.

Destined to hamstring the Confederate cavalry was a government policy which required every trooper to furnish his own mount. He was paid 40 cents a day for using the animal and promised feed, horseshoes, and the services of a blacksmith (a promise which too often could not be kept). The horse was given a fair valuation, and if he were killed in action, his owner was paid that sum. But if the animal were captured, worn out, or otherwise disabled, there was no reimbursement. In either case the trooper must find a replacement, expending the money paid him or his own. His remount might be a horse taken from the enemy in battle or raid, or a dead comrade's. Failing such, he had to be given a furlough to go home and obtain a new mount. It was a long journey to Georgia or Mississippi, for instance, and the search became increasingly difficult.

"For the want of a horse the rider was lost." The dehorsed trooper had two choices. He could transfer to another arm of the service, an alternative few cavalrymen welcomed, or he could join "Company Q." Such collections of horseless horsemen, eating their hearts out longing for a chance to get back into the saddle, were melancholy enough in themselves. The sorry state of "Company Q" was aggravated when it deteriorated into a refuge for a number of riffraff, malingerers, and assorted duty dodgers, well content to sit out the war in a safe place. Finally "Q" had to be disbanded, partly because of its worthless elements and partly because chances of finding remounts became virtually hopeless. Members were drafted willynilly into the artillery or infantry. It was said of true cavalrymen that "they went with a broken spirit."

But in the earlier years of the war the policy of the Confederate government, which considered itself unable to afford the provision of cavalry mounts, though it did supply artillery horses and transport mules, served as readily as it was accepted. "Why," one cavalryman asked, "should it have been thought that the people of Virginia would have held back their horses when they refused nothing else to the government?" [35]

A similar frugality in regard to cavalry mounts beset the United States Government in 1861. When volunteer cavalry regiments were being reluctantly considered, it was suggested that while the War Department would furnish arms, horses and their equipment should be the responsibility of the states and patriotic citizens.[36] The thought of putting up the cash for 1,200 horses per regiment at a minimum of $119 a head, plus saddlery and so on, failed to appeal widely. Only one Union regiment, the 3rd Indiana Cavalry, is recorded to have been mustered in with troopers owning their mounts.[37] In one instance an individual bought horses for an entire troop.[38] Generally the Union cavalry horses were purchased by government contract.

New England and New York were scoured for sturdy Morgans, often first-rate cavalry mounts, descendants of that extraordinary little stallion, Justin Morgan. Surprisingly good, too, were the "Canucks" from north and south of the Canadian border. Like the Morgans, they did not run large. Short-legged, shaggy, with long manes and tails, they were comparative miniatures of their forebears, the huge Norman chargers of the mailed knights. Yet they were good-tempered, enduring, and hardy; they could live on bark and leaves when there was nothing else to eat. Other breeds and crosses came from the Midwest and in ever larger numbers as the Union armies gained control over the horse-breeding regions. For the Blue cavalry there proved to be horses enough and to spare. It was furnished 284,000 during the first two years of the war, although the maximum number of cavalrymen in the field at any time during that period did not exceed 60,000.[39]

Machinations of grafting contractors could not greatly affect that generous stream of supply. They rebranded cavalry mounts, at $119 a head, as artillery horses, which brought $150 each. They palmed off on the government such shipments as the one from St. Louis in which only 76 out of 411 animals were found fit for service by a board of survey. Five were dead on the train's arrival, and 330 undersized or overaged, stifled, ringboned, blind, spavined, or otherwise crippled. Price per head had been boosted $11 over the $119 maximum. The loss to the United States on that one lot was $40,000.[40]

More than financial damage was done by such nefarious contractors, who should have faced a firing squad. Cavalrymen were kept out of action or cut down by the enemy because they had been issued worthless mounts. Luckless troopers took animals given them in anger or disgust, or made a wry jest of it like the Irishman, who looked into the mouth of the mount assigned him, then doffed his cap and made the wretched nag a profound bow. Questioned by his captain as to the reason for his antics, he replied, "Respect for old age, sir." [41] A Massachusetts officer scanned a batch of remounts, turned over to his troop, and caustically remarked: "Such a collection of crow's bait the eye of man never saw. Solomon's song of the war horse was the most bitter satire ever conceived. He may have been wise in his day and generation, but he evidently never saw field service, and they didn't know everything down in Judee." [42]

But most new regiments of Union volunteer cavalry were satisfied with the animals obtained for them by their own officers or honest contractors. The problem for those with a small quota of horse-wise troopers was how one handled the strange creatures.

"Take care of your horse before you take care of yourself"—that was the cavalryman's credo. Water and feed. Groom him thoroughly, first donning a white stable frock to spare your uniform. The 1st Rhode Island, admiring those garments, once wore them, when clean, to church, quoting the Scriptures (Revelations III) in justification: "He that overcometh, the same should be clothed in white raiment." [43]

See to it whenever possible that the horses have adequate shelter. The 1st Maine self-sacrificingly lived up to that charge. In camp at Augusta it built stables, but the men had to weather the tough winter of 1861–62 in tents. Snow was five to six feet deep, and it was often twenty degrees below zero, "cold even for Maine." [44] "Horses cost money—men don't," ran the regiment's comment.

Finally you saddled and bridled and rode the beasts—or tried to. Those first essays at the equestrian art are so vividly chronicled by regimental historians that one suspects that they were among the sufferers. Many of the horses were unbroken, never previously ridden. Selling the government vicious animals nobody else would buy was one of the tricks of crooked contractors.

The ordeal of the 1st Maine, beginning in mid-December, at least helped keep it warm.

Those first mounted drills—will they ever be forgotten, so long as one lives who saw them? Most of the horses had never before been ridden on the back [*sic*], and most of the men knew as little about it as the horses. There was kicking and rearing, and running and jumping, and lying down and falling down, on the part of the horses, and swearing and yelling, and getting thrown and being kicked, and getting sore in various ways, by the men. There was crowding in the ranks, and getting out of place and striving to get back into place, and pushing forward and hanging back, and going backwards and sideways, and all ways but the right way, and all sorts of haps and mishaps, which, though amusing to look back upon now, and amusing at the time to all but the unfortunate ones, were anything but pleasant then to those immediately concerned.[45]

Finally the regiment ventured a review for the Governor. Confusion quickly developed in the ranks of Company K, largely composed of seafaring men, whose commander was an old-time sea captain. When a private's mount backed out of line, the skipper hailed him in his quarterdeck voice, "Come up there! What in hell are you falling astern for?" "Why, captain, I can't get the damn thing in stays!" the trooper shouted. The skipper bellowed back an order: "Well, give her more headway, then!" [46]

Typical, too, were the tribulations of the 2nd New York:

At first we had some exciting times with our young and untrained horses [its historian related]. One of our men received a kick from his horse which proved fatal to his life. Several of our wildest and seemingly incorrigible ones we have been compelled to run up the steepest hills in the vicinity, under the wholesome discipline of sharp spurs, until the evil has been sweated out of them. We find, however, that the trouble is not only with the horses, but frequently with the men, many of whom have never bridled a horse nor touched a saddle. And then, too, these curbed [sic] bits in the mouths of the animals that have been trained with the common bridle, produced a most rebellious temper, causing many of them to pitch up into the air as though they had suddenly been transformed into monstrous kangaroos, while the riders showed signs of having taken lessons in somersaults. . . .

We do not wonder that the chivalrous Black Horse gentry have expressed their contempt of Northern "mudsills and greasy mechanics," and have made their brag that we could never match them.[47]

Bruised and aching troopers grinned ironically when they read such sentences in the manuals as these: "In training the recruit mounted, care should be taken to give him a gentle and well trained horse." [48] "In no case should a horse be punished for timidity." [49] The crowning touch of official naïveté was: "There are other horses which kick." [48]

Following primary grades in the school of the cavalryman came advanced courses. Bareback riding. Jumping. Accustoming the horses to firing and other noises. Field music, manuals advised, should be practiced near the horse-exercise yard (surely on the theory that animals, which could endure the frightful racket of trumpeters learning to blow, could stand anything). A similar practice was observed with bands whose unexpected, sudden blasts could rout a squadron. Horses must be familiarized with their riders, firing from the saddle or swinging a saber to cut at canvas dummies, stuffed with hay, as they rode past. Mounts of standard- and guidon-bearers must be made used to the sight and sounds of flags waving above them and snapping in the wind.

All that and more had to be learned. Gradually man and beast acquired those skills, polishing them in the hard, postgraduate school of field service. Finally beheld was the beautiful spectacle of regiments of cavalry wheeling and countermarching, trotting and galloping, in response to trumpet calls, the horses recognizing and obeying them as quickly as their riders. No less stirring a sight were the horse artillery batteries, cavalry with guns, rushing into position, unlimbering and opening fire.

Facing the cavalry of both armies was service arduous beyond their imagining. Constant picketing and patrols. Jeb Stuart's long, hard-riding raids and those by Union General Kilpatrick which won him the nickname of "Kill-cavalry." The test of battle. A primary method of summing up success or failure, victory or defeat, lay in the condition of the animals on the picket lines. Add up the number of sore backs and lamed legs, exhaustion beyond endurance and weakness from lack of feed, the cases of dreaded glanders and "greased-heel," [50] and you had an answer.

Groom and rub down your mount, trooper. Clean out his hoofs. Hard, monotonous work, but your life may depend upon it. Smooth down mane and hide hair under the saddle blanket—and leave no wrinkles in it. Water and, as "Stable Call" bids, "Give your poor horses some hay and some corn." If the quartermaster hasn't come through with any, forage for it before you think of your own hunger. Do your utmost when you have to picket your horse in the mud to find some dry footing—boards, bricks, bits of tile; standing day after day in muck, he'll finally come down with "greased-heel" or thrush, his hoofs rotting away. Sponge out his nostrils and watch for the telltale running mucous that may mean glanders. Report him for isolation then, or it may spread, and the whole troop will need remounts besides yourself.

When you lie down with saddle for pillow to sleep in the open, with no picket line or tree where you can tether your horse, you can safely fasten him by halter tie rope to your hand. He will walk around you grazing, perhaps awaking you at times by tugs, but he will never step on you. On long, hard marches of a day and a night or more, he will let you sleep in the saddle, carrying you until he founders and drops.[51]

Tend his wounds and cherish him. If he could speak, he would promise you: "In this war, like any other soldier, I will do my best without hope of any war-cross, content to serve my country and you, and, if need be, I will die, calm and dignified on the battle field."[52]

How did cavalry horses behave in combat? They could not understand but obeyed when they were ridden into action. Veterans remembered how they

seemed to share the hopes and fears of battle equally with their riders. When sabres were drawn and the troops cheered, the horses gallantly responded. If a volley came in a charge and the horse was unhurt, he would lower his head and toss it from side to side. In charging infantry, he would charge straight at a man and knock him down; if against cavalry, he would lift his head and forefeet as though going over a fence. A man seldom cries out when hit in the tumult of battle, and a horse shows similar fortitude, or perhaps it is insensibility to pain under excitement. A horse, even with a foot shot off, would not drop. He might be fatally wounded but he would hobble on or stand with drooping head until loss of blood brought him down. They became attached to their riders and to one another and kept their places in the ranks, even when riderless. If one lost his rider and was not wounded, he continued by himself until some movement threw him out, then go galloping here and there, neighing with fear and alarm, but would not leave the field. In battle the horses became as excited as their riders, sometimes becoming quite uncontrollable and carrying them beyond where they wished to go. [Elmer Eugene Barker, "Monuments to Their Horses," in *New York History*, XXX, p. 45f.]

The war's toll of horses ran to many thousands. During eight months of 1864 Union horse losses reached 500 a day; the Army of the Potomac alone used up 40,000.

High as battle casualties ran, other causes made heavier inroads on cavalry strength. Both armies established horse infirmaries in only partially successful efforts to cope with disease. In September, 1862, epidemics rendered nearly half the horses of the Army of the Potomac unserviceable, and the Army of Northern Virginia also suffered severely. On hard campaigns horses went without unsaddling for two or more days—for fifteen in one appalling instance.[53] In October, 1862, a shipment of horses was left in freight cars fifty hours without water or food, then issued for immediate service.[54] Malnutrition and even starvation were not uncommon, as supplies of hay and grain failed, and the stripped countryside yielded no forage. "The horses would eat the bark off trees, would gnaw through the trunks of the slender forest growth and would devour empty bags, scraps of paper, and all the small debris of the camp."[55] Famished creatures chewed the hair from each other's manes and tails.

A captain of Union cavalry, Charles Francis Adams, Jr., in May, 1863, wrote a poignant letter home about the horses' sufferings: [56]

An officer of cavalry needs to be more horse-doctor than soldier, and no one who has not tried it can realize the dis-

couragement to Company commanders in these long and con-
tinuous marches. You are a slave to your horses, you work like
a dog yourself, and you exact the most extreme care from your
sergeant, and you see diseases creeping on you day by day and
your horses breaking down under your eyes, and you have two
resources, one to send them to reserve camps at the rear and so
strip yourself of your command, and the other to force them on
until they drop and then run for luck that you will be able to
steal horses to remount your men, and keep up the strength of
your command. The last course is the one I adopt. I do my
best for my horses and am sorry for them; but all war is cruel
and it is my business to bring every man I can into the presence
of the enemy, and so make war short. So I have but one rule, a
horse must go until he can't be spurred any further, and then
the rider must get another horse as soon as he can seize on one.
To estimate the wear and tear on horseflesh you must bear in
mind that, in the service in this country, a cavalry horse when
loaded carries an average of 225 lbs. on his back. His saddle,
when packed and without a rider in it, weighs not less than
fifty pounds. The horse is, in active campaign, saddled on an
average about fifteen hours out of twenty-four. His feed is
normally ten pounds of grain a day and, in reality, he averages
about eight pounds. He has no hay and only such other feed as
he can pick up during halts. The usual water he drinks is brook
water, so muddy by the passage of the column as to be of the
color of chocolate. Of course, sore backs are our greatest trouble.
Backs soon get feverish under the saddle and the first day's
march swells them; after that day by day trouble grows. No care
can stop it. Every night after a march, no matter how late it
may be, or tired or hungry I am, if permission is given to unsaddle, I examine all the horses' backs myself and see that
everything is done for them that can be done, and yet with every
care the marching of the last four weeks disabled ten of my
horses, and put ten more on the high road to disability, and
this out of sixty—one horse in three. Imagine a horse with his
withers swollen to three times the natural size, and with a
volcanic, running sore pouring matter down each side, and
you have a case with which every cavalry officer is daily called
upon to deal, and you imagine a horse which has still to be

ridden until he lies down in sheer suffering under the saddle. Then we seize the first horse we come to and put the dismounted man on his back. The air of Virginia is literally burdened today with the stench of dead horses, federal and confederate. You pass them on every road and find them in every field, while from their carrions you can follow the march of every army that moves.

On this last raid dying horses lined the road on which Stoneman's divisions had passed, and we marched over a road made pestilent by the dead horses of the vanished rebels. Poor brutes! How it would astonish and terrify you and all others at home with your sleek, well-fed animals, to see the weak, gaunt, rough animals, with each rib visible and the hip-bones starting through the flesh, on which these "dashing cavalry raids" were executed. It would knock the romance out of you. So much for my cares as a horse-master, and they are the cares of all. For, I can safely assure you, my horses are not the worst in the regiment and that I am reputed no unsuccessful chief-groom. I put seventy horses in the field on the 13th of April, and not many other Captains in the service did as much.

Colonel Blackford, of Jeb Stuart's staff, was equally moved by compassion. In his memoirs he told of watching a battery trot past on its way to replenish its ammunition chests during a hot action.

Behind the battery came hobbling as best they could a string of frightfully mutilated horses which had been turned loose as they received their wounds, and who [sic] had followed their comrades when they left the spot where they had been in action. After they had all passed, I saw a horse galloping after them dragging something. Thinking it was his rider as he emerged from the clouds of smoke on the field of battle, I moved to intercept and stop the animal, but to my horror discovered that the horse was dragging his own entrails from the gaping wound of a cannonball, and after passing us a few yards the poor brute fell dead with a piercing scream. The wounded horses of a battery will stay around their mates as long as the battery is in action and then try to follow whatever their condition may be. On many battlefields my pity has been so touched by the sufferings of wounded horses that I would stop and put them out of their pain by a friendly pistol shot. In one case I remember I came near being seriously hurt by a large horse springing forward as he fell and nearly bearing me and my horse down under him as my ball pierced his brain.

As early as the autumn of 1862 General Lee foresaw the danger of the prospective failure of the horse supply and took every means he could to remedy it, steps that could be only mitigations.

He deplored the system of mounting cavalrymen on their own animals but found no way of changing it. All the horses the government could furnish, and more, were needed for the artillery and transportation. Once the small surplus was exhausted, Lee faced a dilemma. No more animals could be taken from the farmers. If their stock was further depleted, crops, already insufficient, would dwindle to the point where neither the army, the civilian population, nor the animals could be fed. Raids and impressments in enemy territory brought in some remounts, sometimes as many as a thousand or two. Yet that was a game which Federal raiders in Virginia could play, too—along with the destruction of crops.[57]

"For want of a horse the rider was lost." The line runs through the history of the Confederate cavalry like a litany. But the fatal hour for the Gray horsemen had not yet struck when Jeb Stuart proudly and confidently marshaled his regiments for review at Brandy Station June 7 and 8, 1863, and pickets were posted at the Rappahannock fords.

CHAPTER 4

Arms and the Cavalryman

━━━

NEW cavalrymen gripped and tentatively swung their recently-issued sabers, a tool of war they had read of but very few had handled. The like of these was the weapon of knighthood in flower, the *arme blanche* of the romances, the blade of "Charles O'Malley" and his Irish dragoons. It flashed bare in a charge like that of the Light Brigade at Balaklava. A sense of martial power flowed from it into the man who wielded it. In 1861 not many suspected that swords, like the lances briefly carried, were on their way toward obsolescence.[58]

The clash of sabers, that most stirring sound in combat, echoed through the Civil War. Though the crack of revolvers and carbines and the thundering cannon of the horse artillery drowned the ring of steel on steel, they did not supersede it. The machine gun, to be the nemesis of cavalry, waited in the wings, little used.[59]

Sabers first issued followed the French pattern. They were later supplanted by the more highly curved model of 1860.

Both sides manufactured and imported sabers. In the first year the South, with its inferior facilities, was compelled to arm its cavalry with whatever blades it could find, some of them heirlooms taken down from pegs over the mantlepiece. An assortment of early American and Mexican War sabers made some troops look like a group of collectors of antique arms. Early shortages in the North led one regiment to turn crude wooden sabers on lathes, replicas that drew laughs from spectators yet proved useful for practicing the manual; when real sabers were issued, the men were able to handle them creditably.[60]

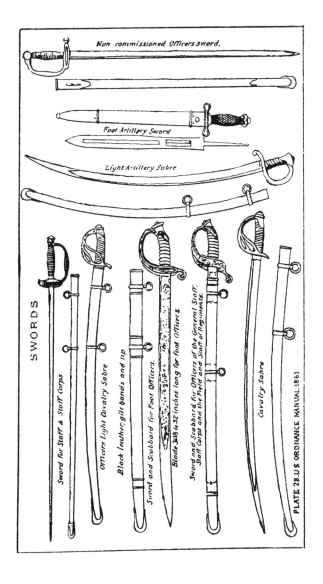

Non commissioned Officers sword.

Foot Artillery Sword

Light Artillery Sabre

SWORDS

Sword for Staff & Staff Corps

Officers Light Cavalry Sabre

Black leather, gilt bands and up

Sword and Scabbard for Foot Officers.

Blade 30½ to 32 inches long for foot Officers

Sword and Scabbard for Officers of the General Staff, Staff Corps and the Field and Staff of Regiments.

Cavalry Sabre

PLATE 28. U.S. ORDNANCE MANUAL 1861

On drill grounds sabers whirled in moulinets (like arms of a windmill), suppling wrists. Thrusts, cuts, and parries were practiced dismounted and mounted. Men of awkward squads were apt to miss slashes at dummies, as they rode past, and hit their horses' ears or legs with unpleasant consequences. The most competent instructors were West Pointers, who had studied fencing at the Academy under the Master of the Sword. Gradually recruits learned to wield the strange weapon. Slung from belts, its rattle and jangle might betray a patrol. And yet when a charging cavalryman had emptied his revolver, and there was no chance to reload, his saber, like the infantryman's bayonet, was his weapon of final resort.

Veterans sharpened theirs, though not to a razor edge, which would nick and turn when parried or striking bone. Swung by powerful men, sabers cut into skulls, deep through shoulders, or lopped off arms. Thrusts delivered by a *beau sabreur* were deadly. Sabers, declining through the Indians wars and with the development and improvement of rapid-fire and automatic arms, would linger as long as cavalry rode, although they tended increasingly to be left behind at bases when troops took the field.

The day of their passing was not yet. Brandy Station saw saber combat, mass and individual, that revived memories of the Napoleonic wars.

The past also lived again when a Confederate troop was temporarily armed with pikes, which had been in the possession of John Brown and his men when they surrendered in the Harper's Ferry arsenal.[61] Lances appeared when the 6th Pennsylvania Cavalry was equipped with them on the recommendation of General McClellan, who on his foreign tour had admired them in the hands of the Russian cavalry and had heard of their skillful use by the Poles, the world's premier lancers.

That weapon was not altogether strange in America. The 2nd U.S. Dragoons once had been armed with it. In 1847–48 it had proved formidable in the hands of Mexican lancers. The Pennsylvanians' slender spears, nearly ten feet long, made a brave display with their three-edged tips and scarlet, swallow-tailed pennons, but the troopers heartily disliked them. They were hazards in wooded country, being apt to be tangled in branches. Soon they were discarded, and the 6th Pennsylvania returned with relief to its original armament of sabers and revolvers.

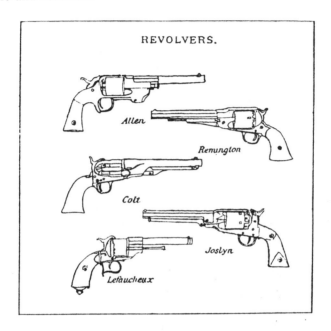

REVOLVERS.

Allen
Remington
Colt
Joslyn
Lefaucheux

The handy revolver, notably the Colt six-shooter, remained a cavalry favorite. In charge and close combat it gave a trooper six quick chances to drop his enemy, but reloading was slow and not easy, especially on a restive horse. Powder cartridges must be inserted in chambers, balls pressed in with fingers and rammed home with a lever, and the cartridges primed by pressing caps on cones. If a cavalryman emptied his revolver and had no time to reload, he must resort to saber or carbine.

Not the hand gun but the shoulder arm took precedence, as dismounted cavalry tactics began to prevail on the battlefield. Here again shortages hampered the South. Numbers of Confederate troopers carried rifles or shotguns, firing buckshot and ball, until factories, imports, or captures from the enemy could arm more with carbines. Those weapons developed from muzzle- to breech-loaders, firing brass cartridges,[62] and thence to repeaters. Against hidebound opposition, requiring President Lincoln's authority to break,[63] the 7-shot Spencer tardily emerged as the king of repeating carbines. Its tubular magazine was inserted through the butt of the stock. The trooper could carry ten extra loaded tubes, making seventy more rounds readily available.[64] In comparison with other small arms of the day the Spencer became in effect a hand machine gun; it gave the Union soldier a tremendous increase in firepower, which the Confederate could not begin to match. Even single-shot, breech-loading carbines could be procured only in limited quantities for the Gray troopers—never more than enough to arm one, perhaps two, squadrons in a regiment, with the deficiency made up by Enfield rifles.[65] When the day came for Southern cavalrymen to face the withering, rapid fire of Spencers, they dubbed them the guns "a Yank could load on Monday and shoot all the rest of the week." It was almost with a sense of hopelessness that they entered combat in the latter years of the war against Blue regiments armed with the deadly repeating carbines the South could obtain only by capture and then but few; and those served no longer than their ammunition, equally scarce, lasted.

Spencers, first tried out by the Army of the West on June 24, 1863, were not issued to the Union cavalry until shortly before the Battle of Gettysburg.[66] There in the hands of Buford's troopers they played an important part in holding the line in the initial engagement of the first day. What their firepower might have achieved had it been available at Brandy Station on June 9 becomes one of history's most interesting might-have-beens.

To be reckoned with in many cavalry combats was another weapon, which was used tellingly at Brandy Station: the cannon of the supporting horse artillery. Here again the industrial North surpassed the South by its manufacture of the best gun for the purpose, the 3-inch Ordnance Rifle. Light in weight (about 815 pounds), its six-horse teams were able to keep up with cavalry, the cannoneers being individually mounted instead of riding on carriages or running beside them as in light artillery. It fired all types of rifle ammunition, and its range with shell was about two and one-half miles. Federal 3-inchers were prized trophies; failing them, the Confederate horse artillery used whatever cannon were available, including the short-range, smoothbore Napoleons. The swift maneuver and rapid fire, which were essential, made horse artillery one of the most dashing arms of the service.

Booted and spurred, in short jackets of blue or gray, often with yellow piping, the Civil War cavalryman was a jaunty figure. For the North the forage cap was regulation; Southerners more frequently wore felt hats. The crested helmet and jacked leather cap of the Revolutionary dragoon, which might have spared many a head cut, were not revived. Troopers quickly acquired the swagger and rolling gait of cavalrymen.

Mounted, the Union horseman at first was far from a picture of martial efficiency. Loaded with regular and extra equipment, he and his mount looked like a combination of a one-man pack train and a moving arsenal. On his person he carried an over-three-foot-long saber in metal scabbard, rifle or carbine, and a revolver, a box of cartridges, another of percussion caps, a cloth-covered tin canteen and a coffee cup, a haversack for rations, plus other devices "recommended to his fancy as useful or beautiful." All that was in addition to heavy clothing, including an overcoat. The combined weight amounted to some 50 pounds.

Another 70 pounds of weight, besides the trooper's own, was heaped upon his unfortunate horse. Fastened to the saddle was the following appalling conglomeration of items:

One or (rarely) a pair of revolvers in thick leather holsters
A pair of saddlebags containing extra clothing, toilet articles, and small belongings. (*Cavalry Tactics*, 1841, republished in 1863, prescribed that the contents of the saddlebags be: pantaloons, shirts, shaving case, handkerchiefs, gloves, socks, a second pair of boots, stable jacket, and forage cap.)
A nose bag, perhaps filled with feed
A heavy leather halter
An iron picket pin with a long lariat or rope for tethering

Two horseshoes with extra nails
A currycomb and brush
A set of gun tools and cleaning materials
A rubber blanket or poncho
One or a pair of woolen blankets
Extra utensils, souvenirs, and so on
Sometimes an eight-pound armored vest

Thus accoutered and armed *cap-a-pie,* the cavalryman seemed to have derived directly from Lewis Carroll's White Knight in *Through the Looking-Glass* who strapped to his horse a deal box, beehive, mouse trap, dish for plum cake, bag of candlesticks, bunches of carrots, and fire-irons. And like the White Knight the trooper so burdened "certainly was not a good rider" but fell off in front, behind, and every now and then sidewise. "The great art of riding is to keep your balance." [67]

When the rider was in the saddle [runs an amusing comment on the Union horseman] begirt with all his magazine, it was easy to imagine him protected from any ordinary assault. His properties rose before and behind him like fortifications, and those strung over his shoulders covered well his flanks. To the uninitiated it was a mystery how the rider got into the saddle; how he could rise to sufficient height and then descend upon the seat was a problem. The irreverent infantry said it was done by the aid of a derrick, or by first climbing to the top of a high fence or the fork of a tree.[68]

Grinning Rebels, who knew better than to pile such impedimenta, even if they had owned it, on their mounts, wondered whether their Federal opposites were lifted into the saddle after the horse was packed, or whether they mounted and then had the paraphernalia festooned about them. The answer was that man and beast were loaded, and then the former was given a leg up by one or two comrades. The last man was heaved aboard by two already-mounted troopers grasping his carbine sling.

Of course, horses were unable to carry such weight for long and broke down under it. The story is told of an Irish recruit who noticed his mount's distress and decided to share the load as an act

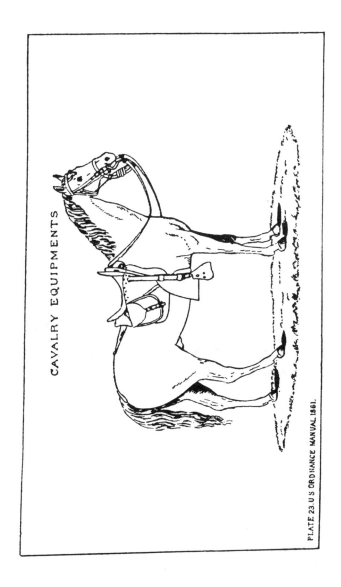

CAVALRY EQUIPMENTS

PLATE 23. U S ORDNANCE MANUAL 1861.

of mercy. He transferred nearly 100 pounds from the horse to his own shoulders, was helped into the saddle, and rode off jubilant over his unselfishness.[69]

Such surplus baggage was the folly of green recruits, and field service shortly put an end to it. "It became a fine art how to lessen the burden of the horse; and the best soldiers were those whose horses were packed so lightly that the carbine was the biggest part of the load. It was a wonder in the first campaign how a cavalryman could get onto or move his horse when equipped for the field. The wonder afterward came to be how a man could live with so meagre an equipment." [70]

The greatest and almost the sole contribution by General George B. McClellan to cavalry, his own arm of the service, was the saddle he developed and which bore his name. It was a good military saddle, so serviceable that its use by the U.S. Army, with only slight modifications, was continued through the First World War. An early fault, rawhide covering which split and galled a rider, was eliminated when it was covered by tanned leather. Confederate cavalrymen often adopted it along with other captured Union equipment. The English roundtree saddle with which many Gray troopers began the war had been pleasant and useful at home, but under campaign conditions it soon made soreback horses. Later on the government provided a saddle easier on the horse but harder on the rider. "Had the Federals been compelled to use such, the pension rolls would be much larger today for 'injuries received in the service,'" ran a caustic, postwar comment from the South.

Otherwise than the saddle he designed, McClellan, despite his tour abroad when he observed the cavalry of foreign armies in action, must be branded the evil genius of the horsemen of the Army of the Potomac from the day he first took over its command to the one when he relinquished it. That is all the more deplorable when one considers his great services as an organizer of infantry and artillery. He was always asking for more cavalry, but when he received it, he allowed the regiments to be split up into details of orderlies and escorts for himself and other general and staff officers

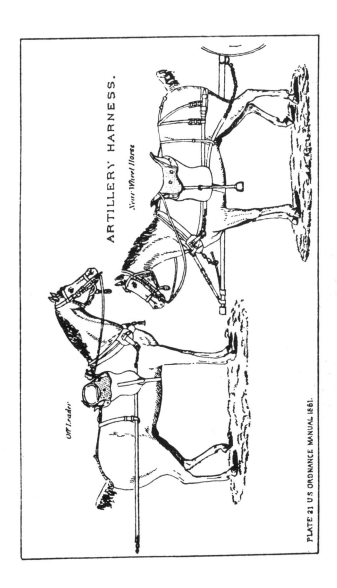

ARTILLERY HARNESS.

Near Wheel Horse

Off Leader

PLATE 21 U S ORDNANCE MANUAL 1861.

and to be scattered among corps, divisions, and brigades for use as couriers and pickets for infantry camps—for almost any purpose except those for which the arm was designed.

Smart regiments, which could furnish fine-appearing escorts, were particularly preyed upon and broken up by details, greatly to their personnel's distress, from colonel to private.[71] A whole regiment assembled was a rare sight. As orders whittled away segments from individual troopers to squads, or to complete troops, the query would run through a regiment, "Whose kite are we going to be tail to next?" [72] It is not surprising that the Confederate cavalry, whose commanders seldom stood for such practices, rode rings around or crushed forces of Federal horse, whose strength had been frittered away by detachment, or who had never served together as a body since leaving training camp.

Long overdue reorganization did not come until the winter of 1862–63, when General Joseph Hooker ordered the horsemen formed into brigades and divisions of the Cavalry Corps of the Army of the Potomac. It was high time. The Union cavalry through no fault of its own had sunk into a slough of inactivity. Hooker himself had succinctly stated the case when in November, 1862, he declared to General William W. Averell: "Well, General, we have not had many dead cavalrymen lying about lately."

The sardonic remark got around. It was picked up and flung at an arm which through late formation and constant attrition from details never had had the opportunity or capability of proving itself. "Whoever saw a dead cavalryman?" gibed weary, trudging infantry at the horsemen who rode past, spattering them with mud.

At Brandy Station both the supporting infantry on that field and Hooker were given a silencing answer when the General's cavalry chief reported 866 casualties.[73]

CHAPTER 5

Commanders and Commands

⚬⚬

If any branch of the military service is feverish, adventurous and exciting, it is the Cavalry. One's heart beats as fast as the hoof falls; there is no music like that of the bugle, and no monotone so full of meaning as the clink of sabres, rising and falling with the dashing pace. Horse and rider become one— a new race of centaurs—and the charge, the stroke, the crack of carbines are so quick, vehement and dramatic that we seem to be watching the joust of tournaments or following fierce Saladin and Crusaders again.[74]

⚬⚬

CAVALRY bred commanders as vivid as the arm itself. The Civil War leaders of horse, like their predecessors, covered a wide range, striking in contrasts. Archtypes of the flamboyant, hell-for-leather cavalryman were Jeb Stuart, Custer, and Kilpatrick; also Hampton and to a lesser extent Fitz Lee and, in his own peculiar way, the able Bedford Forrest. To that company also belonged the Confederate raider and partisan leaders, Ashby, Mosby, and Morgan. The Cromwells of the day—and it is apt to be forgotten what first-rate, hard-hitting cavalrymen were the dour Protector and his stern Ironsides troopers—were those foremost Union commanders of the arm, Sheridan and James H. Wilson, along with such subordinates as Merritt, Buford, Crook, and Mackenzie. In the same category rated the eccentric Confederate, "Grumble" Jones, but his like was as rare among the Gray horsemen as Custer's with the Blue.

Other factors besides leadership contributed to the triumph of the Ironsides over the Cavaliers, but their ultimate victory was overwhelmingly definite.

Brandy Station, in spite of the fact that some foremost leaders had not yet emerged or were engaged in other theaters, assembled an extraordinary galaxy of cavalry commanders and commands.

Jeb Stuart has ridden through countless pages of biography and history with the gallant grace he charged Yankee cavalry. He lived by the sword and lives on by the mightier strokes of the pen. Few soldiers have boasted so many ardent devotees.

West Pointer and Indian fighter. His father-in-law, General Philip St. George Cooke, had remained loyal to the Union instead of joining his native Virginia. The resentful son-in-law yearned to capture the General and would have escorted him to a Southern prison with courtly deference barely cloaking a sense of justice triumphant.

Plumed hat, flaring russet beard, scarlet-lined cloak, superb horsemanship. Surprised at Verdiersville by enemy cavalry, he vaulted into the saddle of his unbridled bay hunter, grazing in a yard, leaped the fence, and escaped. He sometimes carried his two setters, Nip and Tuck, on the back of one of his spirited chargers. Such a rider, whose mount was indeed his "second self," could give full attention to command and combat.

He loved praise and often merited it. Criticism hurt him, and the strictures he met after Brandy Station sorely rankled. No man delighted more in the admiration of fair ladies and to none was it more gladly given—adulation bestowed and received *sans reproche* by the dashing cavalryman whose devoted fidelity to his wife was unquestionable.

Dancing and festivities at any opportunity. Music wherever he went. Bands—his ringing baritone leading songs—the lively twanging of his banjo player, Sam Sweeney, in camp or on the march.[75] Stuart had ranked Sweeney away from his regimental commander. Tunes rippled from his slung banjo—"Dixie," "Jine the Cavalry," "Alabama

Gals," "Oh, Johnny Booker," "Sweet Evelina," "Old Gray Horse"—
they carried Stuart [76] and his troopers through many a campaign. By
his gaieties and music Jeb Stuart relieved the grim business of
warfare with a spontaneity that the organized efforts in later conflicts could never match.

Fond of pomp and panoply Stuart pre-eminently was. But, as did
many other commanders worth their salt before and since Napoleon,
he knew the value to *esprit de corps*. While there was more than a
little vainglory in his showmanship, one can understand his pride
in parading the valiant striking force he had wrought. At times
his love of display passed the bounds of prudence. In the second
of his magnificent reviews at Brandy Station, staged because
General Lee had not been able to be present at the first one, Lee
forbade the gallop past ordered by Stuart, since the horses must be
spared for the hard campaign ahead. Yet the galloping and sham
battling of the first review and the spit-and-polish of both had ex-
acted a toll. Stuart and his troopers were tired and less alert than
usual when Union cavalry crossed the Rappahannock fords at dawn
on June 9, 1863.

J. E. B. Stuart nevertheless ranks high among the great leaders of
horse. It was not his famous raids that built that reputation. His ride
around McClellan's army in 1862 was effective against Federal
morale, but the dent its destruction of supplies made in the Union's
plenty has been described as no more serious than "missing a
second helping of ice cream at Sunday dinner." The circuit around
the Army of the Potomac that kept him from Gettysburg until
late on the second day stands forever as a blot on a bright record.
Elsewhere he excelled as a combat commander, brilliantly fulfilling
cavalry's missions of screening, reconnaissance, and frequent reports
to superiors. His use of his supporting horse artillery, especially
while the gallant Pelham lived to lead it, was notable. At Chancellorsville after the death of Jackson, Stuart took over and commanded Stonewall's corps with high competence.

"He never brought me a piece of false information," was Lee's
glowing epitaph for Stuart. Never uttered was a sequel the Gray

General might have sadly added: At Gettysburg, when I urgently needed information, he was not there to bring it.

Stuart's opposite number at Brandy Station was Alfred Pleasonton, the newly-made commander of the recently organized Union Cavalry Corps. It would be hard to find two more contrasting leaders. West Point, Class of 1844, Pleasonton had served with gallantry as a dragoon officer in the War with Mexico and against the Sioux and Seminoles. A neat, soldierly man, his grave face mustached, he and glamour were utter strangers.

Some of his subordinates said hard things of him, calling him "the *bête noire* of all cavalry officers," "pure and simple a newspaper humbug," [77] which was a great deal less than fair. The fact was that he did not possess the spark and drive a cavalry commander for the Army of the Potomac so gravely needed. No more did his predecessor, Stoneman. One such had been ready to hand in Phil Kearny, but he had been killed at Chantilly while leading an infantry division.[78] The Union cavalry, though it steadily improved under Pleasonton's leadership, had to wait for Sheridan to achieve superiority.[79]

Probably the best estimate of Pleasonton was that of his opponent, Jeb Stuart, who characterized him as a good-looking and fairly able soldier, lacking a bit in the fighting capacity for rough-and-tumble cavalry operations. Precisely that tough quality was demanded at Brandy Station. Granted it, a successful reconnaissance in force might have turned from a drawn battle into a victory.

They who led divisions or brigades of cavalry at Brandy Station rode with pride, the pride inspired by commanding a long column of cavalry. It was a glittering rapier in a man's grasp, flexible and deadly—his to feint with, to parry, and thrust home.

General Wade Hampton, South Carolina planter turned soldier, remained the *grand seigneur,* a lord of the manor in uniform. The Confederacy owed much to his patriotism for the troops he raised and considerably equipped at his own expense. He often provided for destitute families of men of his commands. His qualities of leadership would carry through the war into the trying period of reconstruction to make him Governor of his state, then United States Senator.

A handsome, bearded man with "the air of a great gentleman of an elder time." A six-footer so powerfully built that he looked larger. The power of his legs, if he chose to grip a horse's barrel hard, could make the animal groan with pain. He mightily wielded a straight, two-edged sword fully forty inches long; only the famous blade of the Prussian officer, Heros von Borcke, was longer.

Hampton's fault as a leader was a mania for personal combat, the pure love of a man-to-man fight that could make him forget the duties of command. Before the war he hunted and killed bears with a knife only. Froissart and Malory would have delighted to chronicle his exploits as a swordsman—how he rose in his stirrups, towering above an enemy horseman. His heavy blade hewed with all his great strength behind it, beat down parrying saber as if it were a straw, clove his adversary to the brain. He was famous for that frequent feat: splitting skulls from crown to chin with one blow. To face so formidable a warrior demanded high courage of Yankee cavalrymen, and more than a few dared. At Gettysburg Hampton was the victim of his own favorite stroke when he was charged from behind and took a saber gash in the scalp. The blow lacked his might; he was patched up and rode back into action. In mêlée he was cut twice more in the same place. Blinded with blood, he leaped his mount over a fence to escape besetting enemy. As he soared over the rails, a shrapnel ball struck him in the side. Only then was he forced to quit the field.

Chivalry mingled with ferocity in this leader, who was a crack shot as well as a *beau sabreur*. It was on the march to Gettysburg that Hampton engaged in a duel with a Union cavalryman, revolver against carbine. Both missed in the first exchange. In the second the trooper's bullet ripped Hampton's cape and grazed his chest, but the former had trouble reloading and lifted his hand as if asking a truce. With the courtly tactics of Fontenoy—"Gentlemen of France, fire first"—Hampton raised the muzzle of his weapon and waited. When his opponent was ready, they fired again. The Confederate's bullet shattered the trooper's wrist, extraordinary revolver shooting at a range of 125 yards. The wounded man ran for the woods, and Hampton let him go.[80]

Between Hampton and Fitzhugh Lee, Robert E.'s nephew, lay a certain rivalry. The latter was Jeb Stuart's favorite brigadier, perhaps because the Corps Commander and the South Carolinian were cast too nearly in the same mold. Fitz Lee, with service against the Indians and a detail as instructor in cavalry at West Point, possessed high competence in the arm, dash, and the fighting spirit. "Ladies languished over the jingle of his spurs and ambrosial whiskers." A vigorous man, still in his twenties, he fought through the war, finally commanding the cavalry of the Army of Northern Virginia. In the Spanish-American War he donned the blue again as a major general, one of four Civil War cavalry officers to return to serve in a conflict of more than three decades later.[81]

Tall W. H. F. ("Rooney") Lee was a brave and able cavalryman who deserved more acclaim than he received, for he rode always in the shadow of his great father. When he was wounded at Brandy Station, his brigade was taken over by the less competent Chambliss. The two remaining brigades were led by Beverly Robertson and W. E. ("Grumble") Jones. Both were strict disciplinarians who paid for it in the free-and-easy Confederate service by being defeated for re-election as colonels of their regiments by rank and file unwilling to be ordered around. To continue to make use of their abilities the War Department had to transfer them to other commands. Robertson with his "unsmiling eyes" and "Grumble" Jones, who lived up to his nickname, were objects of Jeb Stuart's hearty dislike and they returned it.

Jones, Stuart's antithesis, was irascible, profane, and contemptuous of all display. The Zach Taylor of the Civil War, he disdained uniform and wore blue jeans, a hickory shirt, and a threadbare homespun coat with shoulder straps sewed on. Only his soldierly qualities indicated his West Point background. Before the war he had resigned from the army and gone to live in the Virginia mountains where, after the death of his wife, he became a recluse until his state's call brought him back to army service. "He could not get along with anybody, could not get along with himself." Yet he was a first-rate cavalryman who looked after his men well and, like them, slept on the ground, wrapped in a piece of oilcloth. Some months after Brandy Station he was court-martialed by Stuart for using disrespectful language to a superior officer and transferred to independent command in southwest Virginia. He was killed in action in the fall of 1864.

In the Union Cavalry Corps John Buford led the 1st Division. The fact that he was clean-shaven except for a mustache brought out the firm lines of a fighter's jaw, inheritance of a long line of soldiers, dating back to the wars of the Scottish border. A fine cavalryman, more tenacious than brilliant, he shone as a master of dismounted tactics. Two of the three brigades under him were led by Colonel Thomas C. Devin, a fighting Irishman who looked like a taller edition of Sheridan, and Major Charles J. Whiting. Over his first brigade Buford had a veteran officer who bore the scar of a wound from a fight with the Apaches in 1857. Colonel Benjamin Franklin Davis had trained the 8th New York Cavalry. When Harper's Ferry was about to surrender to Stonewall Jackson in 1862, Davis had led the 8th and three other regiments out by night and cut a way through enemy troops, capturing a wagon train and 100 prisoners en route. It was said of "Grimes" Davis that he would go far as a cavalry leader, but for him Brandy Station would prove to be the end of the road.

Colonel Alfred N. Duffié, 2nd Division, seemed to have stepped straight out of a French military print. He was a graduate of St. Cyr, had campaigned in North Africa, the Crimea, and Austria, and come to the United States in 1860. As an experienced foreign soldier, his offer of his services had been eagerly accepted by the Union and had proved useful in training the 2nd New York Cavalry. Before battle he dramatically exhorted his men in strongly French-accented English; they smothered laughs but followed. Duffié led with the dash of Murat but without the punch.

One of his brigades was commanded by Colonel J. Irvin Gregg, the second by another foreigner, Colonel Luigi P. di Cesnola. Like Duffié he was a Crimean War veteran. He emigrated in 1860 to New York, where he founded a military school for officers with a student body of 700, then trained cavalry regiments. Dearly loving a fight, his valor won him a Medal of Honor. Soon after Brandy Station he was captured and confined for a year to Libby Prison. On release he returned to duty and won a brigadier generalcy.[82]

General David McMurtrie Gregg, 3rd Division, was another veteran of the Indian wars. It was partly his patriarchal beard but more his awesome dignity that lent him the aspect of an Old Testament prophet who had chosen to discard flowing robes for a blue uniform. To young officers reporting that they thought such-and-such was the case, he would sternly reply: "You should not think, sir, you should know. Go back and find out." His coolness in action emphasized that immense dignity of his. More would have been heard of him if he had not taken such pains to keep out of the newspapers with his stern refusal of any publicity: "I do not propose to have a picture reputation."

Gregg's two brigade leaders, Colonel Judson Kilpatrick and Sir Percy Wyndham, seemed to have been picked as perfect foils to their commander.

Rakish Kilpatrick, with the cavalryman's swagger afoot or in the saddle, had been noted for his speeches at West Point and kept on making them in the field. Yet, when after a harangue he ordered a charge in a voice like a trumpet, he usually led it, grim mouth set, pale eyes flashing. His gingery sidewhiskers flared like his temper, and his tongue could lash like a whip. Men admired or hated him. His light, wiry frame was apparently tireless. Though he asked no more of his troopers than of himself, his demands were often too heavy on men and horses. Long marches and raids, headlong charges and rallies, gave him the nickname of "Kill-Cavalry"; deserved or not, it stuck.[83] With devil-take-the-hindmost abandon, he fought war to the hilt.

Truly a soldier of fortune was Colonel Sir Percy Wyndham, son of a British peer and cavalry officer. Few have fought in so many wars and in so many different arms and branches of various armies.

At fifteen he joined a students' corps in Paris and took part in the French revolution of 1848. He transferred to the navy with the rank of ensign, then to the marines. His next choice was the English artillery, followed by a commission in the Austrian lancers, where he rose to squadron command. A prospect of more action led him to resign and enter the Italian army. From the battles of Garibaldi's campaigns he emerged as a brigadier with decorations and a knighthood.

Inevitably the Civil War drew him across the Atlantic. Appointed colonel of the 1st New Jersey Cavalry, he molded it into a fine fighting unit and led it through a long series of scouts, raids, and battles. It was part of his brigade at Brandy Station, and there he suffered the severe wound that forced his mustering out. The remainder of his extraordinary record included: running a military school in New York City; more fighting in European armies; various unfortunate business enterprises ranging from oil in the United States, a comic magazine in Calcutta, Italian opera, lumber in Mandalay, to cotton in Burma. Reduced to poverty by successive failures, he pawned his jewels and decorations to pay his debts. His final fling was the construction of a large balloon in 1879. Its ascension attracted great crowds, but Wyndham, manning it, did not live to collect. At 300 feet it burst over a lake, and the old soldier, who had survived scores of battles, drowned. "Thus ended a singular and adventurous career." [84]

Two able generals, Adelbert Ames and David A. Russell, led the Union infantry brigades supporting the cavalry at Brandy Station.

The part played by commanders of the horse artillery batteries on both sides has been neglected, except by one historian,[85] in accounts of the battle, as was also the case with the gunners at Gettysburg,[86] notwithstanding the fact that the guns at Brandy Station were splendidly served and became focal points of the fiercest conflict.

One cannot avoid summoning up a departed spirit and speculating how the fortunes of war on June 9, 1863, might have been swayed had John Pelham lived to command the Stuart Horse

Artillery then. For Pelham's wraith hovers over battles he did not survive to fight only less persistently than Stonewall Jackson's. On the talented gunner's record stood such exploits as that at Fredericksburg, when with the one remaining gun of his battery he had held up the advance of Burnside's army for almost an hour; and that was but one of his gallant feats. Fellow artillerymen can picture him in action at Brandy Station. "He would have wandered around Fleetwood Hill—appearing in a dozen positions—and he would have secured his ammunition somehow. He had a winning disposition—enough to get a few extra rounds out of anybody's combat wagons." [87] But three months earlier on the same battleground Pelham had been unable to resist taking part in a cavalry charge and had fallen, mortally wounded.[88]

Although the guns he had commanded did not prevent the crossing of the Rappahannock fords in June, other gunners in gray fought them well under Major R. F. Beckham. And the high traditions of the Federal horse artillery were upheld by Pennington, Martin, and others.

The foot soldier is ever by himself, two-legged, alone. If he wishes, he may flee. What saves cavalry and makes it the most terrible and majestic of military arms is nothing more than formation. To each man's stature is added the height and weight of his mount. He is six-legged, he stands twenty-four hands high, he weighs a thousand pounds. He is merged in mass and movement. The self he finds, frighteningly, before battle, is lost. He is a creature without choice. If he reins in, he is run down.[89]

That massive might and cohesive compulsion combined to engender in cavalry regiments a pride of body, true *esprit de corps*. In some of the Union regiments it had been inherent from the first. Others had only recently developed it, when they were given the chance to serve as a unit instead of being hamstrung by details and detachments.

The unsung Regulars, hard core of the Blue cavalry from the start, possessed that spirit as a birthright. All told, there were only six regiments of them, and four, the 1st, 2nd, 5th, and 6th, fought at Brandy Station, grouped in Whiting's brigade. The first two boasted heritage from the old Dragoons. Plains dust still figuratively whitened their blue uniforms, and for them the Rebel yell was an echo of the Indian warwhoop. On the record of the 2nd U.S. Cavalry, which had been stationed in the South in 1861, stood its refusal of surrender and its long march northward to join Lincoln's army.

The 2nd New York Cavalry, composed not only of New Yorkers but of men from New Jersey, Connecticut, and Indiana, clung to its name of The Harris Light, no doubt to the gratification of Senator Ira Harris of New York. The Senator had helped raise it and, animated by no passion for anonymity, had presented it with a flag bearing his likeness and inscribed "Harris Light Cavalry." Happily the regiment did him proud. The legislator also had a part in the mustering of the 6th New York Cavalry, originally designated the Ira Harris Guards.

A winter under canvas in its native state had at the outset toughened the already durable fiber of the 1st Maine Cavalry. Its seafaring contingent had learned to maneuver their mounts as handily as a dory in a squall. It had not been long in winning rare acclaim from one of the foreign observers, frequently critical of the Yankee horse. "Much of the Federal cavalry was wretchedly made up," he wrote, "but there was a Maine regiment of long-armed swordsmen, whose equals I have never seen." [90] The 1st Maine was known for its fighting quality and its discipline. Soon after its organization its officers and non-coms had signed a pledge of abstinence from the use of intoxicating liquors as a beverage, a pledge that, its chaplain declared,[91] was not sacredly kept by every man but by "numbers." The regiment is said never to have drawn its spirits ration and once refused to accept from an undoubtedly astounded commissary officer a barrel of liquor he had brought thirty miles.

In the case of the 8th Illinois Cavalry the Demon Rum is accused of having drawn first blood. Soon after its organization, ladies bestowed upon it a handsome silk flag that, no sooner unfurled, was torn in half by a gust of wind. Presented at the same time was the somewhat ominous gift of a large box of bandages. One of them was shortly needed when a member of the provost guard cut a hand while destroying a barrel of liquor about to be sold to recruits. A regiment with not a few devout members, the 8th Illinois. At Brandy Station alone two of its troopers suffered a frequently reported Civil War injury: they were "wounded in the Testament." That is, bullets struck the small Bibles they carried in a pocket over their hearts, knocked them down, but otherwise did not harm them.[92]

A credit to its state and the Army of the Potomac was the 1st Massachusetts Cavalry, a regiment with fighting spirit and considerable stamina. After it eliminated the system of electing officers, one of the first units to do so, it was well led. It waged war with the grim severity of a New England conscience. Somewhat symbolic was the presentation by a lady to one of its officers of a pair of socks with the Rebel flag embroidered on their bottoms "so that he could easily tread it under foot." [93]

With equal fervor it was said of another New England regiment, the 1st Rhode Island Cavalry, that on its first campaign in the South it "sniffed the tainted air of Secession." Its historian poetically described its organization:

> Little Rhode Island lifted her guidons, and brave spirits rallied to her recruiting station in Providence. As her territory was small, though her heart was not thus circumscribed, many from the borders of Maine and Connecticut, with a passion for saddles and bridles, sought admission to the cavalier command. Meanwhile the bugles in the White Mountains, answer to the bugles on the shores of Narragansett, called out a splendid battalion, superbly mounted and finely furnished, in their rendezvous at Concord. A peculiar class of men—patriotic spirits and dash, fire, fortitude, and endurance—elected this swift and ardous arm of the service.[94]

The rigors of strict training by Colonel Duffié drove the independent New Englanders to the verge of mutiny, and their officers offered to resign, but in two weeks hot resentment gave way to admiration for the Frenchman who was forging it into a keen weapon. Fortunate, too, in its training was the 1st New Jersey Cavalry. The veteran English soldier, Wyndham, moved its camp out of the mud, released many members from the guardhouse, and taught it to drill, take care of itself, and fight. Only once did the 1st relax briefly. When it occupied a Virginia plantation, freed Negroes flocked to camp. Every New Jersey trooper, though for two days only, enjoyed the luxury accorded some of his Southern counterparts: a body servant and groom.[95]

Among the Pennsylvania regiments, memory of the 6th's misadventures with the lance clung, though it had discarded that weapon long before Brandy Station. Maine cavalrymen called the 6th "turkey-stickers."

Early equipment difficulties had long hampered the 3rd Indiana. Without an issue of saddles, it had resorted to grain sacks stuffed with straw, clothesline stirrups, and halters and tie ropes as bridles. The ideal target for its foot-long, dragoon "horse pistols" was said to be a good-sized barn. Surmounting such early obstacles had made it into the hard-riding, hard-fighting regiment it was.

Before Brandy Station the 10th New York Cavalry foraged a grindstone, and most of its troopers spent a day putting sharp edges on their sabers. There were a few, however, who had heard that the rules of war dictated that soldiers captured with sharpened swords be summarily shot. Those gullibles left their sabers "as dull as their comprehension."[96]

Thirteen of Virginia's forty regiments of horse, plus a battalion, fought at Brandy Station. Attrition had whittled them down from the 650 effectives, first mustered by the strongest units, to from 350 to 500 by 1863. They were fine cavalrymen, still for the most part well mounted. The 1st Virginia, organized by Jeb Stuart, had forgotten its early resentment against the stern training of its fussy West Pointer colonel; it knew now that it was he who had made it into the first-rate regiment it was. It did not matter that the Black Horse Troop of the 4th Virginia had lost the complete uniformity of the color of its mounts. It had created a legend that still lived. Gone, too, was the pride in apparel which had once characterized the 7th Virginia. When its homespun-clad colonel, "Grumble" Jones, furnished it with cheap, coarse clothing obtained from a state penitentiary, insulted troopers had marched in a body to their commander's headquarters and indignantly flung the stuff down in a heap in front of his tent. Now it wore anything it could get. No longer were there any dandies in the 2nd Virginia. Forgotten were the fancy uniforms once worn by the Botecourt Dragoons, which had formed its Company C. The regiment had lost the neat little pincushions, well supplied with pins and needles, which had been presented by ladies when it went to war. It had long since used up another gift made at the same time: bandages and hospital necessities. Its commander's Negro body-servant still was called "The Colonel's Cup-bearer," although these days the cup was filled usually with branch water only.[97]

Among the fine formations from farther south were regiments that bore the old Roman designation, legion, revived under Anthony Wayne in the post-Revolutionary American army: the Jeff Davis Legion of Mississippi, the Cobb Legion of Georgia. Others, which were numbered, were the South Carolina units raised by Wade Hampton and those from North Carolina, brought by Beverly Robertson. Their deeds would be preserved mostly by letters, diaries, and the memories of men. In the South defeat and impoverishment hampered regimental historians, who flourished in the North.[98]

A certain cavalry officer at Brandy Station, though he held no command but served on Stuart's staff, merits special mention. Johann August Heinrich Heros von Borcke became one of the chief chroniclers of the battle and a legend in the Confederate Army.

Son of a Prussian infantry officer, he was given a small horse when he was ten and taught fencing. He grew to a towering 6-foot-4 and was commissioned in the Cuirassiers of the Guard. When the Civil War began, he followed the path to America his countryman, Steuben, had taken in the Revolution. Von Borcke, also a good drillmaster, was welcomed in the Gray cavalry. Jeb Stuart drew him like a magnet. The huge Prussian became the cavalry leader's aide, courier, shadow, and master of revels. Much of the gaiety of Stuart's headquarters was staged by the jolly giant—dances, skits, and *tableaux vivants* in which he loved to pose prone as Tyranny, with a pretty girl's tiny foot on his neck.

In combat, looming high on one of the large horses needed to carry his weight, he was formidable. While his exploits were not as frequent and as full of derring-do as he related them, they were not far from it. He wielded a saber of prodigious length, two-edged, and of excellently tempered Damascus steel, always at his side day or night. Once a rattlesnake woke him crawling over his hand. It reared its head and whirred; evidently, he decided, it "meant mischief." With a lightning motion he whipped out his blade and "severed the reptile in twain." That great saber, swung by "Major Armstrong" as they called him, could as easily, and often did, slice through an opponent's sword arm. A few days after the June battle at Brandy Station enemy fire found the fine target the big man furnished. Then a sharpshooter's bullet pierced his neck, inflicting a wound from which he never fully recovered, though he persisted in returning to action.

A first-class fighting man, Heros von Borcke, for all his bravado. It was familiar ground he rode over on that June day of 1863, and he recalled it in his grandiloquent way when he rallied broken troopers in gray.

" 'Men,' I shouted, 'remember the previous deeds on these very fields. Follow me! Charge!' " [99]

CHAPTER 6

"On These Very Fields"

M AJOR VON BORCKE's shout at the June 9, 1863, Battle of
Brandy Station was a good rallying cry. Surely Jeb Stuart's
troopers grinned at the heavy German accent in which it was delivered, but there was inspiration in the memory of past victories
"on these very fields."

It was on August 20, 1862, that Brandy Station had first fulfilled
its destiny as a battleground.

Lee had defeated McClellan in the Seven Days Battle, blunting
his stab at Richmond. With the rest of Virginia perforce left unguarded, a second Union army of 45,000 under General John Pope
had penetrated beyond the town of Culpeper. Early in August
Lee detached Stonewall Jackson with 24,000 to meet the threat. They
attacked part of Pope's force at Cedar Mountain and drove it northward. Meanwhile orders from Washington had pulled back the
protesting McClellan to unite his troops with Pope's. The strategy
of Lee, following Jackson, was to strike and overwhelm Pope before
the junction of the Federal armies could be effected. Although Pope
was warned by captured copies of Lee's orders and had been considerably reinforced, the Confederate attack with forces daringly
divided would result in the smashing triumph of Second Manassas
or Bull Run.

For that battle the first fight at Brandy Station was a curtain-
raiser, as it was for following engagements on the ground
around Fleetwood Hill.[100] It introduced dramatis personae who
would reappear, characters that would have their entrances and
their exits, some of the latter permanent ones. Now the fields were

first salted with blood and strewn with their first increment of the debris of combat: bits of broken weapons, cast-off equipment, shell fragments, and bullets. Reports began those repeated references to the little railroad town that would make Brandy Station one of the great war names.

August 20 was a hot, dry day. Cavalry squadrons kicked up the dust on the roads, as Jackson's advance guard pressed Pope's retreating Federals. Jeb Stuart led, a new plumed hat sitting stiffly and somewhat self-consciously on his head. As has been mentioned, he had lost the old one, plus his scarlet-lined cloak, when some of Duffié's Blue horsemen surprised him in a farmhouse at Verdiersville. Stuart, who prided himself on being on the other end of surprises, was out today to expunge an unpleasant recollection. He would have preferred other troops for the purpose than those that followed him, for the advance consisted of Robertson's brigade: the 17th Virginia Battalion and the 2nd, 12th, and 7th Virginia Regiments, the last commanded by Colonel "Grumble" Jones. Stuart's dislike for Robertson and Jones was as patent as his fondness for Fitz Lee and von Borcke. Nevertheless he left the brigade in Robertson's hands and retained general direction only. The column crossed the Rapidan, dropped off the 2nd Virginia to guard its upper fords, and pushed ahead.

Blue horse of Pope's rear guard fell back on Brandy Station. Doubtless troopers scanned the sign on the railroad depot and licked parched lips, wondering if there was any good reason around for the name. General George D. Bayard had five regiments: 1st Maine, 1st New Jersey, 2nd New York or "The Harris Light," 1st Pennsylvania, and 1st Rhode Island. Weary men stood to horses after a brief bivouac. They were learning that Stonewall Jackson seldom allowed his opponents a rest.

Dust clouds on the roads to the southeast emphasized that fact. Trumpets signaled, "Mount." Regiments formed in deep echelon in the open country between Stevensburg and Hazel Run. Their artillery opened on the approaching enemy, and Bayard sent dismounted skirmishers forward into the woods.

A Rebel charge came whooping down. Skirmishers scattered and ran frantically for their mounts, being held in defilade, three to a horseholder. That gloomy, hard fighter, "Grumble" Jones, and his 7th Virginia hit Kilpatrick's 2nd New York and broke it. Lieutenant Colonel Joseph Kargé waved his saber to lead his Jerseymen in a countercharge, but there was no iron yet in the regiment. It wheeled, ran, and let its commander and his adjutant gallop alone into the ranks of the enemy, with the former taking a leg wound before they could fight their way out. The other regiments still held. Stuart sent Robertson's squadrons circling around to their right rear. Though they missed the road, a courier brought them back onto it, and in succession the 6th and 12th Virginia and the 17th Battalion rode down on the Union flank. Bayard's men did not wait to cross sabers with them but galloped back under cover of their guns, emplaced across the Rappahannock. Fitz Lee's cavalry and Pelham's artillery, having driven Buford before them, were close to Kelly's Ford now. The Blue horsemen's only salvation was to get across the river fast, which they did. Defeated, with far heavier loss in casualties and prisoners than the enemy, they had at least covered the crossing of the wagons and artillery and given General Pope a breathing spell until Bull Run.

For the Union cavalry it had been the same old story. They had been outgeneraled and outfought. Bayard, who would be mortally wounded at Fredericksburg the following December, was not the leader they needed. Regiments, still suffering from inadequate training and the old policies of misuse of cavalry, failed in the test of combat. A time of redemption and vindication must wait for another ten months.[101]

At Brandy Station the Confederate cavalry, gathering itself for further pursuit, celebrated another of a long string of victories. Stuart fair-mindedly commended both Robertson and Jones, whose 7th Virginia had borne the brunt of the fight. With the *sang-froid* of the Prussian cuirassier he had been, huge Major von Borcke wiped his bloody blade on his horse's mane. "These very fields" were indeed worth remembering. Yankee newspapers, picked up later in the campaign, would concede as much to the enemy. They described, as the redoubtable Heros relished quoting in his memoirs, a Rebel charge "led by a giant, mounted on a tremendous horse, and brandishing wildly over his head a sword as long and big as a fence rail." And the giant's prowess won him a citation by the brigade commander for gallantry in action.

The Brandy Station countryside seldom remained peaceful for long. Clashes of sabers, shots, and trumpet calls, with the agonized shrillings of wounded horses and the more muted cries of wounded men, faded away into stillness, only to be soon revived as redoubled echoes. Waters of the Rappahannock fords, running clear for a time, were muddied again by the hoofs of cavalry mounts and wheels of artillery carriages.

Confederate pickets never left those fords unguarded. Wade Hampton's brigade, standing vigilant sentinel over them, was relieved in the late winter of 1862–1863 by Fitz Lee's, riding up from its camp at Culpeper Courthouse. Robert E. Lee's belligerent nephew, not content with sentry duty alone, took his men over the river at Kelly's Ford and made a swift foray against the enemy cavalry. He caught them unready in the vicinity of Hartwood Church and hit them hard.

For the blue-jacketed cavalrymen it was again the old, dispiriting tale. They had not been sufficiently taught that rudiment of soldiering, alertness. Nor were they able to hold their ground, especially in a surprise attack, against adversaries who had whipped them so often. The Black Horse Troop and its legend still rode. As many of the Federals as could gallop out of the trap fled all the way back to the camps of the V Corps. They left 150 prisoners and a quantity of much-needed horses, forage, and equipment in the hands of Fitz Lee's jubilant troopers.

The smart of defeat provoked orders for retaliation. General William Averell was directed to take his brigade across the Rappahannock and "attack and rout or destroy" the impudent enemy. Detaching 900 men to fend off Rebel patrols north of the river, Averell on March 17 decended on Kelly's Ford [102] with 2,100 men and a battery of horse artillery and drove off the Gray pickets. Although the river was high and swift from spring freshets, it was fordable by horsemen but would submerge the artillery carriages. The Union gunners, more enterprising and efficient from the outset than the cavalry they supported, promptly removed powder charges from the chests and distributed them to the troopers, who carried them across dry in their horses' nosebags, probably slung by their headstalls from the men's necks.[103] Averell, safely over, deployed his line in the fields and woods, with odds of three to one in his favor against any force the enemy could immediately bring up.

He did not have to wait long for Fitz Lee, who came hurrying up from Culpeper Courthouse. His leading regiment charged in column of fours, revolvers spitting. The Blue defense recoiled, and reserves were hastily thrown in to bolster it.

Conflict swayed back and forth. General Stuart and Major John Pelham of his horse artillery, who had been attending a court-martial at Culpeper, galloped toward the sound of the guns. The gallant young gunner officer, whose exploits were famed in both armies, aided Captain Breathed in finding a good position for his battery, then rode toward the cavalry squadrons. A glimpse of the 2nd Virginia, wheeling into line for a charge, was more than he could resist. He spurred his horse and joined the regiment's colonel at its head. Boyish face alight with the joy of battle, he waved his hat and shouted, "Forward, boys! Forward to victory and glory!"

More than a few times Pelham had led his horse artillery in charges, unusual for that arm. There was no need now for him to take part in the onslaught of a well-led cavalry regiment. Certainly if Stuart had been close enough, he would have peremptorily ordered his daring subordinate back. Pelham's life, frequently risked in line of duty, was too precious to the Confederacy to be needlessly hazarded.

A shell exploded over him. Struck by a fragment in the back of his head, he toppled mortally wounded from his mount. A trooper broke ranks, dismounted, and with an officer's help lifted the unconscious young gunner up in front of his saddle pommel, mounted, and escaped from the enemy, who were closing in. Future battles on this ground must be fought without the gallant Pelham's superb handling of the guns of the horse artillery.[104] Fitz Lee, falling back before Averell's superior numbers, formed a line across the road from Brandy Station to Kelly's Ford, a broad, open field in its front. As Blue cavalry advanced over it, the four guns of Breathed's Battery raked it, sounding Pelham's requiem. Their fire lifted to let the impetuous Fitz launch a charge that swept away the defenders and thundered down on their artillery despite a hail of shrapnel and double-shotted canister. It overran and drove off the crews, and only a counterattack saved the pieces from capture. Averell's trumpeters sounded familiar signals for a retreat.

April, 1863, and more brisk fights on and around the now famous plateau. They were postludes to Fredericksburg and preludes to Chancellorsville, both smashing Confederate victories. Yet so far as cavalry was concerned, the scales, weighted so long in favor of the Gray, were beginning to tip slightly toward a balance point. Stuart's Corps had endured a winter of hardships and deprivation. Its men went hungry and ragged. Sickness and poor forage had whittled down its horses, and remounts were scarce or unobtainable. "Company Q," that melancholy organization of dismounted cavalrymen, was growing. One squadron of the 2nd North Carolina would use 143 horseless troopers, not yet relegated to the infantry, as supports in the forthcoming action.

Hard service was teaching the Union cavalry. Its mounts, like the enemy's, had been depleted by glanders and greased heel, by the casualties of Fredericksburg, and the rigors of the Mud March, but replacements came in steadily. General George Stoneman led it now. No more than Bayard had been was he the talented commander the arm required; however, he was fortunate in having under him such able brigadiers as Buford and Gregg. And at long last the Blue horse was about to be given the attention it deserved from headquarters. General Joseph Hooker, commanding the Army of the Potomac since Fredericksburg, was planning reorganization into a Cavalry Corps, but that reformation would not become effective until a short time before the June Brandy Station Battle.

That April saw heavy rainfalls which turned roads into quagmires, sucking at the hoofs of tiring horses and slowing marches. Fog cloaked the fields and the fords of the Rappahannock and the

Rapidan. Cavalry columns of both sides groped through the mist, feeling for contact with the enemy. The eerie white curtain seemed more menacing than night's black one, whose opacity was so often relieved by moonlight. As Hooker's campaign was launched, Stoneman was ordered to pave its way by forcing the Rappahannock fords. He was then to strike for the Virginia Central Railroad, destroying as much of its tracks as he could, while the Gray horse was drawn after him. Hooker would then cross the river and turn the Confederate lines at Fredericksburg where Burnside's assaults had been shattered last December. That would compel Lee to retreat, finding Stoneman blocking roads and burning bridges in his rear—delaying him until Hooker could catch and crush him.

Through the latter half of the month the Federal cavalry attempted to perform its part of the plan. Stoneman marched from Warrenton Junction with Averell's, Buford's, and Gregg's divisions, leaving Pleasonton's three brigades to serve the main army. Buford rode down on Kelly's Ford where sharpshooters of the 9th Virginia Cavalry and one gun of Moorman's horse battery beat him off. Meanwhile Gregg tried to cross at Rappahannock Station upstream and met with the same fate. Another detachment of the 9th Virginia in a blockhouse joined with the 2nd North Carolina, supported by a long-range Whitworth breechloader, in battering him back. Stuart did not need to bring up his reserves.

Buford thrust at the Rappahannock Station railroad bridge April 15, with Gregg managing to cross some of his command at Welford's Ford whence they turned the flank of the defense at Beverly's. For a time the way was open. But Stoneman was slow in following up the break, and Rooney Lee was prompt in countering it with his 9th and 13th Virginia. In a sharp fight they drove the Blue cavalry back across the river with losses in men and horses.

The river rose higher, its fords swimming deep. Stoneman waited in bafflement for eleven days until the waters subsided. Then at last he got 6,700 sabers across. On April 29 slashing troopers galloped down on the outnumbered squadrons of Rooney and Fitz Lee around Brandy Station. This time the cavalrymen in gray could not hold them. They fell back, and the Army of the Potomac crossed the river on pontoon bridges and pushed on to Chancellorsville.

Stoneman was loose for his raid now. He led the bulk of the Union cavalry south, tearing up railroad tracks and cutting telegraph lines. He would not rejoin the army until after the campaign, failing to receive expected orders to do so.[105] Destruction wrought could not compensate for his absence. It left Pleasonton's three small brigades, with one battery of horse artillery, to screen Hooker's advance, and they could cover only the front. Jeb Stuart's hovering horsemen scouted the Blue columns, capturing prisoners and identifying three corps and harrying the flanks.

The great victory for the Confederacy at Chancellorsville was dimmed by its irreparable loss of Stonewall Jackson, mortally wounded by the fire of his own troops at dusk in the woods. So far as cavalry was concerned, it saw a number of sharp actions: gallant charges by the 6th New York and the 8th and 17th Pennsylvania and a fine stand by Martin's 6th New York horse battery. The Gray cavalry bore itself with its accustomed valor but suffered a moment of unwonted panic when in the confusion of a rear guard attack the 1st and 3rd Virginia charged each other. Of significance was General Stuart's competent handling of Jackson's corps when Stonewall was carried from the field. The dashing cavalryman's confidence in himself, a quality never lacking and repeatedly justified, rose still higher—rather too high in light of events of the now imminent June Battle of Brandy Station.

CHAPTER 7

They Shall Have Music

TRUMPET calls, which still seem to linger in the air at Brandy Station and over many another Civil War battlefield, rang out ever more imperiously in June of the crucial year of 1863. Cavalry heard and heeded the notes it considered peculiarly its own, though it shared them with the artillery: "Stables," "Water Call," and "Boots and Saddles," a shorter, swifter summons than "The General" that ordered all arms to break camp and march. "Trot," "Gallop," and the urgent blasts of "Charge." Sometimes troopers, rolling up in their blankets, hearkened to the lovely, poignant strains of "Taps" [106] as they fell asleep, or stood at attention beside a grave while it was sounded for a comrade's last bivouac.

Now and again other horns—cornets, tenors, altos, trombones, and basses—caught up the trumpets' notes in harmony. Cymbals clashed, drums rolled and boomed. At the outset of the war it had not been unusual for a cavalry regiment to have its mounted band, enhancing parades and reviews. Some were mustered out before long; a number survived—some dismounted, some still horsed. At times there were mishaps to the musicians on horseback, as in the case of a trombone player of the 1st Massachusetts Cavalry. Blaring away, he tangled the slide of his instrument in a blackberry vine, which firmly anchored him and his mount while the rest of the band marched on. Whereupon the Colonel glared at the spectacle of military disorder and roared: "What's he doing, sticking that thing in the ground?"

Cavalry bands during the earlier years of the war were likely to be left at Washington and other bases when their regiments took the field. The swifter movement demanded of the mounted arm was then deemed to deny it the infantry's privilege of marching to music that lifted weary men over many a long mile. However, cavalry commanders kept their bands within reach when they could, well aware of the value of music to morale and grateful for another service: many bandsmen served gallantly on battlefields as stretcher-bearers and surgeons' helpers.

GENERAL

With the coming of Sheridan, the cavalry's mounted bands were ordered to accompany the fighting columns and play them into action with their liveliest tunes.[107] At the Battle of Dinwiddie Court House, March 31, 1865, Maine musicians of the 1st District of Columbia Cavalry engaged in a musical duel with a Confederate band. They blasted back and forth across the field at each other, "Yankee Doodle" versus "Dixie," "Three Cheers for the Red, White, and Blue" countering "The Bonnie Blue Flag." With such spirit did they play that a trooper about to charge yelled, "That puts the fight right into me." [108]

The 2nd Virginia Cavalry boasted the only mounted band of any regiment from that state. It rejoiced in a splendid set of instruments, captured from a New York regiment.

Failing "sounding brass and tinkling cymbals," there were voices.

The Civil War was a great singing war, the First World War somewhat less so, and the Second, because of considerably more mechanical transport and other marching conditions, lacking in that notable adjunct to good cheer and *esprit*. Cavalry regiments, like those of

STABLE CALL

other arms, had their quartets and choruses. A favorite ditty of the harmonizing four of the 1st Massachusetts Cavalry ran:

> I asked her if she could and would;
> I thought she'd say she couldn't.
> Instead of that she said she could,
> But rather thought she wouldn't.

But it was to Stuart's Gray horsemen that two true cavalry songs belonged. There was their favorite, "Jine the Cavalry," roared out, with Jeb's baritone leading, on many a ride into battle. Then there was the ballad of the same title, sung to the tune of "The Old Gray Mare." [109] Its stanzas, a new one added for each campaign, were a saga of the service of the cavalry of the Army of Northern Virginia. Their first lines ran:

> We are the boys that went around McClellian. . . .
> We are the boys that crossed the Potomacum. . . .
> And then we went into Pennsylvania. . . .
> Then the big, fat Dutch girls hand around the breadium. . . .
> Old Joe Hooker, won't you come out o' the Wilderness! . . . .

In the Confederate cavalry voices raised in song were often given verve and rhythm by gay and lively chords from Sam Sweeney's banjo. How Stuart ranked Sweeney away from his regimental commander has already been told. It was highhanded of course, but surely some of the spirited dash with which "The Last Cavalier" led his corps to so many victories derived from Sweeney's music. For the Gray horsemen—in camp and on the march and up to the brink of battle—the war was fought to the accompaniment of a truly American instrument.[110]

Sam's masterly playing ran in the family. His elder brother Joel [111] had given concerts in the North before the war and was one of the most celebrated of the blackface minstrels, ranking with that stanch Unionist, Dan Emmett, author of "Dixie," whose appropriation by the Confederacy he bitterly resented.[112] Sam's tunes were always on tap, the lively and the sentimental ones Jeb Stuart loved. "Jine the Cavalry," "Listen to the Mocking Bird," "Her Bright Smile Haunts Me Still," and "Lorena." "The Bugle Sang Truce for the Night Cloud Had Lowered," "Hell Broke Loose in Georgia," "Oh, Lord, Gals, One Friday," and "The Girl I Left Behind Me." Frequently Sam played alone, sometimes with others: with Stuart's servant, Mulatto Bob, on the guitar or the bones, and a couple of fiddlers—all that was needed for a rollicking dance.

Sam's banjo would bring tears or, like the bands at Dinwiddie, put fight into a man. It deserved poetic tribute along with Jeb Stuart, who inspired it.

> With all the actor's grace and quick light charm
> That makes the women adore him—a wild cavalier
> Who worships as sober a God as Stonewall Jackson,
> A Rupert who seldom drinks, very often prays,
> Loves his children, singing, fighting, spurs and wife.
> Sweeney, his banjo player, follows him.
> —STEPHEN VINCENT BENÉT *John Brown's Body*

Sam Sweeney, following his beloved leader until the latter's mortal wounding at Yellow Tavern, then served under Fitz Lee until his own death from smallpox at Hanover Court House.

A lull in a campaign might—and would if Stuart could arrange it—find the Gray cavalry in the vicinity of some hospitable Virginia mansion. It might be one of the homes of Urbana or "The Bower," the residence ten miles from Charleston of the Stephen D. Dandridges with their "flock of attractive daughters and nieces, some very handsome," and all endowed with their full quota of Southern charm. White tents would be pitched and picket lines stretched for the horses. From wagons or saddlebags body servants would unpack officers' best uniforms. Sam Sweeney would tune his banjo, while Mulatto Bob would fetch his guitar and unlimber the clacking bones. Fiddlers, excused from camp fatigues, suppled fingers that had been gripping reins or carbine.

WATER CALL

There would be a dance that night, Jeb Stuart in his glory among the pretty girls. There would be singing and theatricals, with Major von Borcke and Colonel Brien of the 1st Virginia Cavalry, two top comedians, taking the leading parts. Lighted windows drew troopers to listen to the music and wistfully watch the reels, quadrilles, and waltzes. R.H.P.—Rank Has its Privileges. Yet in compensation Stuart would give enlisted men furloughs to go home whenever he could. Meanwhile even a spectator of the gaiety could forget the war for a time.

Once an Urbana party was interrupted in the manner of the famous Brussels ball on the eve of Waterloo. The crack band of the 15th Mississippi Infantry was playing for Stuart's cavalry that evening, and "music arose with its voluptuous swell." An outburst of firing by pickets brought it to a sudden stop. The Yankees were attacking. The hall was emptied in a minute, as officers rushed for their chargers and led their commands into action. Shortly the attack was beaten off. Ladies, disregarding party gowns, tenderly cared for the wounded. After the last bandage was tied, the dance was resumed.

TO HORSE

Naturally there was no Virginia hospitality for Union officers. They must forego festivities until they were granted leave to Washington or other cities within their lines. However, after Brandy Station became a base for the Army of the Potomac in 1864, trains brought wives and sweethearts to balls there, with one of the fine regimental bands furnishing the music.[113]

As time dulled memories of the death of comrades and wounds, veterans still vividly remembered the weather in their campaigns— the drenching rains after Fredericksburg, the heat at Gettysburg— and the music: the calls and fanfares that have rung through martial history before and since Joshua ordered the trumpets to sound at Jericho; the spine-tingling blare of the bands. Stirring songs from the majestic "Battle Hymn of the Republic" to lilting "Dixie." It is small wonder that for old soldiers, returning to Brandy Station after the war for reunions, music lingered in the air. Memories brought back the twang of Sam Sweeney's banjo playing for dances on June nights of 1863 and the massed trumpets that heralded General Stuart's two magnificent reviews.

MOUNTED BAND
(From *Battles and Leaders of the Civil War*)

CHAPTER 8

Pass in Review

A GRAY curtain, the Confederate cavalry, was lowered before the
stage of operations in the days after Chancellorsville. Fighting
Joe Hooker's scouts could find no peephole through it nor were they
able to slip around the wings. But it might be possible to see over
the top of that curtain. Up soared the Federal balloons. They had
served on occasion, yet it was generally recognized that balloons
were "a wretched substitute" for good cavalry reconnaissance.
Besides, the balloonists were understandably prudent enough to
ascend well behind their own lines. Daring Rebel horse batteries,
given a fraction of a chance, could be expected to seize the opportunity to gallop up, unlimber, sink trails, and open with shrapnel
on gas bags too far forward.

Effective aerial observation must wait long years for the reconnaissance plane. However, Hooker learned from his balloon men
that a certain amount of enemy traffic was moving westward. Alert
watchers with field glasses in his lines over along the Potomac at
Fredericksburg reported that the number of Confederate tents
pitched on the heights had diminished. That confirmed the fact that
some troops were being shifted. Lee might be planning to strike
somewhere—perhaps to invade the North again—and there was
always the possibility that Stuart would launch another large-scale
raid. Washington supported the latter prospect. A telegram to
Hooker warned that: "Prisoners and deserters brought in here state
that Stuart is preparing column of from 15,000 to 20,000 men,
cavalry and artillery, for a raid." Uneasiness and apprehension
spread northward. Though the Army of the Potomac presumably

barred the way, Stuart had ridden around it before, and there was no confidence in the War Department that he might not do so again. Authorities advised that the militia of Maryland, Pennsylvania, and Ohio be called out as a second line of defense.

The need for definite information was vital, and there was only one way to obtain it. Burst through the masking curtain.

Pleasonton, commander of the Union Cavalry Corps, was summoned to Hooker's headquarters on June 6, 1863, and given momentous orders.

You will take the three divisions of your corps and its four batteries of horse artillery, he was told, and cross the Rappahannock. Two brigades of infantry with a light battery will closely support you. Once over the river, you will march directly to Culpeper and disperse and destroy the enemy's trains and supplies of all descriptions to the best of your ability. In performing that mission it is of utmost importance that you discover the position and intentions of Lee's army.[114]

In view of the yet unsuspected extent of the Confederate concentration around Culpeper, Pleasonton was headed for trouble. Yet his was a strong force, 10,981 men, and a highly mobile one except for the infantry brigades ill-advisedly attached. The reorganized Federal cavalry was animated by a new spirit and a compelling urge to prove itself at last. Here lay its opportunity. Here was its chance to enable the mighty Army of the Potomac it served—77,208 men and 370 cannon—to redeem Chancellorsville and Fredericksburg.

Meanwhile the curtain had thickened. Stuart, with Hampton's and Fitz's and Rooney Lee's brigades already on hand to guard the fords and screen the movements of the Army of Northern Virginia behind him, now was joined at Culpeper Courthouse by "Grumble" Jones's and Robertson's brigades. Less a brigade detached to cover the movement of one of the Confederate corps, Stuart's strength now had mounted to 9,536 sabers, including the gunners, manning the thirty pieces of a battalion of horse artillery. Surely here was mobile might enough to render the curtain impenetrable, to assure that General Robert E. Lee's masterly strategy should once more baffle and circumvent the enemy.

Undetected, the Army of Northern Virginia began to complete its assembly in the vicinity of Culpeper Courthouse. Longstreet's and Ewell's corps already were there. A. P. Hill was stealthily moving his over from Fredericksburg. Only that diminution of his tents on the heights betrayed the shift, and while it lent suspicion that something was afoot, it revealed nothing further. As the bulk of the cavalry rode a half dozen miles forward to reinforce its guard over the Rappahannock fords, regiment on regiment of Gray infantry stacked arms around the picturesque little town that was the county seat. Light artillerymen parked their guns and grazed their horses. So mustered the splendid army, 54,356 men and 257 cannon, that would drive so deep into Pennsylvania. Outnumbered as before by the enemy, the string of brilliant victories it had won proved how little account it took of odds.

James Ewell Brown Stuart looked upon the array of cavalry, more than he had ever before beheld assembled under his command, and his heart leaped. So must similar sights had stirred great leaders of horse before him from Genghis Khan through Marlborough, Seydlitz, Prince Rupert, and Murat. The bearded brigadiers and their lieutenants—the lean, hard troopers—the tossing manes and swishing tails of the long lines of picketed mounts— sheathed sabers and carbines, ready to hand—the guns, caissons, and teams of the dashing Stuart Horse Artillery. Such a magnificent muster bred an irresistible impulse in the cavalier general. They must be paraded. There must be a full review. General Lee must see it. So must the ladies of the neighborhood and all who could reach it. And at a ball the night before the spectacle the ladies in their best party gowns must be vouchsafed their chance to pass in review.

Orders of the corps command were published, invitations sent. A great burnishing and furbishing got under way.

The Major-General commanding puts on his West Point manner, harassing plain combat colonels, Southern gentlemen who prefer informal war. The negro servants, the spare shirts, the Day & Martin boot-polish, with which the gentlemen rankers rode to battle in '61—they are forgotten things. You see elegant young men greasing their own leather, and shining their metal with wood ashes, and grooming their horses.[115]

As early as May 20 Stuart's staff officers, each required to provide himself with a new uniform and see to it that his mount was properly caparisoned, had been set to work on the pageant. Jeb himself, born actor and showman as he was a born soldier, could step straight into his leading role, costume gorgeous, lines and gestures perfect. Theater and scenery for the Stuart production were nothing short of providential.

The stage for it fairly thrust itself upon him: It was a long wide field in the vicinity of Brandy Station, between Culpeper and the Rappahannock. At the ideal site on this field was a hillock no craftsman could have excelled in design of a reviewing stand. To complete perfection, the field was so close to the Orange and Alexandria Railroad that a halted train would offer seats for spectators, Stuart pitched his tents on nearby Fleetwood Hill, overlooking Brandy Station, to supervise everything, and he set June 5 as the date.[116]

The rank and file indulged in more than its usual quota of soldier grumbling. Such fuss-and-feathers and folderol were all very well before the war when a militia company had nothing much else to do, but now these cavalrymen were veterans with two years of hard fighting behind them and a lot more ahead. A trooper kept himself, his mount, his arms and equipment in as good trim as possible; if he neglected to, he heard from his sergeant. Imposition of all this extra spit-and-polish seemed over and above the call of duty. It was high time a man and his horse, too, were given a chance to rest—they needed it.

Muttered protests and objections from the ranks, shared by not a few officers, met with the usual headquarters disregard. There would be a review by command of Major General Stuart, and that was that.

Turn out an escort to honor an arriving notable, former Secretary of War George W. Randolph. Police camp. Find more fatigue details to pitch extra tents and furnish them, for hotels and hospitable homes could not hold the throng of guests. Harness up ambulance and wagon teams to fetch and carry the ladies from the railroad station after their journeys from as far away as Richmond and Charlottesville. Sweep out and decorate Culpeper's courthouse for the ball.

On with the dance. Music struck up for quadrilles, reels, and waltzes. It could not be said of that evening that "bright the lights shone o'er fair women and brave men" present, for even the resourceful Major von Borcke had been able to provide only a few tallow candles to illuminate the hall. Yet there was gaiety and romance, the more poignant and compelling since this was wartime.

Although a disappointing message had come that General Lee, concerned with supplies for the approaching campaign, could not attend the review, Stuart decided that it would nevertheless be held for the many guests who had come so far to witness it.

At eight o'clock on the following morning skies bright and blue, General Stuart and his staff mounted and rode toward the Brandy Station plain. Plumes nodded, and steeds curvetted. The folds of the General's battle flag flaunted free, as trumpeters sounded flourishes. Big von Borcke admired the lovely ladies waving to the cavalcade from porches and verandahs. Some before taking carriages to follow and watch the review ran to the street to strew flowers in the path of the horses. It was all in the grandest tradition of the pomp and panoply of war—a page out of Homer, Herodotus, or Tacitus. Marshaled on the level ground waited a line of Gray cavalry that extended for a mile and a half. On a flank were stationed the rifles and Napoleons of Beckham's battalion of horse artillery. In Chew's Battery, Acting First Sergeant George Neese worshipfully watched Jeb Stuart advance to review his troops. "The trappings on his proud, prancing horse all looked bright and new, and his sidearms gleamed in the morning sun like burnished silver. A long, black, ostrich feather plume waved gracefully from a black slouch hat cocked upon one side, and was held with a golden clasp which also stayed the plume." [117] There, Neese was certain, rode the most graceful horseman he had ever seen, every motion in harmony with his mount's. While three bands performed their most martial airs, Stuart galloped to a little knoll, wheeled to face front, taking his post under the Stars and Bars, and "sat his saddle like a gallant knight errant."

Notes of trumpet calls soared, and shouted orders seconded them. Regiments in column of squadrons marched past at a walk. A countermarch then at the end of the field, with the trumpets signaling "Trot" until the cavalcade was a hundred yards from the reviewing stand. Now 8,000 sabers whipped from scabbards, flashing in the sunlight. "Gallop" blared. Triumphantly the ordered ranks of splendid horsemen dashed past, the Rebel yell shrilling above pounding hoofs. On the ridge to the left clouds of white smoke wreathed Beckham's guns, opening a furious fire with blank cartridges as if to repulse a charge.

TROT

Watchers gasped, thrilled to the core. So must the Light Brigade have charged at Balaklava while the Russian artillery thundered. "Those feminine spectators who had handsome male companions put their handkerchiefs to their eyes and swayed and gracefully swooned. It was observed, strangely enough, that those girls who had come with parents and those who were attended by awkward swains, did not faint." [118] For that one high moment troopers forgot the toil and trouble the review had demanded. It was, a gunner thought, "enough to make even an old woman feel fightish." An afterglow of splendor lingered on through a second ball danced that evening on the Brandy Station greensward, with great bonfires furnishing far better illumination than the Culpeper candles.

Tired troopers had scarcely begun to relax when on June 7 a second dispatch was received from army headquarters. General Lee, now free, would be pleased to review the cavalry next day. It was of course a command performance, and all the work had to be done over again. Grumbling redoubled, mitigated only by the inherent willingness of the average Confederate soldier to oblige Massa Robert. Most of the ladies had gone home, but dignitaries were arriving from Richmond, and an additional, though critical, audience was assured when General John B. Hood accepted an invitation to "come and see the review and bring your people."

His "people" turned out to be his entire infantry division. Cavalry hosts were worried that some contretemps would result from the rivalry between the two arms and the foot troops' jealousy of men lucky enough to make marches on horseback. As Hood's Texans lined the edges of the field, Fitz Lee begged their leader: "Well, don't let them halloo, 'Here's your mule!' at the review."

Any mishap in horsemanship would promptly draw that gibe from the infantry, who might sound off also with a verse or two of the favorite army song from which it came:

A farmer came to camp one day, with milk and eggs to sell,
Upon a mule which oft would stray to where no man could tell.
The farmer, tired of his tramp, for hours was made a fool
By everyone he met in camp with, "Mister, here's your mule."

Wade Hampton seconded Fitz Lee's plea. If Hood's division set up that shout, the cavalry, Hampton laughingly promised, would charge them. There was considerable likelihood of such banter, since a few mules had intruded into the first review.[119] And one of the unmilitary-looking creatures was about to step on stage at the second. That same Sergeant Neese, who had praised Jeb Stuart's appearance, dismayed the General by parading with his battery, mounted on a sleek mule with extra long ears. One startled glimpse of those ears, and Stuart sent an aide galloping to remove the sergeant and his mount from the scene before the infantry could roar a view halloo.[120]

Another near upset in decorum threatened when "Grumble" Jones's brigade was seen to be unprepared to pass in review. A second aide was rushed from the post of command to require correction. "Grumble," that able but informal soldier, fed to the teeth with a surfeit of parading, glanced up from a comfortably reclining posture on the ground and swore sulphurously at the inquiring aide. But as the indignant young officer left, he heard Jones's trumpets sound "Boots and Saddles," and the brigade took its place in the column.

This time the show was a comparatively tame one. By General Lee's order there was no galloping and no firing by the artillery. Horseflesh and powder must be spared for the hard campaign in store. Yet the march past at a walk was an impressive demonstration of strength and readiness. Lee, observing it proudly, wrote to his wife: "I reviewed the cavalry in this section yesterday. It was a splendid sight. The men and horses looked well. They have recuperated since last fall. Stuart was in all his glory. Your sons and nephews were well and flourishing."

Stuart's glory, which drew that smiling and understanding comment from the superior who depended upon him so greatly, was not always smiled on. Others called it "military foppery," and the usefulness of the reviews as morale builders was discounted. Richmond gossiped about the balls. Jeb and his officers, ran the whispers, had been "rollicking, frolicking and running after girls." (What soldier, given a chance, wouldn't?) A Culpeper lady—one suspects she had not been invited to the dances or, if so, failed to have a good time—caustically wrote Jefferson Davis:

President, allow a rude Southern lady to say General Stuart's conduct since in Culpeper is perfectly ridiculous, having repeated reviews for the benefit of his lady friends, he riding up and down the line thronged with those ladies, he decorated with flowers, apparently a monkey show on hand and he the monkey. In fact General Stuart is nothing more or less than one of those fops, devoting his whole time to his lady friends' company.[121]

But the real cost of the festivities and displays was the energy they had expended and the rest they had denied. Like officers who attended the Brussels ball on the eve of Waterloo, Stuart and his subordinates would have been fitter for a night's sleep. Few had taken the opportunity to relax like that seasoned old campaigner, "Grumble" Jones. Lee's foresight on horse power and powder at the second review could not compensate for the prodigality at the first. The men, bored and weary, had scarcely been dismissed after the June 8 parade when they were put to work packing equipment for an early move on the following morning to cover the advance of the Army of Northern Virginia. Prospect of action aroused less interest than usual in the tired troopers.

Gray regiments bivouacked near the fords and around Brandy Station and Fleetwood Hill where Stuart and his staff were sheltered under two tent flies, with all other baggage already stowed in the headquarters wagons. The Corps commander would have spared no more than a careless glance for the loveliness of the summer scene spread out around him: the green woods and the new-ploughed ground, richly brown; the fields of fragrant clover and golden wheat, ready for mowing. Not pastorals but martial epics for Jeb Stuart. He must have smiled to himself at the glowing memory of the gallop past on the plain yonder, and his eyes, gazing north, held the vision of battles ahead.

"Reveille" and "Boots and Saddles" tomorrow were to launch his brigades on their ride northward. Dispositions for the night placed them in readiness for an early start on the first stage of the march that led to Gettysburg.

Over near Oak Shade Church, north of the Little Hazel River and about seven and a half miles northwest of Fleetwood, was encamped Fitz Lee's brigade. Fitz was ill and had temporarily turned over command to Colonel Tom Munford of the 2nd Virginia. Four other regiments from that state completed the brigade. They, with eight other Virginia regiments and a battalion in other brigades, betokened the great contribution of the Old Dominion to the Confederate cavalry.[122] Some two miles west of the junction of the Hazel and the Rappahannock and close to Welford's Ford lay Rooney Lee's brigade, all Virginia except for one North Carolina regiment.

1ST VIRGINIA CAVALRY REGIMENT, C.S.A., 1861-62
(Drawing by Frederick P. Todd)

Lower on the larger river a more important crossing place, Beverly Ford, about a mile and a half above the railroad bridge, was guarded by Jones's command. It was a strong one: four regiments and a battalion, called the Laurel, from Virginia. Its main body was bivouacked two miles inland along the Brandy Road. Between "Grumble's" troopers and his river pickets were parked four of the six batteries of Beckham's horse artillery. Pelham would not have placed them in that position, in danger of being overrun by a sudden attack driving in the pickets. But Pelham was dead, and the Gray artillery, despite its many able gunner officers, would not look upon his like again.

Kelly's Ford, near which he had been mortally wounded, was four miles below the railroad span. Pickets there were Robertson's men, the two North Carolina regiments that furnished them being stationed some distance to their rear where they could graze their horses in the meadows dotting the five miles between the Barbour farm and Stevensburg. Still farther back than Robertson in that area of good pasturage rested Hampton's brigade of three regiments and three equivalent units termed legions. They were chiefly from North and South Carolina.

Such was the cavalry, outposts now and forthcoming advance guard of the Army of Northern Virginia, which, assembled for invasion, waited poised only six miles to the rear around the town of Culpeper.

That mighty array close at hand, General Lee in command, would have lent Jeb Stuart confidence in the unlikely event the reliant and usually alert cavalryman needed any such reassurance. More important was his conviction that there was no enemy within striking distance. Not a Blue patrol had been sighted all the day of June 8. Nothing contradicted the belief that well to the north the country was empty of any of Hooker's horsemen. The unenterprising Yankees would have to be sought out tomorrow as on many earlier occasions.

As a proper precaution the fords were guarded. Otherwise, except for being prepared to move forward in the morning, Stuart paid little attention to his dispositions. His troops were scattered, good grazing dictating the bivouacs of the brigades, not a need of close support in meeting an attack. If he noted that potentially perilous position of the horse artillery, he neglected to correct it. One cannot avoid believing that Stuart, had he expected an enemy incursion, would not have left the two most vital approaches in the care of his least trusted brigade commanders: Robertson at Kelly's Ford and Jones at Beverly.

As the pleasant summer evening darkened into night, Gray cavalrymen, except for the pickets at the fords, slept deeply. A bright moon set about two o'clock of the morning of June 9, 1863. The stars shed faint radiance. Gradually a heavy haze began to settle down on the river, blinding sentries and dulling sound. All was quiet on the Rappahannock.

CHAPTER 9

March to Battle

RATIONS, forage, and ammunition were issued in the encampment of the Cavalry Corps, Army of the Potomac, at Warrenton. Throughout the regiments officers and non-coms made a last check of men, mounts, and equipment. Bugles and trumpets sang "The General" and "Boots and Saddles." As the last notes died away, musicians wiped their lips with the backs of their hands and slung their instruments, shifting them back to a comfortable position. Strict orders forbade any more windjamming until they rode into action. Nor would any fires be allowed. Standards and guidons were furled and cased to conceal any betraying glint of color, and making dust or noise was to be avoided as far as possible. This was to be a surprise attack.

BOOTS AND SADDLE

It was about noon on June 8 that the long blue column swung off along the road to the southwest. Troopers exchanged knowing glances. Some of these regiments had ridden this way before. They were headed for Kelly's Ford and Brandy Station.

Thud of hoofs, rumble of artillery wheels, and the steady tramp of infantry boots. Pleasonton could take pride in this command of his,[123] and it had begun to be proud of itself since the fight last March at Kelly's Ford when it had borne itself well. Ranks, though not full for all units, were nearer so than they had been since the first muster. A three-battalion (squadron) regiment should, according to cavalry tables of organization, total 1,189 officers and enlisted men.[124] Failure to come up to authorized strength, often due to the faulty replacement system, was not so important as the fact that gaps, otherwise caused, had now been filled. Details of a regiment's smartest men, absent so long in Washington and at army headquarters to serve as escorts and tickle the vanity of some general, had been pulled back and were present for duty—no longer showpieces but fighting men.

Brigadier General John Buford's stubborn Scot's jaw must have relaxed a little as he surveyed his 1st Division. Colonel Benjamin Franklin Davis led the 1st Brigade: Illinois, Indiana, and New York cavalry regiments and Batteries B and L (combined into one unit), 2nd U.S. Artillery. These were the regiments that "Grimes" Davis, refusing to surrender with other forces at Harper's Ferry, had led out by night through a Confederate cordon in a daring escape, gathering in an enemy wagon train en route. The 2nd Brigade under Colonel Thomas C. Devin comprised two New York, a Pennsylvania, and a West Virginia regiment. Except for the 6th Pennsylvania, once lancers, Major Charles J. Whiting's reserve brigade was all Regulars: two fine old regiments, the 1st and 2nd, and two younger ones, the 5th and 6th, plus Battery E, 4th U.S. Artillery. Their ranks were somewhat thinned by combat, and there was no great prospect of filling them, for there was no bounty for enlistment in the Regulars. War correspondents mentioned them infrequently, concentrating on troops from the states their newspapers served. For them the title of the later Harrigan and Hart song could be reversed to read: "I Don't Belong to the Volunteers. I'm Only a Regular." But theirs was an honored name. In their keeping lay the gallant, tenacious tradition of the United States Army, and they were faithful to their trust.

France in the dapper person of Colonel Alfred N. Duffié led the 2nd Division, and Italy its 1st Brigade, commanded by Colonel Louis P. di Cesnola, with his regiments from Massachusetts, Ohio, and Rhode Island. Colonel J. Irvin Gregg's 2nd Brigade comprised three regiments from Pennsylvania, supported by Battery M, 2nd U.S. Artillery.

Another Gregg, General David McM.—he of the patriarchal beard—headed the 3rd Division. A breeze ruffled the flaring, ginger-colored sideburns of Colonel Judson Kilpatrick, riding before the 1st Brigade: one Maine and two New York regiments plus Orton's Company, District of Columbia Cavalry. More luxuriant were the striking whiskers—true Dundrearies [125]—of the commander of the 2nd Brigade, Colonel Sir Percy Wyndham, veteran of three foreign armies and various branches of their service. His troops were a Maryland, a New Jersey, and a Pennsylvania regiment, with the 6th New York Battery in support.

Slanted rifles jutted from the long column. There marched seven regiments of infantry and a light battery—3,000 men—under Generals Adelbert Ames and David A. Russell. With mixed emotions cavalrymen surveyed the foot troops, both a handicap and a stanch standby. On the former count the doughboys slowed the rate of march, and since this attack evidently was earmarked as a swift foray, a lightning stroke, and a rapid withdrawal, they were a decided impediment. On the other hand, if Pleasonton ran into enemy cavalry in superior force, perhaps also supported by infantry, and with the river at his back was assailed in front and flanks, his own riflemen could prove to be his salvation. They would cover him until he could cross and re-form, while his artillery in turn protected their retreat. In any event the foot was present on orders from headquarters. It could no longer be argued that they hampered the mobility of a vital reconnaissance. Whether the Union cavalry was now capable of executing successfully a mission of its own was still a question in the light of past performances. Hooker could not be blamed too much for hedging.

From Warrenton southwest to Kelly's Ford was some twenty miles. The column covered the greater part of the distance, not an inordinately long march but wearing and dusty in spite of care taken. Fortunately the preoccupied enemy was raising his own dust and a good deal more of it. Across the Rappahannock the approaching troops in blue sighted heavy clouds. The dust of Stuart's review for Lee and of Hood's division marching on and off the field had not settled before it was augmented by that of the Confederate cavalry taking its several stations and preparing for the next day's advance. Troopers of the 1st Maine considered the extent of the dust being kicked up yonder and nodded grimly to each other. Obviously there was hot work in store.

Dusk fell, then dark. "Horse, foot, and dragoons," in the old army phrase, obeyed the quiet order, passed along the column, to halt. They were not far from Kelly's Ford, but far enough to be safe from observation unless the enemy probed across the river. He appeared to have no such intention. Pleasonton's scouts crept forward cautiously to points where they could observe the farther bank of the Rappahannock. Crossings were picketed, to be sure, but the guards showed no signs of activity. They were tired, reviewed to a fare-thee-well. Uppermost in their minds was the thought that they would be passing over the river tomorrow, through these shallows where they stood sentry, to spearhead the advance of the Army of Northern Virginia. There was no suspicion that soon they would be desperately defending the fords instead.

As the scouts reported back, the Blue regiments underwent a considerable amount of shifting into position, "poppycocking" they called it, grumbling heartily. It was, however, not needless maneuvering. Pleasonton, having estimated the situation, had passed down his battle orders through his division commanders.

Buford's division with Ames's infantry was to move out first, crossing the Rappahannock at Beverly Ford, and drive thence for Brandy Station, four and one-half miles distant. The other two divisions and Russell's riflemen, initially under Gregg's over-all command, were to cross by nearer Kelly's Ford, while Buford's earlier attack distracted attention from them. Then Gregg's troops would divide.

Duffié, taking a southwesterly direction, was ordered to push as far as Stevensburg to find out whether the enemy occupied the road between Chancellorsville and Culpeper, and whether he had any troops on the march along that road, and to cover the left against any offensive movement on their part. In the meanwhile Gregg, with his division, was to proceed toward Brandy Station in order to strike the rear of the cavalry which Buford was to attack in front, while Russell, bearing to the right in order to make short work with his infantry, would endeavor to assist the latter between the railroad and Beverly Ford.[126]

A good battle plan, considering the dearth of information on enemy strength and dispositions and assuming that surprise would be achieved. Lee, Jackson, and Stuart had often effectively used such bold division of striking forces in the classic pincers or nut-cracker movement. "This Pleasonton, for more than a year, has been studying the art of war with his schoolmate Jeb Stuart, and he is capable of learning." [127]

Marshaled for tomorrow's attack, growling troopers were at last allowed to water and feed their mounts and eat their own cold rations, ham and hardtack, with vain visions of coffeepots bubbling over fires to make a hot brew that would put strength into a man. Over in the 6th Pennsylvania Cavalry a group of officers finished their mess. Unspoken thoughts of the battle ahead filled every mind. Friends leaned close in the moonlight. "In case anything happens to me, will you write ———?" "Of course. And if I don't come through, will you ———?" The regimental chaplain sensed the quiet interchanges. It would be his duty to pass on such messages, both those directly confided to him and those of the friends who would not live to keep their promises. He remembered the solemn and earnest prayer he offered that night.[128]

You will not picket your horse, the word was passed. Unsaddle but don't unbridle. Loop reins over an arm and lie down and get some sleep. Veterans, spreading blankets and pillowing heads on saddles, obeyed promptly and cynically. There would be little enough of that sleep. In a few hours sergeants and corporals would be shaking them awake, booting the rears of reluctant ones. Roll out, trooper. Rise and shine. Stand to horse. Hurry up and wait— the old army game. Sure enough, they were roused at midnight and told to be ready to move out at 3 A.M.

Darkness before dawn, vitality at low ebb, combat ahead. They breed moments of self-doubt, of mingled hope of survival and premonition of death. Soldiers of all wars have known those moments and their weight on the spirit. Passage of time intensifies them, and only daylight and action can dispel them. For the Union cavalrymen before Brandy Station consciousness of past defeats made the burden heavier.

They stared into the blackness, looking east for the first glimmer of dawn of the ninth day of June, 1863. Men, far out of earshot of enemy pickets though they were, spoke in undertones. Hands sought saber hilt, carbine, and revolver butts, for reassurance, and fingers slipped under girths, testing their tightness. Horses snorted and stamped restively. Riders patted their necks, quieting them.

Over in Buford's lines sounded whispered commands. Leather creaked as troopers swung into saddles. A muffled tread of hoofs and rumbling artillery wheels. The 1st Division, accompanied by General Pleasonton, was off for Beverly Ford. Enviously the 2nd and 3rd heard their comrades leave and set themselves to endure more wearing waiting.

The skies began to look a little lighter. With vast relief Gregg's men mounted and rode for Kelly's Ford. They were scheduled to reach it simultaneously with Buford's arrival at Beverly. At any moment now they would hear his carbines opening upriver. They themselves, as the half-light revealed their approach, would shortly face enemy fire from the farther bank.

But no flashes cut through the dawn. Blessedly a thick fog had settled down on the Rappahannock, masking the attack.

CHAPTER 10

A Ford Is Forced

JOHN BUFORD'S timing for the march of his 1st Division to Beverly Ford was carefully estimated. Four miles an hour at the walk should bring him to the river just as dawn was breaking. That gait made less noise than a trot and, most important, would leave the horses fresh and unblown for the attack. Furthermore, the pace must be accommodated to the rate of march of Ames's brigade of infantry.

Troopers must have shivered a little when they thought of the chill water, not yet warmed by the summer sun. This would be no leisurely, unopposed passage such as Walt Whitman painted in words in "Cavalry Crossing a Ford." [129] "The splashing horses loitering stop to drink"... "The brown faced men" and their "negligent rest on the saddles"... "Scarlet and blue and snowy white, the guidon flags flutter gayly in the wind." No, they must rush the river under fire, with pounding hoofs kicking up a drenching spray that would spatter following files. Even so they would be lucky compared to the poor infantry, wading through wet to the waist or higher and pushing on in soggy clothing and squelching boots.

Colonel Benjamin Franklin Davis headed the vanguard. Buford could not have picked a better man—a born leader and a veteran of the Indian Wars. Sometimes, they say, old wounds ache a little before a new battle. Perhaps that morning "Grimes" Davis felt his scar from a fight with the Apaches. Now a brigade commander in fact though not yet in rank, he was rated as one of the most promising of the Federal cavalry commanders and slated to rise high. Behind him rode his former regiment, the 8th New York he had trained so well; then comrade regiments of the Harper's Ferry exploit.

Davis had funneled his brigade into column of fours to keep within the shallowest part of the ford and retain formation when it emerged on to the narrow road on the farther side. Now the New Yorkers' leading troop rushed it, horsemen spurring reluctant mounts into the water. They dashed through in a cloud of heavy spray.

Close behind Davis rode two supernumeraries, Captain Ulric Dahlgren and First Lieutenant George A. Custer, aides-de-camp to Generals Hooker and Pleasonton, respectively. A pair of gallant and fearless young officers, seekers after glory both and finding it and finally the grave where its path led—Dahlgren nine months later on a raid to Richmond with Kilpatrick from this same vicinity of Brandy Station, Custer not until the Little Big Horn. Pleasonton would commend those two for their valor today and award to Custer the honor of carrying back his report and a captured Rebel battle standard to headquarters. From this passage of the ford onward both young cavalrymen were in the forefront of the fiercest fighting.

At the sudden apparition of bluecoats bursting through the fog, startled pickets of Company A, 6th Virginia Cavalry, Jones's Brigade, snatched up their weapons. Carbines and revolvers cracked in rising crescendo. They closed in on the constricted column, fighting desperately. If they could not halt or at least delay this surprise attack, the rest of the brigade would be caught before it could saddle up. Beckham's exposed batteries, unharnessed and unhitched, would be overrun.

It was a valiant stand A Company made. It took losses but it bought precious time with them.

Davis and his men would not be blocked. They drove down the road in a flying wedge. It flung the Virginians into the fields and swept them back toward the edge of the woods which skirted the open ground north of St. James Church.

In the meanwhile the rest of the 6th Virginia had got to horse in a marvel of swift reaction such as only veterans could manage.

Major C. E. Flournoy and 150 troopers galloped down on the rapidly advancing Yankee column.

Foremost elements of the Blue and Gray crashed head-on, horse against horse, body to body. Yells and clash of sabers and rattle of revolvers. The 8th Illinois was coming up front into line with the New Yorkers, while the 7th Virginia was hastening to the support of the 6th.

Some distance in front of his column, momentarily checked, Colonel Davis reined in and waved his saber to rally his men. "Stand firm, Eight New York!" he shouted back.

A Confederate officer, Lieutenant R. O. Allen, rode down on the isolated Union commander. Saving the one shot left in his revolver, the lieutenant cantered to within sword's length before Davis heard him and turned. The colonel's saber swung through an arc that would have cut deep into neck and shoulder. It slashed through empty air. His adversary in a lightning motion had swung below the side of his horse. From that position he fired. The bullet drilled Colonel Davis through the brain. As his body slid from the saddle, furious New Yorkers converged to avenge their leader on his slayer and a sergeant and private who had joined him. They killed the sergeant, but Lieutenant Allen and the trooper galloped clear.

Chaplain Gracey of the 6th Pennsylvania bent over a stretcher being carried to the rear. "Who is that, boys?" "Colonel Davis, sir." "Is it possible? Is he wounded badly?" "A Minie ball through his head, sir." The chaplain, as he left to rejoin his regiment, said a brief requiem. "God have mercy on the brave, noble, patriot-soldier, the hero of Harper's Ferry." [130]

The 1st Union Brigade pressed on. Its weight thrust the 6th Virginia aside, thirty men and horses down, heavy casualties for an under-strength regiment. Up on its left at that critical moment galloped the 7th Virginia, led by its picket company. Having been relieved at the river a few hours before, the pickets had their horses haltered in camp and ready to hand. Comrades pounded after them, many coatless and bootless, some, not having taken time to saddle, riding bareback. In a whooping charge Lieutenant Colonel Thomas Marshall flung his regiment on the bluecoats.

Young John N. Opie rode in the first set of fours galloping down the road, a tight rein on his wild-eyed, hard-mouthed mare. She took the bit regardless and bolted. All his strength could not restrain her.

My horse did what I too well knew she would do—that is, she shot out from the column like a thunderbolt and rushed down the road with the rapidity of lightning. I looked around behind me, and no one was in sight. I pulled with all my strength and vigor; I hallooed, "Whoa! whoa! whoa!" but to no purpose, as her mouth was fixed against her breast. I thought of killing her, but I had nothing but a sabre, as three days before, someone had stolen my six-shooter. I expected, every moment, to rush upon the enemy. I again pulled with superhuman vigor; I hallooed, "Whoa! whoa!" but all in vain; she still rushed madly on. I thought of jumping off but that would never have done.

I turned a bend in the road, and there, across my path, was a double line of cavalry. My hope was that, seeing a single horseman, they would understand the situation and not fire; but I suppose they thought it was the devil, as my horse was black as night, and was running at the rate of about forty miles an hour. At any rate, I saw them raise their carbines, then a line of smoke, then a crash; when, heels over head, both horse and rider tumbled through the air and fell, headlong, in a pile on the side of the road. My right leg felt as if paralyzed, but, seeing and feeling no blood, upon examination I found that a ball had struck the toe of my boot and plowed a furrow through the sole.

I jumped up, still having my sabre in my right hand, my horse lying by my side dead, not having uttered a groan or made a struggle. I found, the next day, when I went to get my saddle and bridle, that four bullets had penetrated her. How I escaped remains a mystery, as I was only twenty yards distant from the enemy, and received the fire of several hundred men. After I arose to my feet, I heard the boys charging down the road. In a moment they were opposite me in the road, when another volley was fired; a man dropped dead at my feet, Lieutenant

Morton, of Company "H." I seized his horse and mounted him, and joined in the charge. We broke the Eighth New York.[131]

The charge crumpled against the stone-wall resistance of the rest of the 1st Brigade, backed by the 2nd. As the 8th Illinois smashed against the onset, Sergeant Henry Pearson was bowled out of his saddle by the impact of a bullet, fired almost point-blank, that struck him over the heart. No more than shaken and shocked, he picked himself up and managed to remount. The ball had thudded into his pocket Bible, his mother's gift. He was only "wounded in the Testament."

Yelling Blue troopers, Illinois, Indiana, West Virginia, more New Yorkers, and Pennsylvania, battered back the Gray horse, sharpshooters scourging the retreat. In resurgence the Union regiments drove for Beckham's exposed batteries. The Stuart Horse Artillery was within an ace of capture. Considering the subsequent splendid service of its guns, the fate of the battle can be said to have hung in the balance at that moment.

But the artillerymen had been granted just respite enough while the 6th Virginia still held and the 7th rushed to reinforce it. Captain James F. Hart's Battery had been parked close to the road. Cannoneers manhandled two of its pieces into position and opened with canister on the advancing Blue cavalry. It was a gallant sacrifice stand. They would be well lost if they could cover the withdrawal of the rest of the artillery.

For the bulk of the gunner battalion there was not a second to spare for fumbling or lost motion. With the deftness of long practice drivers threw harness on the nervous teams and hitched, then clambered into saddles. Cannoneers, saddling their own horses, limbered the guns, mounted in their turn, and rode hard after the column of carriages as the battalion rolled. Major Beckham's field desk, jolted from a careening wagon, was the only loss when the galloping batteries whirled away, executed front into line at St. James Church, and prepared for action.

The two howitzers left behind, loaded and fired at top speed, swept the road with bursts of canister from flaming muzzles. Nothing could live in the path of those spreading cones of lethal balls. Blue horsemen, not sparing time to dismount sharpshooters and pick off the gunners, charged them, not in a suicidal frontal assault but fanning out around the flanks. Cannoneers swung trails right and left, muzzles veering, to meet the onrushes. They could not cover a wide enough arc—they could not fire fast enough—to blast back the encircling waves. Sabers slashing, cavalrymen flooded the gun positions. Crews fought them with revolvers, thrusting rammer staffs, and swinging trail handspikes.

A thunder of hoofs shook the ground, as General "Grumble" Jones rushed in the 11th and 12th Virginia and the 35th Battalion to the rescue of the artillerymen, beating back their assailants. Limbers dashed up. The near-lost howitzers were hooked on and pulled out to add their fire to that of the cannon in front of the church. Covering the two battered regiments that had borne the brunt, the Gray cavalry commenced a fighting retreat.

Buford had met with prompter and stronger resistance than he expected in view of the initial success of his surprise assault. But now all his troops were over the river and pressing onward. Ames's infantry was delivering a well-directed fire from the edge of woods. Parts of the 2nd and Reserve brigades were in action or support.

Pleasonton sent off to Hooker his first report, marked 6 A.M., from Beverly Ford.

"Enemy has opened with artillery, and shows some force of cavalry. Had a sharp skirmish. Colonel Davis, commanding Second Brigade [It was the 1st Brigade], 1st Division, led his column across, and is badly wounded." [132]

The 1st Division had taken a check but not a serious one. Yet it was a matter of grave alarm that so far no sound of Gregg's guns had been heard downriver—he was one hour late in striking Kelly's Ford—and the success of the whole operation depended on the closing of that jaw of the pincers. Nevertheless Buford must press his attack—must press it at the risk of all the Confederate cavalry, along with infantry that might be marching up from Culpeper, converging on his division with its back to the Rappahannock. Surely Gregg would soon be in action. On that everything must be hazarded.

CHAPTER 11

Target: Charging Cavalry

•-•

JEB STUART was drinking his morning coffee at his head-quarters on Fleetwood Heights when he heard the first shots from the direction of Beverly Ford. Whether the brew was good coffee, captured from the Yankees, or the Rebel article, plentifully adulterated with chicory, it must have turned to gall in his mouth. That firing, whatever it amounted to—a light, hit-and-run raid or an attack in force—meant surprise, the unforeseen, the unprovided-for. Every report sternly reproached a cavalry commander charged with the duty of screening the concentration of the Army of Northern Virginia. Here was turnabout, the cavalry boot on the other foot: the despised enemy horsemen usurping a Stuart pre-rogative.

The General wasted no time on rankling reflections. There would be enough of them later, prompted by criticism from Richmond where a newspaper branded the Federal onset for what it was: an absolute and complete surprise.[133] Aides and couriers were standing to horse when a galloper from Jones dashed up with the word that the enemy was across the Rappahannock at Beverly Ford and advancing in strength. Stuart rushed out orders for reinforcement of the struck brigade and sent his wagon train rolling toward the safety of Culpeper. Then he rode rapidly toward the rising din of battle.

Already those good soldiers, Hampton and Rooney Lee, were marching to the sound of the guns. The former hurried forward four regiments to take post on Jones's right. Robert E. Lee's tall son "had advanced from Welford's down the river toward the firing, and had gained a strong position on the Cunningham farm, with excellent cover for his dismounted men behind the stone fence which runs northwest from near the overseer's house, with his artillery on the hill behind, near the Green house, and open ground around him in every direction." [134]

Meanwhile Jones, yielding to odds against him, was falling back slowly and stubbornly. He turned to one of the battery commanders: "Captain Chew, I am not in command today, but do you see that gap in the woods yonder? I think the Yankees are bringing a battery there. If they do, give them hell." [135] There had probably been a temporary suspension from command as a disciplinary measure for Jones's unreadiness to pass in review yesterday. In any event he paid little attention to it beyond that remark.

Stuart found Jones's and Rooney Lee's Virginians and North Carolinians in line of battle, forming an angle in front of St. James Church. The former's regiments, to the right, had their backs to the railroad and were facing generally north, while Lee faced east. To the fore were the sharpshooter companies of each regiment, dismounted, Lee's with their carbines leveled over the fine cover of the stone wall. Saber companies waited poised in the rear. On the hill near the Green house Beckham's gunners rammed charges down muzzles, and shells burst in the woods where the Blue infantry was maintaining a hot fire. Hampton was galloping up from Brandy with four of his regiments and legions.

It was a strong defensive position Jones and Lee held. An enemy attack with dismounted skirmishers and mounted men vainly tried to crack it. Before the withering fire of the sharpshooters, mowing down the horses, the assault recoiled to the woods.

Now the angled Gray lines transformed themselves into a launched spearhead. Rooney Lee's troopers fanned out to threaten the Federal right and rear. Wade Hampton, arriving, extended his right to lap half around the enemy's left in the woods. If this onslaught were not stopped, it would be the fate of the Union 1st Division, not the Confederate Cavalry Corps, to be clamped in pincer jaws.

Volleys, rippling along the Blue front, suddenly ceased in the center, as cavalry squadrons emerged from the trees onto the open

6TH PENNSYLVANIA CAVALRY

(Drawing by Harry C. Larter, Jr.)

field. The sun sharpened the colors of standards and guidons now unfurled. Trumpets, muted no longer, blared "Trot," "Gallop," "Charge." With a rolling tattoo of hoofs the 6th Pennsylvania and the 6th Regulars hurtled across the eight hundred yards that separated them from the Rebel artillery on the hill.

GALLOP

Only the discarded lances of the Pennsylvanians, leveled with scarlet pennons whipping, would have made that charge a grander spectacle.[136] The 6th, happily rid of those weapons, was content with drawn sabers. Beside them rode the steady ranks of the hard-bitten Regulars.

Up on the hill gunners of the Stuart Horse Artillery saw them galloping forward. Target: advancing cavalry. Artillerymen could not ask a better one—one that demanded their most rapid rate of fire and with no shots to be wasted. Only a short time before two of these crews had met Blue horsemen at close quarters and nearly lost their guns and their lives. The batteries must break the charge in mid-course. Smoking pieces leaped back in recoil—were swabbed, loaded, sighted, barked again.

> I see the shells exploding leaving small white clouds, I hear the great shells shrieking as they pass,
>   The grape like the hum and whirr of wind through the trees, (tumultuous now the contest rages,)
>   All the scenes at the batteries rise in details before me again,
>   The crashing and smoking, the pride of the men in their pieces,
>   The chief-gunner ranges and sights his piece and selects a fuse of the right time,
>   After firing I see him lean aside and look eagerly off to note the effect;
>   Elsewhere I hear the cry of the regiment charging, (the young colonel leads himself this time with brandish'd sword,)

I see the gaps cut by the enemy's volleys, (quickly fill'd up,
no delay,)
I breathe the suffocating smoke, then the flat clouds hover
concealing all; . . .
And ever the sound of the cannon far and near, (rousing
even in dreams a devilish exultation and all the old mad joy in
the depths of my soul.)
WALT WHITMAN, *Drum-Taps,* "The Artilleryman's Vision"

Artillery Captain James F. Hart watched that valiant charge
come on, stirred by admiration. His guns were taking counterbattery fire from the Union artillery now, but he could not tear his
eyes from the splendid sight down there in the field. Shells, exchanged for canister as the range narrowed, were taking the Blue
cavalry in enfilade as well as frontally. Saddles emptied. A color
sergeant reeled and toppled from his horse. As he fell, another
sergeant caught the sinking banner from his hands and carried it on.

"Never," Hart remembered, "rode troopers more gallantly than
those steady Regulars, as under a fire of shell and shrapnel, and
finally of canister, they dashed up to the very muzzles, then through
and beyond our guns, passing between Hampton's left and Jones'
right." [137]

Charging ranks swept back the first Rebel lines into the woods.
But they had done their utmost—they could go no farther—nor
could they hold. From right and left Gray cavalry closed in on
them. The Regulars thrust them back briefly, opening a gap, and
the two 6th's burst through it, with a battery riddling their ranks
at a range of fifty yards.

CHARGE

Doughty Chaplain Gracey, no man to be left behind, was riding
with his Pennsylvanians. The scene etched itself vividly in his
memory.

The noise is like deafening thunder; whistling shot and screaming shell fall all around us, or go crashing through the trees, or bury themselves in the ground, sending a shower of limbs, twigs, barks, leaves, and earth, all over us, while the air seems filled with the wickedly-whistling Minie balls. It seems impossible that any of us shall ever get out of this alive. Earnest prayers ascend for Divine protection. We lie close to our horses' necks, and hug still closer as the crashing shot and shell pass within a few feet or inches of us. Our horses are alarmed and excited, and hurry us through the woods, jamming against trees, tearing through brush, and at other times impenetrable thickets, tearing our clothes and sometimes our skin; but we heed not these little impediments, give the horses the spurs, and in a few minutes are out on the open plains again.[138]

How many they had left behind they would not know until the roll was called. Pennsylvania's Major Robert Morris was missing. Following troopers had seen his mount hit and crash down, with the officer beneath it; he had been captured and would die in Libby Prison. Only such of the wounded as could ride had been brought back, supported on the horses. Beaten back but not shattered, the two 6th's reformed as Pleasonton's [139] trumpeter sounded the "Rally." A dash of Rebel cavalry cut off and made prisoners of some of the rearmost files, but artillery fire ripped it and sent it scurrying away.

It was high noon now, and they had been fighting since dawn, first with the full weight of surprise favoring the Union, then with the scales tipping back to balance and beyond, as more and more Confederate reinforcements galloped into action. Four batteries were engaged on each side. Beckham's guns after their narrow escape had delivered a telling, massed fire from the hill, but several of them had fallen silent, damaged in recoil. Shells of the well-served Federal horse artillery were taking toll of the Gray cavalry. So were Ames's infantry sharpshooters in the clump of woods. It would be tough to scour them out; however, a sweep to the rear of their sheltering cover would cut them off from the ford while the cavalry they supported was driven into the river.

Jeb Stuart gathered his brigades for the kill. This daring raid by a single enemy division, apparently unsupported, was as impudent as it had been unexpected. More, it was amazingly formidable. The Yankee horse was displaying such fighting qualities and tenacity as Stuart and his subordinates had seldom seen before. No matter. He would soon have the bluecoats on the run as on so many previous fields.

All ranks in the Union 1st Division, from Pleasonton and Buford down, had been straining their ears vainly for hours. Where was Gregg with the other two divisions? The whole operation of course depended on the closing of that second jaw of the vise. Only that could relieve the rising, relentless pressure on the first. Time ticked by, and no sound of distant firing cut through the din of battle deafening the combatants. If sound there was, wind from the south blew it away from them. So in a greater battle, some soldier students of military history must have reflected, Napoleon listened anxiously for the coming of Grouchy's guns at Waterloo, guns that came too late.

Nothing seemed to remain but to stiffen resistance and prepare for a fighting retreat back across the Rappahannock.

CHAPTER 12

"The Yankees Are at Brandy!"

G ENERAL GREGG with his 3rd Division, Duffié's 2nd, and Russell's infantry had been late in striking Kelly's Ford. The delay, which would have grave consequences, was due to Duffié's slowness in getting his command in motion, despite his superior's imperative orders. One precious hour late the bluecoats rent the shrouding fog and splashed through the Rappahannock. Gray pickets, as startled as their comrades at the upper ford had been, loosed off hasty rounds at the head of the charging column suddenly upon them.

If Jeb Stuart in the hectic days ahead let his mind revert to Brandy Station, he may have ruefully asked himself why he had allotted the guarding of such an important outpost as Kelly's Ford to Beverly Robertson, a subordinate upon whom he placed little dependence. The same question could not have arisen in regard to the other brigadier who grated on him. "Grumble" Jones's defense at Beverly Ford had been as stanch and stubborn as any commander could demand. The stationing of Robertson at Kelly's should have haunted Stuart's conscience; nor could it be soothed by an answer that he expected no attack. Although no one could have long opposed the surprise onslaught that forced the ford, the posting of the aggressive Hampton, for instance, in that danger area would have told another story for the following action. Robertson's subsequent tactics nearly lost the day for Stuart. A measure of the distrusted brigadier's failure is the fact that his command took so little part in the Battle of Brandy Station that it suffered not a single casualty.[140]

Robertson's pickets, not reinforced, could not hold, but their brief resistance enabled their brigade, two North Carolina regiments, to saddle, mount, and form. Properly the brigadier dispatched couriers to inform his superior of the enemy incursion. They seem, inexplicably, to have gone astray, for Stuart's first notification that the Federals had appeared in his rear would come from Jones; his second via one of Robertson's scouts, not the couriers.

Gregg brushed the pickets aside and forged ahead. He found that Robertson had deployed his men in dismounted line of battle across the road that runs from Kelly's Ford via Newby's Shop and Fleetwood to Brandy Station. If Gregg had chosen to continue on that avenue of approach, it would have brought him in on the right flank of Confederate troops hotly engaged with Buford around St. James Church. He might have shelled Robertson's road block, charged, and smashed through. Surely Sheridan would have done just that, but Sheridan was still in the West.

Gregg's decision was to leave Russell's infantry with artillery support to contain Robertson, while he and the two cavalry divisions swung almost due south, away from Buford's battle, on another road.

Robertson watched the long column of Blue troopers go clattering southward. Again he sent couriers to report the movement to Stuart, but he took no further action. No scout detachment galloped off to keep Gregg under observation, nor was a stronger force dispatched for a swift onset on the flank of the departing Union cavalry—a force that could have been spared even from that small brigade, confronted only by slow-moving infantry. The Confederate leader, judging it best to keep his command intact, simply maintained his road block and waited for orders.

Time flitted irretrievably past, as Gregg trotted away on his long detour. It was a good four miles to a road fork at the Willis Madden house, a veritable Robin Hood's barn that day. There the General took his 3rd Division, Kilpatrick's and Wyndham's brigades, northwest on the road to Brandy Station, with another five miles or more to cover. He sent Duffié's 2nd Division, Cesnola's and Irvin Gregg's brigades, off on the left fork to Stevensburg where their

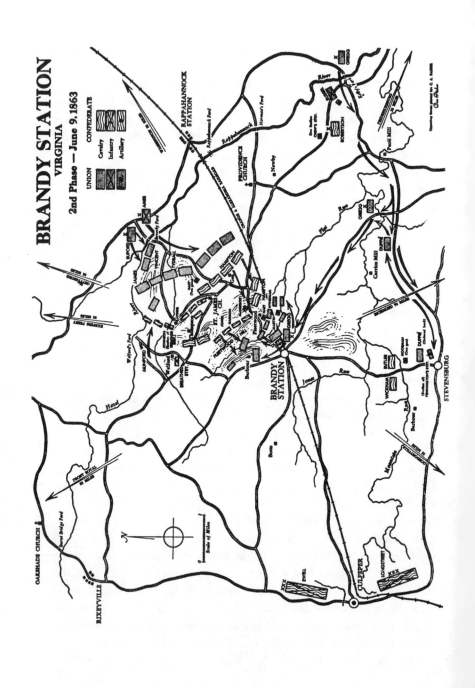

BRANDY STATION
VIRGINIA
2nd Phase — June 9, 1863

UNION | CONFEDERATE

Cavalry
Infantry
Artillery

RAPPAHANNOCK STATION

PROVIDENCE CHURCH

BRANDY STATION

STEVENSBURG

CULPEPER

RIXEYVILLE

OAKSHADE CHURCH

N

Scale of Miles

orders were to angle sharply right on an almost due north road that also led to Brandy.

The three-prong attack Pleasonton had planned for his three divisions was under way. Yet those prongs were spread out now as if on the antlers of a gigantic stag. Buford's was blunted and in danger of being broken. The other two were still miles from being embedded in the enemy.

Duffié's vanguard impetuously trotted straight through Stevensburg on the road west which would lead it away from any part in the combat. Time was lost while it was recalled and doubled back. Then the division prepared to turn north as ordered. Not long before that road had been open clear through to Brandy and all the way to Culpeper. Now it no longer was. Gray cavalry determinedly blocked it with results that will be narrated in a following chapter.

Gregg was off on his wide detour, skirting Robertson's road block; Duffié given check by another one north of Stevensburg. No wonder Pleasonton and Buford listened vainly for the sound of the guns of their comrade divisions.

It was not from the stationary Robertson but, as has been mentioned, from Jones that Stuart received first warning that a fresh force of Federal cavalry was rapidly approaching and threatening the rear. Alert troopers on the far right of Jones's line had spotted Gregg's vanguard and promptly reported it.

Jeb Stuart had already been surprised once today. The thought that it could happen twice was too humiliating to be credible. Disbelief came readily in view of the disliked source of the information. The General dismissed Jones's messenger with the curt answer:

"Tell General Jones to attend to the Yankees in his front, and I'll watch the flanks."

"Grumble's" reception of his superior officer's reply was a characteristic explosion.

"So he thinks they ain't coming, does he? Well, let him alone. He'll damn soon see for himself." [141]

Back on Fleetwood Heights Stuart had left Major H. B. McClellan of his staff in charge of a message center. There a scout from one of Robertson's North Carolina regiments brought a second warning. Yankee cavalry coming and almost at Brandy!

McClellan, not knowing the man, was doubtful. Ride back, he ordered the scout, and make sure you have not mistaken some of our troops for the enemy. In five minutes the man came pelting back, pointing behind him. Look yonder, sir. You can see for yourself.

"And so it was!" McClellan recalled. "Within cannon shot of the hill a long column of the enemy filled the road, which here skirted the woods. They were pressing forward steadily upon the railroad station, which must in a few minutes be in their possession. How could they be prevented from also occupying the Fleetwood Hill, the key to the whole position? Matters looked serious!" [142]

One of his gallopers rushed the alarm to Stuart. Still incredulous in spite of his trust of McClellan, Jeb barked an order to Captain Hart of the artillery. "Ride back there and see what this foolishness is about!" [143] Scarcely had the gunner officer started when a third messenger, one of Stuart's own headquarters clerks, rode up with a shout, "General, the Yankees are at Brandy!" An outburst of sputtering carbine fire confirmed the now undeniable.

Vital phases of a battle can hinge on a single, small, fortuitous incident. Now it was the chance presence near Fleetwood of one cannon. Under command of Lieutenant R. W. Carter, it had been withdrawn from the line of Beckham's batteries and moved back to the foot of the hill because its ammunition was almost exhausted. It was only a six-pound howitzer, light ordnance in a war where double its caliber was standard; the Confederacy, hard-pressed for artillery, used any that came to hand. But to desperate Major McClellan, alone on Fleetwood except for his messengers and with the Blue horse converging on him, that howitzer was providence on wheels. He rushed off a courier for it.

Carter galloped his piece to the crest and unhooked. Its crew flung open the lid of its limber chest, which contained a few defective shells and some roundshot, and loaded. The howitzer flamed and banged. They fired slowly, making the precious rounds last as long as possible. Courier after courier raced off to Stuart.

It was all important to gain time [McClellan realized], for
should the enemy once plant his artillery on this hill it would
cost many valuable lives to recover the ground, even if that
could at all be accomplished. We must retain this position or
suffer most seriously when enclosed between the divisions of
Buford and Gregg. But the enemy was deceived by appearances.
That the head of his column should have been greeted with
the fire of artillery as soon as it emerged from the woods must
have indicated to General Gregg the presence of a considerable
force upon the hill; and the fact that his advance from Kelly's
Ford had been entirely unopposed, together with his ignorance
of what had transpired with Buford, must have strengthened the
thought that his enemy, in force, here awaited an attack.[144]

Colonel Sir Percy Wyndham's 2nd Brigade was leading: 1st New
Jersey, the regiment he had trained; 1st Pennsylvania and 1st Maryland, with the 6th New York Battery. It had swept through Brandy
Station and galloped full tilt to seize dominating Fleetwood Hill.
As Carter's little howitzer spat at the head of the column from the
eminence, Wyndham's right hand rose in the halt signal. The
brigade reined in. Dismount, deploy, and advance as skirmishers. Let
the New York guns unlimber and open.

From the summit a slow fire of dud shells and roundshot from
one howitzer had robbed the Federal onset of its impetus. Yet none
can altogether blame Wyndham, a brave and experienced foreign
veteran, for his caution. He had every reason to believe that the
hill was strongly held. The desultory cannonade could be a ruse,
enticing the Blue cavalry to charge into the blast of massed
batteries kept silent till the range was point-blank. Even if that
piece on the hill were a lone gun, fresh in minds was the recent
feat of Pelham, who in a similar situation at Fredericksburg had
held up the advance of a full corps of Burnside's for almost an
hour with two guns, then with one when its fellow was knocked out.

So once more an artillery stand bought precious time. Stuart,
convinced of the second Yankee attack at last, was rushing up the
reinforcements implored by McClellan to save Fleetwood. He
ordered the nearest brigadier, Jones, to pull the 12th Virginia and

the 35th Battalion out of the line fighting Buford and gallop hard for the hill. On their heels rode Jeb himself. Regiments of Rooney Lee's and Hampton's also were urgently summoned, two of the latter already on the way. But even Jones had one mile and a half to go, and "minutes expanded seemingly into hours" while the anxious McClellan, his last courier dispatched, awaited the aid that must come quickly or be useless.

Artillery Lieutenant Carter's last round was expended now. He began to limber up his howitzer to withdraw, mission gallantly accomplished.

Colonel Wyndham, no longer deceived, mounted his troopers and charged at the head of the 1st New Jersey, his Dundrearies streaming back like pennons. The Blue waves surged up the slopes, lapping the crest, the bright sun glistening on their drawn sabers.

Gregg made ready to fling in the full weight of the rest of his division. Shed now was the patriarchal mantle which seemed figuratively always to cloak the dignified General. As he galloped, he swung his gauntlets over his head and hurrahed. He snapped out an order to his adjutant, Captain Weir, to rush an order to Kilpatrick to charge at once. Weir put his mount at a fence. Twice it refused. Lieutenant Meyer, coming up behind, took the jump, giving the balky animal a lead that carried it over. The adjutant delivered his message, and Kilpatrick's brigade, 1st Maine, 2nd and 10th New York, and a District of Columbia company, was marshaled to ride hell-for-leather in a race for the Fleetwood ridge with the converging Gray horsemen.

Major General Alfred Pleasonton, U.S.A. (*Library of Congress Collections*)

Major General J. E. B. Stuart, C.S.A. (*Library of Congress Collections*)

Lieutenant General Wade Hampton, C.S.A. (From *Battles and Leaders of the Civil War*)

Brigadier General Fitzhugh Lee, C.S.A. (*Library of Congress Collections*)

Brigadier General W. E. Jones, C.S.A. (*Library of Congress Collections*)

Brigadier General Alfred N. Duffié, U.S.A.

Brigadier General David McM. Gregg, U.S.A.

Brigadier General John Buford, U.S.A.

(Photographs on this page reproduced from the Collections of the Library of Congress)

Brigadier General Judson Kilpatrick, U.S.A.

Brigadier General Percy Wyndham, U.S.A.

Duel between a Union cavalryman and a Confederate trooper. Drawing by W. E. Trego. (From *Battles and Leaders of the Civil War*)

The advance of the cavalry skirmish line. Drawing by Edwin Forbes. (From *Life Studies of the Great Army*)

Union horse artillery battery galloping into action at Brandy Station. Drawing by Edwin Forbes. (*Library of Congress Collections*)

A cavalry charge. Drawing by Edwin Forbes. (From *Life Studies of the Great Army*)

The bugle call, by William M. Hunt. (From *Battles and Leaders of the Civil War*)

Camp of the 18th Pennsylvania Cavalry at Brandy Station. (*Library of Congress Collections*)

Charge of General Buford's Cavalry Upon the Enemy near Beverly Ford, on the Rappahannock, by A. R. Waud (*Harper's Weekly,* July 4, 1863).

"This sketch had to be made across a meadow intersected by four ditches, in jumping which some horses fell, their riders getting trampled underfoot. At the other side of this field the ground rose to the woods, which also extended along the right flank. On the left of the road, upon the ridge, was a house used as Stuart's head-quarters, afterward captured—to its left a battery which shelled our men till they closed upon the rebs, the case and canister killing more of their men than ours.

"On the right of the road three battalions were drawn up on column of companies, supported by a brigade in line of battle, and on the left a regiment was posted. Against them General Buford sent two regiments. These had to come out of the woods and form under fire from the batteries. The Sixth Pennsylvania, formerly Lancers, led the charge, which was directed against the centre battalion. The Sixth fell upon these with great gallantry, and, regardless of the chances of flank attack from the other battalions, drove them, fighting hand to hand, through the brigade in reserve, and then wheeling about, passed round the battalion on the right, and resumed position for another charge. The regiment on the left advanced and charged to take us on the flank, but had not the courage to come hand to hand."

Sam Sweeney. (*Courtesy Los Angeles County Museum*)

Sam Sweeney's banjo. (*Courtesy Los Angeles County Museum*)

CHAPTER 13

The Blocked Division

GREGG and his 3rd Division, galloping to the storming of Fleetwood, must have confidently expected Duffié and his 2nd to come up on their left, turn the Rebel right, and drive through to Culpeper.

Veterans remembered that the clear air of that ninth day of June carried sound well. It was possible, despite the north wind, for Gregg and his men to have heard artillery fire to the south in the direction of Stevensburg, but their ears were filled with the pounding of the hoofs of their mounts and the cheers of their charging squadrons. For the moment none could have heeded the distant shots that heralded a third battle within a battle.

General Stuart had begun taking overdue precautions. Before ordering Wade Hampton into action against the attack over Beverly Ford, he had directed that one of that brigadier's regiments be detached to guard the rear at Brandy Station. Hampton sent the 2nd South Carolina Cavalry, commanded by Colonel Matthew Calbraith Butler. Butler had marched his regiment to the railroad town when scouts reported that the enemy was advancing from Stevensburg. Without waiting for orders he wheeled and hurried south to intercept, notifying Stuart who sent Colonel W. C. Wickham's 4th Virginia to reinforce him.

Of the three southerly approaches to Brandy, Butler and Wickham were about to attempt to block one. Robertson, facing Federal infantry, was holding another. None of them knew that Gregg was thrusting between them by the middle, unguarded route.

Butler, a nephew of the Perry brothers of U.S. Navy fame,

handled his regiment as skillfully as his uncles had fleets. Like light scouting craft preceding frigates were the two detachments he rushed off to Stevensburg to develop the enemy's strength and delay him if they could. The first galloped up in sight of the town as Duffié's vanguard passed through, then countermarched. The second under Lieutenant Colonel Frank Hampton, General Wade Hampton's younger brother, came up as a bluecoat squadron was forming east of Stevensburg. The young colonel had only thirty-six troopers but he led them forward in a whooping charge which drove the squadron back upon the main body.

He then fell back upon his regiment, which Butler had put in position, dismounted, and deployed in the woods along the road. The cover concealed the force's mounted men, drawn up across the road and ready to charge again. They awaited Duffié's attack.

It was not long in coming, but it was hesitant and tentative and it failed to clear the woods. Confederate Enfields blasted it back.

Wickham's 4th Virginia was up now, guided by Captain W. D. Farley, one of Stuart's aides, over a narrow byroad that ran through a dense copse of pine. Wickham was senior to Butler but did not immediately assume over-all command.

Now with combat about to be rejoined occurred another of those chance incidents that sway the fortunes of battle.

The 1st Union Brigade (1st Massachusetts, 6th Ohio, and 1st Rhode Island) was suffering from Butler's galling rifle fire from the woods along the road. In Captain Tewksbury's Massachusetts squadron angry troopers soon had enough of taking it without action. They shouted to their commander to lead a charge. Steady, men, he cautioned. As yet he had been given no direction to advance. But the clamor for a charge spread through the ranks until it seemed to be an order passed down from officers through non-coms.

Sabers jerked from scabbards in a rasp of relief, the squadron charged. Captain Lee Higginson's two companies followed, swept into the vortex. Rhode Island cavalrymen flooded along the right of the road, with more Massachusetts on the left and Ohio dashing straight ahead.

Tewksbury's eighty troopers of that impromptu assault [145] struck the enemy first. The Captain, knocked from his saddle, remounted and led on. They went through Frank Hampton's twenty—the rest of his men dismounted to guard flanks—like a whirlwind. Hampton slumped over his horse's neck with a mortal wound, a pistol ball in the stomach. The Blue avalanche caught the 4th Virginia at a disadvantage, entangled in the pine woods where it was trying to form line of battle, and cut it in two. Part of that hitherto stanch regiment was stampeded and fled in panic. [146] Its officers could not rally it. It left the ground strewn with dead and wounded and fifty-three prisoners in enemy hands.

If a cavalry charge is glorious, a cavalry rout is dreadful. Pressing upon one another, strained to the utmost of their speed, the horses catch an infection of fear which rouses them to frenzy. The men, losing their places in the ranks, and all purpose of formation or hope of combined resistance, rush madly for some point of safety upon which it may be possible to rally. . . . Splashing through the pools of mire, breaking down fences, darting under trees, with clang of sabers and din of hoofs, officers wild with shame and rage, shouting themselves hoarse with unavailing curses, and the bullets of the enemy whistling shrilly overhead, the mingled mass sweeps on, until utter exhaustion stops them, or their commanders, struggling to the front, can indicate a place to form.

Such, although that vivid description relates to the flight of a Federal regiment on another field, [146] was the rout of the 4th Virginia squadron.

Captain Tewksbury, having shot the man who had unhorsed him, rode after the rout. A guidon bearer whacked the breath out of a fleeing Rebel with its lance and captured him. Troopers gave chase to a two-horse ambulance, full of stores, and forced it into a ditch where it overturned. They flung themselves on its contents—medical stores, liquor, tea, and coffee—and helped themselves, "avoiding the medicines," until Duffié peremptorily recalled them to meet a Confederate counterattack. [147]

Colonel Butler, one flank exposed by the flight of the Virginia squadron, re-formed his regiment and advanced across the little stream of Mountain Run. Carbines sputtered in a fierce fight with Union skirmishers. Butler was now supported by one cannon, sent by Stuart, but it was outgunned by Battery M, 2nd U.S. Artillery, Lieutenant A. C. M. Pennington. Those close-shooting gunners pumped shells into the Gray ranks. Pennington, field glasses at his eyes, spotted two mounted officers: Butler and Stuart's aide, Farley. He snapped an order. The gunner of one of his pieces laid carefully and fired. The shell struck the ground about thirty paces in front of the horsemen and ricocheted. It smashed into Butler's right leg above the ankle, then ploughed through Farley's horse and sheared off his right leg at the knee.

My horse [Butler wrote] bounded in the air and threw me, saddle and all, flat on my back in the road, when the poor fellow moved off with his entrails hanging out toward the clover field where he had been grazing in the early morning, and died there, as I was afterwards informed. Farley's horse dropped in the road, terribly lacerated, and Farley fell with his head on his horse's side.[148]

Colonel Butler's foot was dangling by a shred of skin (its loss would not keep him out of the Spanish-American War), but he managed to reach the more gravely wounded aide to help him put on a tourniquet. Regimental surgeons arrived with an ambulance and placed Farley in it in spite of his protests that the Colonel be cared for first. The younger man, given his severed limb at his request, clutched it to him as he was taken to a farmhouse where he soon died. Butler later was carried from the field.

The tide of victory was running strong for Alfred Duffié. He had suffered few casualties, considerably less than the enemy, and lost only one man captured, a trooper whose horse ran away with him into the Rebel ranks. The three regiments of his 1st Brigade had rocked back the two opposing him, routing one squadron. And he had not yet brought into action the three Pennsylvania regiments of

Colonel J. Irvin Gregg's 2nd Brigade, but only its supporting horse battery, Pennington's.

Now was Duffié's moment. Call up Irvin Gregg and with the weight of fresh horsemen smash through the cracked blockade toward Culpeper! The brave and stubborn South Carolinians and Virginians still holding the road could not withstand a determined assault any longer. There is every reason to believe that Duffié was about to deliver it.

The 1st Brigade made no second charge. No summons went back to Irvin Gregg. He remained in reserve, wasted strength that should have been used then or earlier. His total casualties throughout the battle amounted only to one man wounded and four missing, and his service was reduced to covering the retreat across the river at the end of the day.

It was galloping couriers from General David Gregg that hauled back Duffié from the brink of triumph. Rejoin me at once, ran the urgent order. Return by the route you came. Had a staff officer, given powers of discretion, brought the message, he might have been persuaded to allow the 2nd Division to burst through the thin barrier on the road and ride hard for Brandy on the most direct route. "Duffié was on the point of scattering his badly hurt opponents when ordered to rejoin Gregg by the roundabout route over which he had come. . . . Had Duffié been kept where he was he most certainly would have broken through into the Confederate rear just when Gregg needed him most." [149] But the orders delivered by the staffer allowed no option.

So perforce the French officer serving the United States turned his back on glory. He had hesitated and was lost. For his division Pleasonton would not ask, as he did for the other two, that it be allowed to inscribe Brandy Station on its guidons.

Duffié wheeled his regiments and retraced his course to the point where he had branched off on the road to Stevensburg. Then he swung north toward Fleetwood Hill where Gregg was having the fight of his life.

CHAPTER 14

Combat for a Hill

T HE summit of Fleetwood Hill, drenched by the sun, was a glittering gauge of battle. As Gregg's 2nd Brigade commander, Colonel Wyndham, charged up its slopes at the head of the 1st New Jersey, standards and guidons snapping in the wind, its crucial crest stood almost deserted. Carter's lone howitzer had fired its last round and was pulling out, its mission valiantly performed. Now the only garrison was a single staff officer, Major McClellan, his last courier dispatched with desperate appeals for help. He watched yards reel by under the galloping hoofs of Wyndham's upsurging regiments. Once in possession of that dominating hilltop, they would hold a natural citadel.

At the last, supremely tense moment McClellan from his vantage point sighted a column in gray approaching at the trot. It was Colonel A. W. Harman's 12th Virginia, followed by Colonel Elijah V. White's 35th Virginia or Laurel Battalion. "Grumble" Jones, as ordered, had sent those two units of his command, battle-weary from fighting Buford all morning yet still eager for action.

They must not have understood the urgency of their summons, for they were at the trot, and that gait would never bring them to the summit in time.

McClellan spurred recklessly down the hill to meet Colonel Harman. For God's sake, charge! They're right on you!

The 12th Virginia in column of fours pounded up the slope. Its leading files reached the crest with Wyndham's charging line fifty yards short of it. Unfaltering the Virginians plunged down to meet the enemy. Their column was a slender spear thrust into the broad sweep of a scythe. Jerseymen mowed down the Gray regiment's vanguard. They flung the rest of it in disorder back over and down the hill. On they rushed, 1st Maryland and 1st Pennsylvania fanning out at their heels. Smashing into the 35th Battalion, they cut it in two.

Major von Borcke of Stuart's staff had been as incredulous as his commander of the report that the Federals were at Brandy. A glimpse of Fleetwood swiftly disillusioned him. It was, he admitted, a sight that made the blood run cold in his veins—the heights and Stuart's headquarters "perfectly swarming with Yankees, while the men of our brigades were scattered wide over the plateau, chased in all directions by their enemies."

It was high time for one of the big Prussian's deeds of derring-do, exploits he described vaingloriously in his memoirs. Some of them he performed to the hilt, for unquestionably he was a man of dauntless courage; others, however, must be taken with more than a grain of salt. Now he dashed toward a breaking Confederate regiment.

I rode up [he related] to the Colonel, who seemed to have lost all presence of mind, and threatened to arrest him on the spot, and to prefer a charge of cowardice against him if he did not at once lead his men on to the attack. This had the desired effect, and with a faint cheer the regiment galloped toward the enemy; but two hostile regiments starting to meet us, the space we were charging over diminished with increasing rapidity, until at last, when only a hundred yards apart, our disheartened soldiers broke and fled in shameful confusion. Carried along for a moment by the torrent of fugitives, I perceived that we were hastening toward a gap in a fence, which had been made to facilitate the movements of our artillery, and soon outstripping the rest by the fleetness of my charger, I reached the gap, and placed myself in the centre, calling out to them that I would kill every man who tried to pass me, and knocking over with the flat of my sabre two of those who had ventured too near me. This had the effect of arresting the flight for a time, and I then managed to rally around me about a hundred of those same men whom, on this identical ground, I had on a previous occasion led to victory. "Men," I shouted, "remember your previous deeds on these very fields. Follow me —charge!" and putting spurs into my charger's flanks, the noble animal bounded forth against the Federals who were now close upon us, but whose lines, by the length of the pursuit, had become very loose. The very same men, however, who had fought so gallantly with me before had lost all self-confidence, and after following me a short distance, they turned again to flight, abruptly leaving me quite alone in the midst of the charging foe. A great hulking Yankee corporal, with some eight or ten men, immediately gave chase after me, calling on me to surrender. Not heeding this summons, I urged my horse to his highest speed; and now turning to the rear myself, and clearing the fence at a part where it was too high for them to follow, I soon left my pursuers far behind. I had not galloped many hundred yards further, however, when I overtook Captain White of our Staff, who had received a shot-wound in his neck, and was so weak as scarcely to be able to keep himself up in the saddle. Having to support my wounded comrade, whom I was determined to save, retarded my pace considerably, and several times the shouts and yells of the Yankees sounded so close at our horses heels that I gave up all hope of escape. Suddenly, however, the Yankees gave up the pursuit and I was enabled to draw bridle after a very exciting run.[150]

The Confederate regiments, which had responded to McClellan's appeal to save the hill, had indeed been repelled and rocked back by Wyndham's assault. Although they were by no means so demoralized as von Borcke alleged, they had undeniably failed in their effort to hold the high ground.

Fleetwood was in Union hands. Three guns of Captain Joseph W. Martin's 6th New York Battery were at its foot, and one of them was being hauled up to keep the crest secure. Pleasonton's 12:30 P.M. dispatch to Hooker was guardedly exultant.

General Gregg has joined me, and I will now attack the enemy vigorously with my whole force. Prisoners report that

Stuart has 30,000 cavalry here. Both Lees, Jones, and Hampton are with him. We have had a sharp fight, and have lost heavily, as we had the whole force in front of one half of my command. Colonel Davis, Eighth New York, and Captain Canfield, Second (U.S.) Cavalry, are killed. Major Morris, Sixth Pennsylvania Cavalry, a prisoner, with a number of others. We have about 100 in hospitals wounded; Major Beveridge, Eighth Illinois, among the number. Buford and Ames have driven their whole force out of their strongest position. It would be well to send a good force of Fifth Corps toward Brandy Station, if it can be spared.[151]

Jeb Stuart galloped toward the key hill, which rose above the smoke of battle like an island in a spume-flecked sea. Having left regiments to hold off Buford, he rushed a courier to Hampton to pull out of the line and recover Fleetwood. But sight of bluecoats on the slopes had been all Hampton needed to anticipate the orders he knew his superior would surely give. His horsemen swept across the field in magnificent order. Cobb's Legion in advance—1st South Carolina in echelon—1st North Carolina—the Jeff Davis Legion—Hart's horse artillery rumbling abreast of the long lines of cavalry—sections of McGregor's and Chew's batteries. Stuart waved them on with a shout, "Give them the saber, boys!"

They charged in close column of squadrons, some straight on, others diverging to thunder along the ridge. The high-pitched Rebel yell, *woh-who-ey,* heralded their coming, and was answered by the ringing, deeper-toned Yankee *hoo-ray* until the breathless shock of contact drowned cheers with the clash of steel.

Jones's half-shattered troopers rallied and re-formed. Harmon was carried off severely wounded, but his regiment and the Laurel men closed in on the enemy with Hampton's gray waves. Thrice a New Jersey guidon was lost and thrice recaptured, twice by its owners, once by the 1st Pennsylvania. Charged front and rear, Jersey was hard pressed. Its commander, Lieutenant Colonel Virgil Broderick, led a dash to cut a way out. His saber pierced a Gray trooper, who leaped convulsively from his saddle and crashed to the ground. Revolvers spurting in retaliation killed Broderick's horse. At once Trumpeter Wood dismounted and turned his mount over to the officer. As the little musician cast about for another horse, a Confederate rode down on him and took him prisoner. While Wood was being marched to the rear, he snatched up a carbine from the ground. Though it was empty, he bluffed his captor into surrender, disarmed and dismounted him, and in turn drove him rearward.[152]

RALLY

Colonel Broderick was fighting his last fight. Five assailants ringed him, sabers swinging. The gallant officer, a skilled swordsman, cut down one of his adversaries. A swerve saved him from the blow of a second. He caught a third's slash on his blade and drove its point into the wielder's forehead. Although he managed to parry the next man's blow, the force of it beat his saber out of his hand. He drew his revolver and fired into the cordon, the bullet dropping a horse in his path. As he spurred through the gap, his own mount stumbled and fell.[153] Broderick, struck by a bullet and deeply gashed by a sword cut, was probably dead before he hit the ground. His second in command, Major John H. Shelmire, was killed about the same time; his body lay across an enemy's.

Senior officers, singled out, were meeting death or wounds in this close-quarters fighting. The brigade commander himself, Colonel Wyndham, was sitting his saddle a little unsteadily, bleeding from a leg wound. He would not leave the field to have it dressed until 4 P.M. when weakness from loss of blood forced him out of action.

The 1st New Jersey, its colonel and major down, was deep in trouble, and Kilpatrick had not yet come up on its right to free it from the pressure that was grinding it down. Its sister Maryland and Pennsylvania regiments had their hands more than full. Fortunately for Jersey, its dilemma was not yet realized by the Gray cavalrymen who had it virtually surrounded. Embattled Jerseymen charged again to hew out an avenue of escape. In their way stood a section of McGregor's battery which had unlimbered to go into action. Primarily because the artillery blocked an outlet, not in an effort to capture it, the bluecoats rode yelling down on the guns. In the brief, furious fight that raged among the cannon, two lieutenants were cut down and killed defending them. A gunner swung his rammer staff to bowl a horseman out of his saddle. But Jersey flooded over the position and carved through an exit.

Lieutenant Henry C. Meyer, Gregg's aide—he who had led the adjutant's recalcitrant mount over a fence—was caught in the fringe of the conflict. He saw a Confederate officer sabering a Marylander who was begging for quarter. In the heat of combat the officer showed no mercy. Meyer galloped to the rescue.

> I tried to shoot him [Meyer declared], but the ball from my pistol missed him and hit his horse. This did not take immediate effect. Finding that I was about to be cut off, as Wyndham's command had been repulsed and Kilpatrick had not arrived, and having only one charge left in my revolver, I had to allow the officer to ride up to and strike me, so to be sure of my aim. As I presented the pistol, it missed fire, and as soon as he could recover his seat in the saddle, he struck at me. I had, however, fallen down on the neck of my horse, so the point of his saber cut into my collar-bone, but the weight of the blow cut a two-quart pail, that I had borrowed that morning to cook coffee in, nearly in two. Before either of us could recover control of our horses, I had gotten my sabre in my hand, which had been hanging from a knot, as was the custom. He then struck at me the second time which blow I parried. His horse then sank under him. I was then being crowded into a corner, where a fence joined a building, by four of his followers, one of whom was dismounted. The latter I saw shooting at me. Urging my horse, he jumped a fence, then a ditch beyond it. This enabled me to escape with only the loss of my hat.[154]

Meyer had been particularly anxious to avoid capture, since he carried copies of all General Gregg's orders on his person—let alone the dismal prospect of a sojourn in Libby Prison. He was free now, his wound painful but not dangerous thanks to the buffer pail. After the battle, when he explained the circumstances that ruined the utensil to its lender, he was greeted with a complaint instead of congratulations on his luck. "Well," sourly demanded the pail's owner, "how do you suppose I am going to cook my coffee?"

Again artillery, this time Union, made a valiant stand. Martin's 6th New York Battery, through some confusion of orders, had advanced only one of its three-inch rifles to Fleetwood's crest and then pulled it back to join two others at the base. (Another section had been detailed to support Kilpatrick.) They dropped shells around the Barbour house, supporting Wyndham's charge, until the intermingling of horsemen in blue and gray forced them to hold fire.

Suddenly a new target presented itself. Wyndham's Brigade, battered back, had fought its way out of encirclement and was streaming off in retreat toward Brandy. Hampton, mustering all regiments within reach, was storming up the counterslopes of the hill. Over its summit into Captain Martin's vision loomed lead pairs of artillery teams. They swung rapidly around, guns unlimbered, and Gray cannoneers swarmed around them—sections of Chew's and McGregor's batteries. Puffs of smoke from muzzles were answered instantly by the three rifled pieces of the 6th New York. A hammering artillery duel began.

Troops of other arms watched artillery in action with a certain amount of envy and admiration. Under the heaviest counterbattery fire crews served their pieces coolly, aiming with deliberation. As they fired and loaded, they often sang. Pelham's French gunners from New Orleans always roared out *La Marseillaise*. If a cannoneer fell, there was only a brief pause in the clockwork precision of their drill; another took over the fallen man's duty. It could be, reflected the envious, that the gunners were fortified with a little stimulant. "They were the only ones remaining in the army who always had brandy, and for that they were much indulged." [155]

Chew's First Sergeant Neese saw round after round rammed into the gun he commanded until after the one hundred and sixtieth shot at top speed fire would flash around the cascabel, and the piece be disabled, burned out at the breech. Meanwhile he kept it banging away under hot bombardment from the enemy. "At one time," he recalled, "the Yankee gunners had such perfect range and distance of our position that their shrapnel and shell exploded fearfully close to me and seriously wounded two of my cannoneers and raked the sod all around me. . . . Whizzing shot, howling shell, exploding shrapnel, and screaming fragments filled the air that hung over Fleetwood Heights with the music of war." [156]

Detachments of cavalry supporting Martin mustered for sally up the hill against the Rebel guns. Yonder on the crest they loaded with canister. Muzzles were depressed to take the oncoming horses in the knees with their blasting charges. Hastily the cavalry abandoned the idea of an attack.

Now two squadrons of Colonel White's 35th Virginia Battalion came sweeping around the west side of the hill in sudden onset. They rode savagely down on the New York battery. Its cavalry support melted away.

Captain Martin and his thirty-six cannoneers, worthy of laurels won at Chancellorsville, stood to their guns. Load with canister! Numbers One rammed home the deadly, short-range charges. Lanyards jerked, and spraying cones of balls burst from muzzles, blasting back the horsemen. The New Yorkers had time for only one round per piece. Virginia came on again, encircling them front, flanks, and rear, thrusting into the position. There was no chance to swing the guns around. Cannoneers battled with revolvers, rammer staffs, and trail handspikes. The licking, slashing sabers were too many for them. They were cut down and overridden. White's troopers pistoled the limber horses.

Martin knew now that his guns were doomed. They could neither be defended much longer nor could they be pulled out, with the teams down in tangled harness struggling in their death agonies. The battery commander ordered his guns spiked or wedged by rounds jammed the wrong way into muzzles. He had only men enough left to hold off the enemy moments longer while their comrades disabled the pieces and destroyed fuses.

Captain Martin and six of his men, most of them wounded, fought their way out. The rest were killed, wounded, or captured, and thirty-two horses were dead. The guns were lost with honor, Pleasonton would declare in his report, which asked that the 6th New York Battery be permitted to place the name of this battle it had fought so well on its guidon.[157] The Confederate cavalrymen, driven off by a new attack, did not long keep the trophy guns or those of the other section, also temporarily taken. Union horsemen recaptured them, but could not hold them long enough for Martin to bring up the teams and limbers of his caissons and pull them away to safety, and they were ultimately abandoned on the battlefield.

Jeb Stuart had won back Fleetwood Hill, but how long could he retain it? The contest for that key point, he would officially admit,[158] had been "prolonged and spirited" and it was far from over. Conflict was widening, rising in crescendo. To the northeast Rooney Lee was being attacked again by Buford. Nothing had been heard from Butler since he had marched south to meet the threat from Stevensburg. Part of Gregg's assault had been repulsed but it was rallying, and another Blue brigade, Kilpatrick's, was hurtling into the Confederate left. Today the Union cavalry Stuart had beaten so often was displaying amazing *élan* and stamina.

CHAPTER 15

Draw Sabers! Charge!

•–•

WHEN Judson Kilpatrick received his orders from Gregg to attack, he had formed his brigade in echelon of regiments parallel to the railroad tracks. In the lead was the 10th New York, then the 2nd New York or Harris Light, then the 1st Maine, with a section (two guns) of Martin's ill-fated New York Battery as artillery support. Those orders came a little late—seconds were counting at that point in the battle—a tardiness partly due to the balky horse of the adjutant carrying Gregg's directive, one of those little things that influence a battle.

The impetuous Kilpatrick, battle flag streaming beside him, flung his squadrons at Fleetwood Hill, just lost to the enemy through the repulse of his fellow brigade commander, Wyndham.

Lieutenant Colonel Irvine rose in his stirrups and shouted to his 10th New York, "Gallop! Charge!" For the eager troopers, drawn sabers flashing, hoofs of speeding mounts pounding beneath, this was fulfillment. Hither had led the long road from the cavalry recruiting station, the rigors of training camp, the march to the front, the first skirmish, the series of conflicts with too many bitter defeats—the long road that had brought them now to Brandy Station.

Lieutenant R. B. Porter, acting adjutant, rode on his colonel's left. He felt the blood throbbing hot in his pulses. "Who," he wondered, "can describe the feelings of a man on entering a charge? How exhilarating, and yet how awful! The glory of success in a charge is intoxicating! One forgets everything, even personal safety, in the one grand thought of vanquishing the enemy. We were in for it now, and the nerves were strung to the highest tension." [159]

They crashed into a Gray countercharge that swept down on them, revolvers spurting. Porter saw saddles emptying around him. At once it was hand-to-hand combat.

Then followed an indescribable clashing, banging and yelling.... Two or three stalwart rebels crowded past me, intent on the capture of Colonel Irvine. I was of apparent little account in their desperate efforts to reach him. We were now so mixed up with the rebels that every man was fighting desperately to maintain the position until assistance could be brought forward. The front squadrons broke to the right and left to allow the rear squadrons to come upon the enemy fresh. In an instant everything was mixed up and confused, and Irvine a prisoner. I made desperate efforts to rally enough of our boys to attempt his recapture, but it was of no avail. Every man had all he could do to attend to himself. I found myself with but two or three of our men near.... Just then a big reb bore down on me with his saber raised. I parried the blow with my saber, which, however, was delivered with such force as to partially break the parry, and left its mark across my back and nearly unhorsed me. One of our boys probed my assailant from the rear, and he dismounted. It was plain I must get out then, if ever. The only avenue of escape was over a high embankment of the railroad, and a reb squadron was advancing on that point, not far away. The rebel commander gave orders not to kill my horse, probably deeming me already a prisoner. Two jumps of the horse brought me to the embankment. Every reb in that squadron fired at me, but strangely enough, the only bullet that found its mark was the one that burned my upper lip so badly that I thought it had been carried away. But the next jump of the horse was over the embankment and out of their reach.

Two flank companies of New Yorkers, galloping to capture a Confederate standard, were cut off. Lieutenant Robb and Trooper Evans put their horses at a ditch in an attempt to escape, but the officer's failed to clear it and fell. Evans saw two pursuers ride down on the fallen man. One sabered him, the blade entering his back near the right shoulder and coming out at his breast.

His horse scrambled out of the ditch, and the Lieutenant clung to him for something like fifty or one hundred feet when he relaxed his hold and fell to the ground. While he was struggling in the ditch, I turned and shot one of the rebels, the bullet taking effect in his arm. He cried out, "O God, I'm shot!" Just then as I was about to dismount to assist the Lieutenant, a little rebel officer made a cut at me with his saber and struck my hat clean from my head. I thought it best to get out of that place, and I made a break for the woods.[160]

The rest of the regiment was also having to get out of that place, borne back by the enemy's fierce onslaughts. In difficulty, too, was the 2nd New York, hit by a flank attack and raked by artillery fire. It wavered. Kilpatrick, steadying the ranks, directed a short withdrawal to re-form.

Lieutenant J. Wade Wilson's section of the 6th New York Battery, which had begun the advance on the hill at the column's rear, had been ordered to its front by the brigade commander. Wilson left the road, obliqued to the right, and moved up fast. Living up to the best traditions of horse artillery, he let nothing stop him. His carriages plunged through a morass, careened down into and out of several deep ditches, and crashed through a fence. From the ridge he opened with percussion shells on enemy cavalry. Twice Kilpatrick sent him farther forward. The gunner officer limbered to the front, dashed ahead, unlimbered, and blazed away again.

In its third position, squarely on the crest, the section was left exposed when the brigade drew back to re-form. Instantly the 6th Virginia charged and overran it. Galloping horsemen raced past to strike the Blue cavalry beyond. Some of their number swerved and swooped down on the isolated guns, seemingly as good as captured.

It was the lot of horse artillery to face such desperate situations, as had already been demonstrated several times in this battle. Lacking the protection which infantry gave light artillery, the horse batteries could depend only partially on their own cavalry to stave off an enemy assault. In the swirl of mounted combat they must at times, as at the present moment, be left unguarded. Only their mobility, the cannoneers being individually mounted, could save them—were they free to pull out. If encircled, the choice was surrender or stubborn, last-ditch resistance.

Such a defense Wilson and his gunners now made.

At this time [the Lieutenant declared] was displayed the heroism of the section, and valor of which any command and country may be justly proud. In reversing, one of the gun-limbers was nearly capsized, one wheel being in the air and the axle nearly vertical. Perceiving this, I ordered the cannoneers to dismount and restore to its position the limber. We were surrounded by a squad of rebel cavalry, firing with carbine and pistol. The order was scarcely needed, for the cannoneers had seen the peril of their gun, and, anticipating the order, had dismounted to restore it; and with revolvers in hand, they defended the gun as if determined to share its destiny and make its fate their own. The bearer of a rebel battle-flag was shot by Private Currant, who would have recovered it but for the great difficulty of approaching the color with a lame and skittish horse upon which he was at the time mounted. The flag was taken by the 1st Maine Cavalry.[161]

With the coming of reinforcements, Wilson was able to pull his guns, ammunition almost exhausted, out of their perilous position.

The 1st Maine, the Brigade's rearmost regiment, was advancing in fine order when it was met by Kilpatrick as it emerged from the woods. Those ginger sidewhiskers bristling, he barked a question at the regimental commander, Calvin S. Douty.

"Colonel Douty, what can you do with your regiment?"

"I can drive the Rebels," came the answer.[162]

Go in and do it then, Kilpatrick brusquely told him.

Maine sailed into action. Always, because of the number of seafaring men in its ranks, such nautical terms were part of its speech, cropping up even in the regimental histories. The 1st Maine "put in" to a town as a vessel puts into port. If it came to a halt, it "hove to." Troopers who failed to bring their horses up into line had "fallen astern." When a column was ordered to move faster, it was said to have been given "more headway."

More headway was given the 1st now as, days of depletion by detachments and details happily vanished, it made its first charge as a whole regiment.

And now opened before them, and of which they were a part, a scene of the grandest description [recalled one of the regiment's historians who rode with it]. They were nearly at the right of a large open field of undulating ground, with woods at their right. At the left, as far as the eye could reach, were to be seen bodies of Union cavalry advancing with quick movements toward the enemy's cavalry, who were also in full sight, and apparently as active. Officers grouped with their staffs, and squads of orderlies could be seen in different localities, some quietly watching the tide of battle, others moving in various direction. Orderlies and staff officers were riding at full speed in every direction, helter-skelter, apparently, as if the success of the whole engagement depended upon each one. A little to the right of the front, near a house surrounded by extensive shrubbery (known as the "Barber House," where General Stuart had his headquarters), was a rebel battery, which turned its attention to this regiment as it emerged from the woods. The whole plain was one vast field of intense, earnest action. It was a scene to be witnessed but once in a lifetime, and one well worth all the risks of battle to witness. But the boys could not stop to enjoy this grand, moving panorama of war. On they went, amid a perfect tangle of sights and sounds, filled with such rare, wholesouled excitement as seldom falls to the lot of man to experience; and thoughts of danger were for the time furthest from their minds. Even the horses seemed to enter into the spirit of the occasion, and strained every nerve to do their full duty in the day's strange deeds, obeying the least motion of rein or spur with unusual promptness, as if feeling the superiority of their riders in this terrible commotion.

A railroad cut breaks the formation somewhat, and for a moment checks the advance; but that is soon crossed, and the regiment re-forms with no loss of time and is again on the charge. Nearly in front is the Harris Light Cavalry, charging

upon the battery, while swooping down upon them is a rebel
force, coming across the field from the woods in a diagonal
direction. For a moment the result is in doubt, and then the
Harris Light breaks, and the men scatter and flee. The force
that drove them keeps on its way, now coming directly for the
First Maine. The First Maine falters not, but keeps on its
course. A shell from the battery on the right comes screaming
with harsh voice along the line, apparently directly over the
heads of the men, and seeming so near as to make it impossible,
almost, for the left of the regiment to escape its effects, and
bursts a quarter of a mile away. Some of the men cannot help
dodging a bit as this goes by, and the others try to laugh at them,
but make poor work of it, as they thoroughly appreciate the
feeling which prompts such a movement. This is followed by
another and another, in quick succession. On they go. And
see! the rebel force that a moment before has driven the Harris
Light now breaks and is in full retreat, and the charge has
turned to a chase. Now goes up a cheer and a yell that must
startle the very stones, as the excited boys ride over them.
One defiant rebel, scorning to run from the "cowardly Yankees,"
remains firm in his position as the regiment reaches him, turning neither to the right nor to the left, breaking through the
ranks of two companies in their headlong speed, and nearly
escaping recognition and capture in the excitement. At one time
two rebel troopers are riding along in the ranks of the First
Maine, as coolly as though they belonged there; and no one
who sees them thinks of capturing them. On goes the regiment,
driving the enemy from the battery, and passing by the lonely
and now quiet guns that a moment before were so loudly talking. On they go, faster and faster, if that were possible, over
fences and ditches, driving the enemy a mile or more. Oh, it
was grand! and many a man who was in that charge has at
times fancied that if it were allowed to choose, he would say,
"Let me bid this world good-by amid the supreme excitement
of a grand, exultant, successful cavalry charge like this!"

The regiment at last halts; the companies are re-formed and
counted off, and are ready for another race. A portion dismount and open fire with their carbines, while the enemy's

bullets make lively music about their ears. Lieutenant-Colonel Smith now finds himself the senior officer (Colonel Douty being in another portion of the field), and assumes command. He finds himself with a small command, alone. The enemy is in his rear, and no other Union troops are near. His command has been scattered somewhat, but the men are coming up and joining him fast. As soon as he has force enough to make the attempt to return, he wheels the command, gives the order "Forward!" and again the regiment starts, going back over the same ground it has just driven the enemy from. It appears that when the gunners left the battery, as the regiment swept upon it, they simply stepped into the woods at the right, where they remained till the regiment had passed, when they returned and again took possession of their guns, and turned them upon the regiment, and were joined by a large force of their cavalry who had taken refuge in the same woods, as well as by some from the other parts of the field. The regiment had passed on and left the guns alone, supposing, if any thought was taken of the matter at all, that the remaining regiments of the brigade would come to its support, and could take care of the battery after it had been tamed.

The regiment, which was now between two fires, kept well together, and rode straight for the battery as if to attempt to recapture it, and then, just as the gunners were going to fire, Colonel Smith suddenly changed directions to the right. In a moment the regiment was out of the line of fire, while the grape and cannister which was intended for the little force passed harmlessly by in the rear, tearing up the ground where the Maine boys had just been; and before the guns could be reloaded and brought to bear upon them again, the boys had cut their way out. Never was the fact more clearly demonstrated, that in a battle it is the safest, as well as the best, for each individual soldier to stick to his command, than it was here; for those who remained together got off the field with small loss, while of those who scattered, many were taken prisoners, some were obliged to cut their way through small bodies of the enemy, some met their death in this endeavor, some escaped by taking Stuart's headquarters; and all took great risks.[163]

Troopers, whom the alert Lieutenant Colonel Charles H. Smith had saved from a cannon blast by his swift maneuver, held together and beat off repeated charges. But one foray cut off Captain Benjamin F. Tucker, took him prisoner, disarmed him, and sent him to the rear under escort of three cavalrymen. They rode on his right and left and behind him. The officer's imagination must have pictured the prison doors of Libby clanging closed behind him, and it was no pleasant prospect. Out of the corner of an eye he noticed that the guard on his left was carrying his saber carelessly. Tucker suddenly leaned over, wrenched the blade away, and ran its owner through. He whipped it free and with a sweeping backstroke cut down the captor on his right. As he fell, Tucker wheeled his mount in the same arc with his slashing blow. Before the Rebel in the rear could react, he found the point of a saber, ready to thrust, presented at his heart. Prudently he surrendered. Tucker herded him back along with the horses of his victims.[164]

Kilpatrick turned from the 1st Maine's valiant onset to rally the rest of his brigade. "Back, the Harris Light! Back, the Tenth New York! Re-form your squadrons and charge!" he shouted. They surged up the hill in answer.

Once more Fleetwood Hill was covered with blue uniforms.

"The moving finger writes; and having writ, moves on."

That which it had several times inscribed for both sides at Brandy Station and poised before setting down an aftermath—not half a line thereof to be canceled or a word of it washed out by tears—was, Here is opportunity, fleeting, evanescent. Seize it now or never.

Jeb Stuart's faulty dispositions and failure to forestall surprise had been the first lapse. Robertson let chances slip when he remained inactive in the position he took after the enemy crossing at Kelly's Ford. Fitz Lee's brigade, in the illness of its commander, was slow to quit its bivouac ground and strike a blow when it was needed. Telling infantry support from the Army of Northern Virginia (at the possible cost of revealing its concentration) might have been rushed up from Culpeper, only a half-dozen miles distant. Robert E. Lee had been informed early in the morning by Stuart that the enemy had crossed Beverly Ford and was attacking. "Lee suspected that the move was simply a reconnaissance, and he wrote Stuart where he could get infantry in case he needed it, but urged him to conceal the presence of Confederate foot if it was possible for him to do so." [165] Confident in Stuart's ability to handle the situation, Lee took no action until late in the afternoon when the continued roar of the guns testified to fierce and prolonged fighting. Then he ordered an infantry brigade to report to Hampton, while he in person rode toward the field. By that time the battle was virtually over. No Gray infantry took part, although Federal reports stated that it had arrived by railroad and was a decisive factor in Pleasonton's withdrawal. The presence of the main army so close at hand constituted, however, a highly reassuring backstop. Jeb Stuart would have scorned to call for help except as a last resort, but there it lay if needed.

Opportunity had knocked oftener at the door of the Union forces, as she does for the aggressor. They had not answered when Gregg's attack was delivered late because of Duffié's slowness in bringing his division to Kelly's Ford; when Gregg himself failed to crash through Robertson's road block and instead made his detour to ride to Brandy by an unguarded route; when Duffié hesitated before the crumbling barrier of Butler's and Wickham's troopers and was recalled to rejoin by the long circuit that kept his division out of action at a decisive moment; when Kilpatrick's charge came too tardily to prevent Wyndham's repulse. Now another and a last knock sounded where Buford's 1st Division was striving mightily to punch a hole through the weakened Confederate lines and strike the rear of the troops hotly engaged with Gregg.

CHAPTER 16

Crisis in a Dust Cloud

~~~~~~

FOR Buford's men, fighting since dawn, charge had followed charge, interspersed with dismounted action. They were bone-weary and hungry, few having had any sustenance all day except a swallow of water from canteens. Yet most were aware neither of fatigue nor hunger. Battle buoyed them up. Cavalry and infantry drew on reserves of energy when the Brigadier called on them for still another effort. Now was their chance, and probably the last one since the day was waning, to clamp the upper jaw of the vise against Gregg's to the south.

Gray ranks in front of them had thinned. Both Jones and Rooney Lee had ill spared regiments sorely needed to reinforce Fleetwood. The latter because of the withdrawal of Colonel L. L. Lomax's 11th Virginia was compelled to shorten his line by falling back to higher ground. There he held a strong position: horsemen under cover, dismounted sharpshooters behind a stone wall, and Breathed's Battery on an eminence with a fine field of fire.

Buford massed his troops and launched them against Lee. Ames's stout brigade of infantry attacked with spirit, the 2nd and 33rd Massachusetts and the 3rd Wisconsin leading, the 86th and 124th New York in support. Rolling volleys mowed down Lee's riflemen under Colonel John R. Chambliss and broke them. Numbers of prisoners were rounded up.

There was still another charge left in the 6th Pennsylvania Cavalry. It rushed through the gap Ames had made, overrode the sharpshooters behind the stone wall, scattered them, thrust onward. But Lee's mounted men had been stationed where they were for

2ND U.S. CAVALRY
(Drawing by Charles McBarron)

just such an emergency. Colonel R. L. T. Beale's 9th Virginia drew sabers and countercharged. They hurled the Pennsylvanians back on the stone wall and battered them against it like sledge on anvil. Most of the close-beset Blue horsemen leaped or scrambled over the barrier. They fled, pursued at a gallop, losing most of the prisoners they had taken, until a rain of shells from a Federal battery lowered a protective curtain behind them.

It was the turn of the 2nd U.S. Cavalry now. The gallant tradition behind the regiment lent it as strong an impetus as its spurs. It crashed into the flank of the triumphant 9th Virginia and flung it back in savage, hand-to-hand combat. Wesley Merritt, commanding the 2nd though ranking only as a captain—he was destined to become one of the ablest cavalry leaders of the war—had his hat sliced from his head in a duel with a Confederate officer.

In few battles have the fortunes of war swayed so swiftly back and forth as at Brandy Station. "At this juncture, the Second North Carolina Regiment, dashingly led by its young Colonel, Sol. Williams, reached the hill, and swept the regulars back, pursuing them almost to the mouth of the cannon." [166] The 10th Virginia, raising the Rebel yell, joined the Carolinians' headlong assault. Into action on Lee's left rode Colonel T. T. Munford with three regiments of Fitz Lee's brigade, "long delayed in coming by reason of some uncertainty in his orders." [167]

But Colonel Williams had fallen with a pistol ball through his brain, and Rooney Lee was swaying in his saddle, one leg gashed by so grave a wound it could no longer grip leather. Casualties mounted on both sides, but the stubborn Buford drove on for a junction with Gregg on blue-crowned Fleetwood Hill. Some elements of the two commands made contact. Another turn of the screw, and the vise would be closed.

Dust churned up by thousands of hoofs, dust far thicker than the smoke of battle, swirled around Fleetwood Hill and its slopes. Men gasped and choked as they drew it into their lungs. It covered uniforms with a cloak of disguise. Not a few Union cavalrymen escaped capture because they seemed to be wearing gray. Revolver and carbine fire sank into diminuendo. In the dense clouds combatants, unable to recognize an enemy, seldom dared shoot for fear of killing their own men. The clang of the saber, now become the pre-eminent weapon as horsemen fought face to face, rang ever louder. Most of the dead, strewn over Fleetwood after the battle, were found to have perished by the sword.

Only those who stood apart and watched from the fringes could catch glimpses of the conflict in all its fury. One such was Captain W. W. Blackford of Stuart's staff, his duty to act as a dispatch rider and observe for his commander. Blackford in fascination watched "a passage of arms filled with romantic interest and splendor to a degree unequaled by anything our war produced." He saw "the lines meet on the hill. It was like what we read of in the days of chivalry, acres and acres of horsemen sparkling with sabers, and dotted with brilliant bits of color where their flags danced about them, hurled against each other at full speed and meeting with a shock that made the earth tremble." [168]

He was spared little time for the spectacle.

During the action [he declared], in galloping from one point of the field to another carrying orders, friend and foe were so mixed together and all so closely engaged that I had some capital pistol practice, and emptied every barrel of my revolver twice at close range. I could not tell with certainty what effects my shots had, for galloping by one cannot take a second glance, but at a target I seldom failed to hit a hat at that distance and in that manner. Pistol practice from the saddle at a gallop was our favorite amusement on the staff and it is surprising how accurately one can shoot in this way.[169]

General Stuart, throwing in his regiments, showed himself the superb battle leader he was, veteran of scores of cavalry fights, the commander who had so ably taken over a corps when Stonewall Jackson was wounded at Chancellorsville. Blackford rode to him now with a report on the appearance of Federal infantry for which he had been especially detailed to be on the lookout. Through his field glasses he had sighted Ames's foot troops advancing with

Buford's drive toward Fleetwood. Stuart in countermeasure at last called for infantry support, dispatching his staff officer on the six-mile ride to Culpeper. General Lee, as previously related, had anticipated the need and started a division toward Brandy.

Meanwhile Fleetwood was about to be stormed once more by the Gray cavalry.

Now the crisis, the moment of decision.

Big, bearded Wade Hampton flourished his long, skull-splitting saber and led his squadrons in a thundering charge along the ridge from the direction of St. James Church. To the right and fore galloped the Cobb Legion under Pierce Young. Black's 1st South Carolina in echelon to the left. Then the surging ranks of Baker's 1st North Carolina and the Jeff Davis Legion. Hart's guns rumbling in their wake.

The battery swung out to find an open field of fire. Its commander's right arm lifted. A clenched fist punched toward the enemy. The blast of a trumpet, soaring above the din, repeated his signal for action front. Teams wheeled, and cannoneers slipped from saddles to unlimber the pieces. Limbers and led horses trotted rearward. The cannon roared. Three salvos of shrapnel at a range of two hundred yards burst among the Blue cavalry holding the summit.

Toward the mangled havoc wrought by the shells plunged the charging horsemen in gray. Young and Black led their surging waves straight uphill. The other regiments circled to smash into flank and rear. Horses, nostrils distended, snorted and catapulted forward. Riders bent low over their necks, sabers outthrust, tensed for the moment of impact.

Mort à cheval, au galop [170]—the cavalryman's fate. If a man must fall in battle, how meet death more gloriously than astride a galloping steed charging into the midst of the foe? So officers and troopers of the Gray and Blue died on Fleetwood Heights that afternoon as they joined combat in milling masses and desperate single encounters.

It was the Union that finally gave way. Stuart had sent Lomax's

THE HAMPTON LEGION
(Drawing by Frederick P. Todd)

11th Virginia sweeping around the hill. That strong regiment made the last charge of the day, brushing aside opposition and riding over Martin's silenced guns, to threaten the enemy's rear and his line of withdrawal through Brandy Station. More of Beckham's artillery took position on the ridge Hampton was scouring.

Gregg's bolt was shot, and Pleasonton's orders for a general retreat were as welcome as they were wise and timely. The Blue squadrons ebbed down the slopes of Fleetwood, harried by the fire of the Rebel cannon above them. Galling as it was, that cannonade proved a blessing for its target. Hampton, flushed with success, had been about to launch another charge when the barrier of bursting shells dropped between him and the enemy. Before he could rush a command to the artillery to cease firing, Gregg's men had reached the cover of the woods.

Buford, conforming in the retreat, pulled back as rapidly as he could, his horsemen shielding the gallant infantry who had served him so well. Foot and horse, ambulances with the wounded, splashed through Beverly Ford. Was it only twelve hours ago that they crossed it? It must have seemed incredible to men who slumped in their saddles as exhaustion from almost constant combat suddenly struck them.

Gregg's 3rd Division, covered by the fresher troops of the 2nd, made good their crossing of the Rappahannock, this time by the railroad bridge, and the Cavalry Corps of the Army of the Potomac marched back unpursued to its base. The Battle of Brandy Station was over.

Gray troopers next day buried the dead, their own and the enemy's, on the battlefield they held undisputed.

> Comes before me the unknown soldier's grave, comes
> the inscription rude in Virginia's woods,
> Bold, cautious, true, and my loving comrade.

> WALT WHITMAN, "As Toilsome I Wandered
> Virginia's Woods"

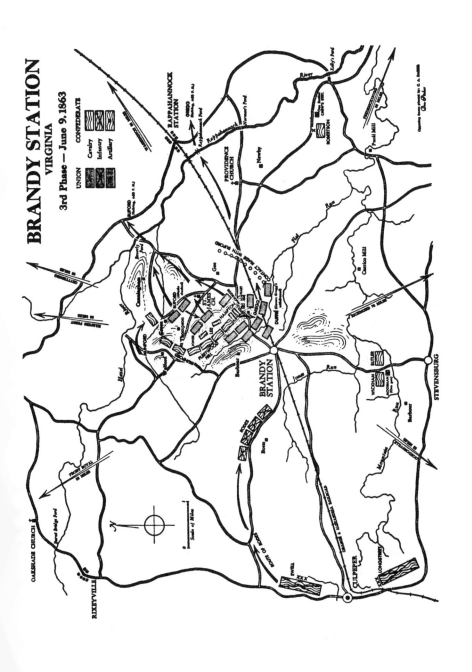

BRANDY STATION
VIRGINIA
3rd Phase — June 9, 1863

UNION | CONFEDERATE

Cavalry
Infantry
Artillery

General Stuart the previous night had ordered his headquarters camp pitched on Fleetwood. It was a point of pride to place it on the eminence he and his men had fought so hard for and finally won. However, a visit quickly dissuaded him. He found the earth "was covered so thickly with dead horses and men, and the bluebottle flies were swarming so thick over the blood stains on the ground that there was not room enough to pitch the tents among them." [171] Even after the burials on June 10 the once pleasant greensward was noisome, with flocks of turkey buzzards gorging themselves on the bodies of horses. Such has been the aftermath of many a "famous victory" before and since Blenheim.

Brandy Station—whose victory? Or was it a drawn battle?

A count of casualties supplies no answer. Official records [172] give the following figures: Union killed, wounded, captured, or missing —866; Confederate—485, excluding the 35th Virginia Battalion where losses were heavy and whose inclusion would have brought totals closer. In any case an attacking force ordinarily suffers more severely.

Even less are rival claims a criterion. Pleasonton's report of June 10 stated he believed he had prevented "Stuart from making his raid, which he was to have commenced this morning," an estimate based, he said, on his opponent's captured orders and letters.[173] The Union commander was completely wrong. No such captures had been made except for Major Beckham's field desk, unlikely to have contained such papers.[174] Stuart at the time contemplated no raid. His duty was simply to screen the concentration of the Army of Northern Virginia for whose northern invasion General Lee did not receive approval until the arrival of a letter from the Confederate War Department dated June 10.[175]

Stuart's claim to a victory was made in his most "flamboyant" [176] manner. The congratulatory order [177] he issued to his command declared:

Comrades! two divisions of the enemy's cavalry and artillery, escorted by a strong force of infantry, tested your mettle and found it proof-steel. Your saber blows, inflicted on that glorious day, have taught them again the weight of Southern vengeance. You confronted with cavalry and horse artillery alone this force, held the infantry in check, routed the cavalry and artillery, captured three pieces of the latter without losing a gun, and added six flags to the trophies of the nation, besides inflicting a loss in killed, wounded, and missing at least double our own, causing the entire force to retire beyond the Rappahannock. Nothing but the enemy's infantry, strongly posted in the woods, saved his cavalry from capture or annihilation. An act of rashness on his part was severely punished by rout and the loss of artillery. With an abiding faith in the God of battles, and a firm reliance on the saber, your successes will continue. Let the example and heroism of our lamented, fallen comrades prompt us to renewed vigilance and inspire us with devotion to duty.

However the order affected the Gray troopers, it would at least give no information or comfort to the enemy if he happened to read it. "Tell it not in Gath, publish it not in the Streets of Askelon."

But what verdict would be rendered by Robert E. Lee? So Stuart and all of the Army of Northern Virginia undoubtedly wondered.

When General Lee rode up from Culpeper toward the close of the battle, he met his severely wounded son Rooney being carried to the rear. The anxious father paused to learn with relief that the wound was not mortal and to make certain that good care was being taken of his third-born. With the Federals in full retreat across the Rappahannock, the battleground lay in the hands of his cavalry, and possession could be considered nine points of the law of victory. Stuart's screen had not been penetrated, and the Union high command could be assumed to continue in the dark as to Confederate intentions. Lee's comment, in response to Stuart's report, dealt with the means by which those objectives had been achieved: the conduct of the action. "The dispositions made by you," ran his letter to Stuart, "to meet the strong attack of the enemy appear to have been judicious and well planned. The troops were well and skillfully managed, and with few exceptions

conducted themselves with marked gallantry." [178] That was "reassuring if not quite so laudatory as might be desired." [179]

Lee's adjutant, Walter H. Taylor, summed up the battle fair-
mindedly in a personal letter: "Altogether our cavalry is justified
in claiming an advantage, although neither side can be said to have
gained a great deal. It was nearly an even fight." [180]

It had not been the purpose of the Union Cavalry Corps, making a
reconnaissance in force, to hold ground but to develop the strength
and discover the designs of the enemy. In those respects it largely
succeeded.[181] The considerable force of Confederate cavalry it encountered confirmed suspicions that offensive action by the Army
of Northern Virginia was in preparation. Hooker planned counter-
action. Another tangible result of Pleasonton's sudden and unexpected attack, formidably sustained in a day-long battle, was the
grave concern caused in the Confederate War Department. Richmond could be menaced by another such raid. The invasion of the
North by the army might now leave the capital more dangerously
exposed than originally envisioned. In consequence the authorities
displayed extreme reluctance to spare reinforcements greatly needed
by General Lee. Troops withheld and some substitutions of untried
brigades would have highly unfortunate repercussions at Gettysburg.

And the Confederate cavalry had been markedly hurt at Brandy
Station, not in its self-esteem, for with few exceptions it had
comported itself with its accustomed valor, but by the losses it
suffered. Officers and troopers who had fallen, most of them veterans,
further drained the South's dwindling manpower. Serious, too, was
the number of horses killed or crippled; their replacement at this
point in the war was increasingly difficult and gradually approaching the impossible. In contrast the North could well afford its
heavier casualties in the battle and restore the regiments' strength
in men and mounts with comparative ease.

But Brandy Station's culmination towered far above any question of victory or defeat. Surely some of the combatants sensed it
as they battled through that long day. In the retreating Blue
column it must have seeped, a heady stimulant, into minds dulled

by fatigue. They had quit the field but in good order, and for hour on hour these troopers, once contemptuously branded Yankee shoemakers and mechanics on horseback, had faced the Rebel cavalry and fought it to a standstill. The specter of the Black Horse Troop was laid at last. No longer could comrades of other arms jeer, "Whoever saw a dead cavalryman?" Let them go look at the graves on Fleetwood.

Stuart's adjutant had not considered deeply enough when he wrote that neither side had gained a great deal at Brandy Station. The Union cavalry's gain in self-confidence was priceless. Thenceforth they would never lose it, and it bred final victory.

Recognition and acknowledgment of the new spirit by the enemy set a seal upon it. If Jeb Stuart, "disconcerted and disillusioned," would not outwardly admit it, the tribute to be rendered by a member of his staff and his future biographer was all that could be asked. Major McClellan, whose prompt and gallant action saved Fleetwood from the first Union assault, would write:

> One result of incalculable importance certainly did follow this battle,—it *made* the Federal cavalry. Up to that time confessedly inferior to the Southern horsemen, they gained on this day that confidence in themselves and in their commanders which enabled them to contest so fiercely the subsequent battlefields of June, July, and October.[182]

> For the first time in the war [another of Stuart's biographers declared] blue cavalry had come over in dangerous force, provoked combat, inflicted heavy damage, and gotten away in good order. The gray troopers would no longer have it all their own way. Those Yankees, they conceded, could always fight. Now they were learning to ride and fight at the same time. In Brandy Station, Gettysburg was foreshadowed, and Sheridan, and the last scene at Yellow Tavern.[183]

Henceforth cavalry regiments in blue, which fought on that Virginia field, would look up with deep pride at an inscription blazoned on their fluttering guidons: Brandy Station.

CHAPTER 17

"He Has Sounded Forth the Trumpet"

THERE could be no resting on laurels gained at Brandy Station for the cavalry of either side—no resting after that battle, and little for the remainder of the war. On June 10, 1863, one of Lee's corps marched from Culpeper and led off the invasion of the North.

Stuart screened the advance of a column through the Shenandoah Valley, guarding the Blue Ridge gaps. And Pleasonton rode to meet him, reconnoitering and, in his turn, screening the counter-moves of the Army of the Potomac. The antagonists clashed in fierce engagements, mounted and dismounted action, at Aldie, Middleburg, and Upperville.

The Federals held the field at the end of the fight at Aldie, but success was marred by the debacle of the unfortunate Duffié. Detached to make a reconnaissance with the 1st Rhode Island, he was cornered by Robertson and Chambliss and his regiment shattered. Only Duffié, four of his officers, and twenty-seven troopers managed to cut their way out of the cordon and escape. At both Middleburg and Upperville Stuart was rocked back, suffering more than five hundred casualties and forced to retreat. All three encounters sustained and increased the confidence the Union cavalry had won at Brandy Station. Now they were convinced, as was the enemy, that it had been no brief candle but a beacon that would light them through the duration of the conflict.

Another important consequence of the Fleetwood fight took place at this point. Criticism by the Richmond press was stinging Jeb Stuart. It challenged him to perform an exploit that would restore his damaged reputation. "Probably inspired by this," [184] Stuart put forward his plan of riding around the rear of Hooker's army, as he had McClellan's, and harassing its crossing of the Potomac. He would take three brigades (his favorite ones) and leave two with the Army of Northern Virginia. Not only the strength he withdrew but his personal leadership would be gravely missed.

How Stuart executed that plan, stretching Lee's permissive orders, has often been described. Suffice it to say that it delayed him from reaching Gettysburg until the afternoon of the second day, his troopers and horses weary. The two brigades remaining with the army had not been effective in providing sorely-needed information, a service in which Stuart excelled—and was not there to give. His was a long, roundabout march from Brandy Station to Gettysburg, and its making reaped no redemption but sowed some of the seeds of defeat.

Gettysburg saw the stubborn defense on July 1, 1863, by Buford's Division, armed now with the new Spencer repeating carbines, and its fine scouting as the battle developed. On the third, Stuart and his cavalry attempted to circle the Federal right and strike the enemy's rear. Gregg and his men rode to meet them. Again was waged such desperate combat, charges, and countercharges as Brandy Station had known. But the ridge east of town was not another Fleetwood. It was the Gray horse, battered back, that finally retreated that day and left the high ground to their adversaries. A little later that day a great charge on the Confederate right flank was made by Farnsworth's and Merritt's men of Kilpatrick's Division over rough terrain, delivered in the belief that Meade would counterattack after Pickett's repulse. It has been compared to the charge of the Light Brigade at Balaklava, and it was as rashly ordered, as bravely pressed, and as definitely shattered. But it had driven two miles deep into the enemy's lines over stone walls and against artillery and rifle volleys. None of the regiments that launched it had fought at Brandy Station, yet they were plainly fired by its spirit.[185]

Blue and Gray cavalry clashed again around Brandy Station in September, October, and November of 1863.[186] During the winter of 1864 the vicinity definitely became Union territory, headquarters of the Cavalry Corps of the Army of the Potomac, then also of the II Corps, confronting the enemy based at Orange Court House. Hooting locomotives of the Orange and Alexandria Railroad hailed the station often. Its sidings held many cars loaded with supplies for transfer to dumps or the wagons of a vast park. Reluctant troopers left huts to squelch through quagmires of red Virginia mud to the picket lines where cold, rain-drenched horses, which turned their rumps to the biting wind and weathered it, were well cared for and well fed. The recruits of '61 were cavalrymen now. Mounts of most regiments had dry footing, layers of brick or plank covered with straw, renewed in the swallowing mud. Consequently these days there were far fewer crippling cases of greased heel, scratches, and thrush.

Gradually refinements and comforts appeared, as Brandy Station became a permanent camp. Sheds and stalls, blacksmith and wheel-wright shops. A field hospital, soon expanded by the Sanitary Commission. A stockade with shelters for prisoners. Brick fireplaces for generals' tents. Rustic cottages built by the Engineers. Accommodations for visiting wives and sweethearts. Once more the battle-ground was the scene of parades, reviews, and balls such as Jeb Stuart had staged in that bygone June of 1863.

It was from Brandy Station that the Army of the Potomac marched in 1864 to Petersburg and the siege that marked the opening of the last act in the drama of the great conflict.

From that little town of the mellow name the Cavalry Corps of the Army of Northern Virginia had begun its march to final defeat. It had made gallant history and it would make still more. But from the June battle onward it rode downhill, down slopes steeper than Fleetwood's, toward surrender at Appomattox.

Valor was not enough. They were whittled down and overwhelmed by their opponents' tremendously increased fire power from the repeating carbine, which they could not obtain except by capture; then only a few and with little ammunition. Losses in men and mounts became irreplaceable. Those that remained were weakened by scanty rations and forage, difficult both to obtain and to transport, once available. They could no longer live off the country in the theater of war, ravaged by repeated enemy raids—notably the fertile Shenandoah Valley. One by one the leaders fell. A bright flame was quenched when Stuart was mortally wounded at Yellow Tavern. Never afterward would the Gray horse be the same. The doughty "Grumble" Jones was killed in action. Rooney Lee, captured in his home as he lay recuperating from his Brandy Station wound, was not exchanged for some time. Such stalwarts as Fitz Lee and Wade Hampton, the latter recovered from desperate wounds sustained at Gettysburg, led on till the end.

Paramount were the facts that from Brandy Station on the Confederate cavalryman was matched in fighting quality and the skills of the arm by his Union counterpart, and that a new commander took over the Cavalry Corps of the Army of the Potomac.

Phil Sheridan, the bowlegged infantryman [187] from the western front, that hot-tempered, hard-driving, splendid leader of cavalry. The Gray horse had had its Stuart from the beginning, but the Blue had waited long for Sheridan. He came none too soon. After Gettysburg the Federal horsemen were threatened by a dangerous decline to something like their former status. Among the talents of General George Gordon Meade, commanding the Army of the Potomac, the ability to use cavalry effectively was markedly lacking. Regiments were scattered again to guard wagon trains and serve as pickets.

Leave such duties to infantry, Sheridan insisted. Keep the cavalry together and employ it as a cohesive striking force. Not until Grant took over the army command and backed him up did Sheridan in a measure get his way. By the fall of 1863 he headed and soon was able to fight to the hilt with three divisions—10,000 men. Returns of March, 1865, for his cavalry in the Army of the Shenandoah and the Army of the Potomac showed 591 officers and 12,836 enlisted men present for duty, with an aggregate strength, present and absent, of 38,623.[188] Although many absences were necessary and unavoidable, those returns show that various evils of detachment had not, even then, been corrected. Sheridan could call upon only a little over one-third of his assigned forces for immediate battle. However, that third—officers, troopers, and mounts—was ready for combat.

The cavalry battles of the last year of the war—Five Forks, Yellow Tavern, Winchester, and the rest—are outside the province of this book. At last with the victorious Sherman forging up from the south, Grant—Petersburg and Richmond his trophies—pressed pursuit of the retreating remnants of the Army of Northern Virginia. Their campaigns were a large-scale Brandy Station, the closing of the jaws of a vise. Again the threatening jaws never met. A gap remained through which Lee might have slipped to join still-resisting Confederate troops to the southwest and prolong the war for a time. Sheridan flung his cavalry squarely across that last line of retreat, and that was the end.

Surely at the finish of that last, long, fighting march there were Union cavalrymen who looked up at their guidons, as a breeze unfurled their folds. Now a new and a final legend would be emblazoned on a stripe of those miniature American flags, bullet-torn and shell-rent: Appomattox. It would stand as a shining sequel to an inscription on a higher stripe: Brandy Station.[189]

There are few markers on the battleground beside the Rappahannock, not designated as a National Military Park. One plaque near Kelly's Ford commemorates the gallant Pelham. Yet memories so vivid they needed neither monument nor parked cannon drew back veterans, who had worn the gray or the blue, to the scene of that mighty clash of cavalry on June 9, 1863. Years after the war, when bitterness had faded, both sides came there together. At a joint reunion in August, 1906, only one Yankee managed to attend. His one-time enemies crowded around him on Fleetwood Hill, joking. You fellows outnumbered us here in '63, they told him, but it's the other way 'round today. Speech, speech! The lone Union trooper refused until they dragged him to the platform but then came through nobly. "Comrades, if I may call you such," he declared, "I desire to say that this is the second time in my life that I have visited Brandy Station, and each time I experienced a warm reception." [190]

They would ride again, some of those cavalrymen who sheathed sabers in 1865, through the Indian wars, and a handful along with their sons in Cuba and the Philippines in the war with Spain. Their grandsons would follow Pershing into Mexico. Those bred in the tradition of the cavalry would chafe when regiments of their beloved arm were disbanded in the First World War and find what consolation they could in serving in the horse-drawn field artillery, and as machine gunners and military police. Thereafter only tokens of the past remained: the crossed sabers insignia with a tank superimposed and the continuance on the army list of the names of famous cavalry regiments, armored now, names that are imperishable. Yet more than a token are the tactics, the dash and *élan*, that the horse soldier bequeathed to his heirs, the armored columns and the air squadrons. In them his spirit still lives.

The Blue cavalry and horse artillery of the Army of the Potomac and the Gray of the Army of Northern Virginia—they who fought the mounted arm's greatest battle in our history that day nearly a century ago by the Rappahannock fords—they have all ridden on. Hoofbeats have long since faded, and the glint of their sabers has vanished in the mists of time. Yet surely in the halls of Valhalla they still tell of Brandy Station to fellow cavalrymen who rode there before them.

Appendix A

HISTORICAL SKETCH OF THE U.S. CAVALRY

FAIRFAX DOWNEY

AMERICAN cavalry made its first important appearance in the Revolution. Although with little previous experience (horsemen had served only occasionally in the Colonial Indian wars), it developed from a social into a military organization, learned the true cavalry spirit, and trained able leaders and troops. Its actions and campaigns, though greatly limited by the amount of open country available, set an example for the future development of the mounted arm.

As the area of conflict shifted to the treeless plains of Mexico and the western frontier, cavalry came into its own. It reached a high point of achievement in the Civil War, when first the Confederate and then the Union horse won a world reputation, and in the wars with the Indian tribes of the West.

Horsed or afoot and finally motorized, yet still wearing cavalry's insignia and fulfilling its functions, U.S. Cavalry has fought on three continents, on prairie and mountain, in swamp and jungle, on distant islands. Some of the most glorious traditions in American military history were established by cavalrymen—by famous commanders from Light-horse Harry Lee to Pershing and Patton and by the men they led, from the dragoons of the Revolutionary legions to troopers in olive drab. Honored, too, are cavalry mounts, from celebrated chargers such as Sheridan's Winchester, Jeb Stuart's Star of the East and Virginia, Custer's Vic and Dandy, and Keogh's Comanche to troop horses—Morgans, mustangs, and Philippine and Manchurian ponies. Often as true of the U.S. Cavalry was the tribute the Conquistador, Bernal Díaz, paid the steeds with which Cortez vanquished the Aztec Empire: "For, after God, we owed all to our horses."

An American cavalry action, a raid by a dozen troopers on a British outpost in New Jersey, brought back prisoners with vital information enabling General Washington to win the Battle of Princeton. Those twelve dragoons were half of all the cavalry Washington then had—members of the Philadelphia City Troop, foxhunters and good riders—good soldiers, too, as the General granted, "tho' gentlemen of fortune." From such small contingents he built up his cavalry, mustering horsemen in New England, the Middle States, and the South. Mounted and trained, uniformed and paid (one South Carolina troop received its pay in "large and small" Negroes, and rolls show its captain due 39¾'s slaves), the arm was increased to four regiments of dragoons of the Continental Line, several separate legions on the Roman model, consisting of both cavalry and light infantry, and troops of the irregular horse such as stanchly fought the well-mounted Tories in New York. Long before they were reinforced by cavalry of our French allies, American troopers were able to fight British veterans on equal terms.

The first American Chief of Cavalry, then called Commander of the Horse, was the Polish Count Pulaski, who was mortally wounded in a charge at the siege of Savannah. Brilliant and dashing leaders appeared in Light-horse Harry Lee, father of Robert E., and in William Washington.

American cavalry distinguished itself in the New Jersey campaign and particularly in the South against the formidable British cavalry commander, Colonel Banastre Tarleton. Some effective use, as at Kings Mountain, was made of mounted riflemen who rode to battlefields and then fought dismounted. Finally cavalry helped pen Cornwallis in on the Yorktown peninsula, forcing the British surrender.

Cavalry's promising career came to a full halt after the Revolution when the entire army was disbanded except for an artillery detachment at West Point. At times troops or regiments were reactivated but soon mustered out for reasons of economy, and for periods of years the United States was without any regular mounted force. However, cavalry in active intervals fought in Mad Anthony Wayne's Indian campaigns in the Middle West and with Harrison at Tippecanoe. One of our few land victories in the War of 1812, the Battle of the Thames, was won by a charge of Kentucky cavalry. Dragoons, mounted and dismounted, also served against the Creeks and Seminoles in Florida.

Until shortly before the Civil War, the American cavalryman still was called a dragoon after his European prototype. He wore a crested helmet as protection against saber strokes, short jacket, and breeches in high jack boots. His weapons were sword and pistol unless he belonged to the mounted rifles. On frontier service he was a picturesque fellow, bearded and with flowing locks (as late as 1851 only cavalry regiments were allowed to wear mustaches). The hard-fighting, hard-drinking dragoon regarded himself as belonging to an elite arm of the service, far superior to mere infantry. His border wars put mounted troops on a permanent basis in the army.

In the War with Mexico, United States Cavalry met Santa Anna's lancers and charged his batteries. One regiment, the 2nd Dragoons, whose service dated back to the Seminole War, took part in virtually every engagement from Palo Alto to Chapultepec, winning fourteen battle streamers for its standard. Doniphan led a cavalry expedition deep into the Southwest, and Stephen Kearny and his dragoons, shifting to mules when their horses wore out, made a tremendous fighting march of more than a thousand miles from Santa Fé through to the California coast. From Taylor's and Scott's campaigns and later Indian combats emerged cavalry commanders who would serve in the great conflict that followed. Brilliant reconnaissances, mounted and dismounted, were made by Robert E. Lee, then an Engineer officer but later lieutenant colonel of the 2nd U.S. Cavalry. His able cavalry leaders in the Civil War, J. E. B. Stuart and Fitzhugh Lee, won their spurs in fights with the tribes of the Southwest and West, as did their great opponent, Phil Sheridan, whose original arm was infantry.

[The service of cavalry in the Civil War, partly covered in the main text, is here omitted.]

Ten regiments of Regular cavalry, two of them composed of Negro troopers called by the Indians "buffalo soldiers" because of their wooly hair, fought in the wars on the tribes of the West and Southwest that extended from 1865 to 1890. Only cavalry could clinch victory by pursuing and rounding up the hostiles and attacking their winter lodges, though many a hard-fought field was won by the steady fire of the infantry. Indian cavalrymen in the U.S. Army, such as the Pawnee and Apache scouts, were invaluable. Several regiments of Indian Cavalry had served in the Union Army in the Civil War.

The service of our cavalry in the Indian Wars included such episodes as: the feat of Mackenzie and the 4th Cavalry who invaded Mexico, defeated Indian raiders in a sharp fight, and rode back across the border, a mighty march of 145 miles in 28 hours; Crook's conquest of the Apaches and his use of pack mule trains to supply his cavalry; the pursuit of Chief Joseph and the Nez Percés who fought one of the greatest rear-guard actions of all time; the Little Big Horn campaign and the wiping out of Custer and a third of his 7th Cavalry.

Regular and volunteer cavalry served in Cuba, Porto Rico, and the Philippines in the Spanish-American War. At Las Guasimas, Cuba, Fighting Joe Wheeler, former Confederate cavalryman, led a charge on the Spaniards, turning the clock back with a yell, "Come on, boys. We've got the damn Yankees on the run!" Wood's and Roosevelt's Rough Riders fought valiant dismounted actions but had to be extricated from a tight corner on San Juan Hill by the Negro 10th Cavalry.

Two troops of the 6th Cavalry rode with the American contingent quelling the Boxer Rebellion in China. Horse marines became a fact when Marine Corps companies were mounted to patrol in Manchuria. Lieutenant Pershing led a troop against the Moros in the Philippines and rose to command the 1916 expedition into Mexico after Villa. Black Jack's aide, young Lieutenant Patton, rode down and killed a Mexican general with his pearl-handled revolver.

U.S. Cavalry reached a strength of twenty-five regiments in 1917, but trench warfare and the machine gun of World War I forced conversion of most of them into field artillery. Only one regiment, the 2nd, saw action in 1918 as a mounted command, fighting in the Aisne-Marne sector, at St. Mihiel and the Meuse-Argonne.

The advent of mechanized warfare in the First World War and its dominance along with the dive bomber in the Second sealed the doom of horse cavalry. Remaining mounted regiments became field artillery. Commanding armored columns, such former cavalry leaders as George Patton exchanged chargers for jeeps and tanks.

The mounted arm's tradition died hard; Bill Mauldin satirized it when he drew an old cavalry sergeant pistoling his broken-down jeep. The last unit to fight mounted was the 26th Philippine Scouts, and that regiment, after its withdrawal from Lingayan Gulf to Bataan, was compelled to destroy its ponies and fight on foot. Horse cavalry no longer exists in the U.S. Army today. The stirring trumpet call, "Boots and Saddles," is sounded only on carriers as a signal to pilots to man their planes. Yet cavalry's spirit, its name, and its functions survive in the Armored Force where, Army Regulations state, "the histories, battle honors, insignia, coats of arms, and colors of the cavalry organizations shall be transferred and perpetuated."

NOTE. The author is indebted to Rowland P. Gill for the following amendments: After World War I the 1st-12th Regiments were retained mounted until the 1930's. In World War II the 124th Cavalry (Texas National Guard) served in India-Burma.

Appendix B

CHARLES LEVER, *Charles O'Malley, the Irish Dragoon,*
I, 243-245.*

AS we came on the scene became one of overwhelming excitement; the masses of the enemy that poured unceasingly from the town could now be distinguished more clearly, and amid all the crash of gun carriages and caissons, the voices of the staff officers rose high as they hurried along the retreating battalions. A troop of flying artillery galloped forth at top speed, and, wheeling their guns into position with the speed of lightning, prepared for a flanking fire to cover the retiring column. The gunners sprang from their seats, the guns were already unlimbered, when Sir George Murray, riding up at our left, called out:

"Forward; close up; charge!"

The words were scarcely spoken, when a loud cheer answered the welcome sound, and at the same instant the long line of shining helmets passed with the speed of a whirlwind; the pace increased at

* The charge described in the extract took place in the Battle of the Douro, May 12, 1809, during Wellington's Peninsular Campaign of the Napoleonic wars.

every stride, the ranks grew closer, and, like the dread force of some mighty engine, we fell upon the foe. I have felt all the glorious enthusiasm of a fox-hunt, when the loud cry of the hound, answered by the cheer of the joyous huntsman, stirred the very heart within, but never till now did I know how far higher the excitement reaches when, man to man, saber to saber, arm to arm, we ride forward to the battle-field. On we went, the loud shout of "forward" still ringing in our ears. One broken, irregular discharge from the French guns shook the head of our advancing column, but stayed us not as we galloped madly on.

I remember no more; the din, the smoke, the crash—the cry for quarter mingled with the shout of victory—the flying enemy—the agonizing shrieks of the wounded—are all co-mingled in my mind, but leave no trace of clearness or connection between them, and it was only when the column wheeled to reform, behind the advancing squadrons, that I awoke from my trance of maddening excitement, and perceived that we had carried the position, and cut off the guns of the enemy.

"Well done, 14th!" said an old gray-headed colonel, as he rode along our line; "gallantly done, lads!" The blood trickled from a saber cut on his temple, along his cheek, as he spoke; but he either knew it not, or heeded it not.

"There go the Germans!" said Power, pointing to the remainder of our brigade, as they charged furiously upon the French infantry, and rode them down in masses.

Our guns came up at this time, and a plunging fire was opened upon the thick and retreating ranks of the enemy; the carnage must have been terrific, for the long breaches in their lines showed where the squadrons of the cavalry had passed or the most destructive tide of the artillery had swept through them. The speed of the flying columns grew momentarily more; the road became blocked, too, by broken carriages and wounded; and, to add to their discomfiture, a damaging fire now opened from the town upon the retreating column, while the brigade of Guards and the 29th pressed hotly on their rear.

The scene was now beyond anything maddening in its interest. From the walls of Oporto the English infantry poured forth in pursuit; while the whole river was covered with boats, as they still continued to cross over. The artillery thundered from the Sierra, to protect the landing, for it was even still contested in places; and the cavalry, charging in flank, swept the broken ranks, and bore down upon their right squares.

It was now, when the full tide of victory ran highest in our favor, that we were ordered to retire from the road. Column after column passed before us, unmolested and unassailed; and not even a cannon-shot arrested their steps.

Some unaccountable timidity of our leader directed this move-ment; and while before our very eyes the gallant infantry were charging the retiring columns, we remained still and inactive.

How little did the sense of praise we had already won repay us for the shame and indignation we experienced at this moment, as with burning cheek and compressed lip we watched the retreating files. "What can he mean?" "Is there not some mistake?" "Are we never to charge?" were the muttered questions around as a staff officer galloped up with the order to take ground still further back, and nearer to the river.

The word was scarcely spoken when a young officer, in the uniform of a general, dashed impetuously up; he held his plumed cap high above his head as he called out: "14th, follow me! Left face—wheel—charge!"

So with the word, we were upon them. The French rearguard was at this moment at the narrowest part of the road, which opened by a bridge upon a large open space, so that, forming with a narrow front, and favored by a declivity in the ground, we actually rode them down. Twice the French formed, and twice were they broken. Meanwhile the carnage was dreadful on both sides; our fellows dashing madly forward where the ranks were thickest, the enemy resisting with the stubborn courage of men fighting for their last spot of ground. So impetuous was the charge of our squadrons that we stopped not till piercing the dense column of the retreating mass, we reached the open ground beyond. Here we wheeled, and pre-pared once more to meet them, when suddenly some squadrons of cuirassiers debouched from the road, and, supported by a field-piece, showed front against us. This was the moment that the remainder of our brigade should have come to our aid, but not a man appeared. However, there was not an instant to be lost; already the plunging fire of the four-pounder had swept through our files, and every moment increased our danger.

"Once more, my lads, forward!" cried out our gallant leader, Sir Charles Stewart, as he, waving his saber, dashed into the thickest of the fray.

So sudden was our charge that we were upon them before they were prepared. And here ensued a terrific struggle; for, as the cavalry of the enemy gave way before us, we came upon the close ranks of the infantry at half-pistol distance, who poured a withering volley into us as we approached. But what could arrest the sweeping torrent of our brave fellows, though every moment falling in numbers?

Harvey, our Major, lost his arm near the shoulder; scarcely an officer was not wounded. Power received a deep saber-cut in the cheek, from an aide-de-camp of General Foy, in return for a wound he gave the General; while I, in my endeavor to save General Laborde, when unhorsed, was cut down through the helmet, and so stunned that I remembered no more around me; I kept my saddle, it is true, but I lost every sense of consciousness; my first glimmering of reason coming to my aid as I lay upon the river bank, and felt my faithful follower Mike bathing my temples with water as he kept up a running fire of lamentations for my being murthered so young.

"Are you better, Mister Charles? Spake to me alanah; say that you're not kilt, darling—do now. Oh, wirrah! what'll I ever say to the master? and you doing so beautiful! Wouldn't he give the best baste in his stable to be looking at you today? There, take a sup; it's only water. Bad luck to them, but it's hard work beatin' them; they're only gone now. That's right—now you're coming to."

"Where am I, Mike?"

"It's here you are, darling, resting yourself."

"Well, Charley, my poor fellow, you've got sore bones too," cried Power, as his face swathed in bandages, and covered with blood, he lay down on the grass beside me. "It was a gallant thing while it lasted, but has cost us dearly. Poor Hixley—"

"What of him?" said I, anxiously.

"Poor fellow! he has seen his last battle-field. He fell across me, as we came out upon the road; I lifted him up in my arms and bore him along above fifty yards; but he was stone dead—not a sigh, not a word escaped him; shot through the forehead." As he spoke, his lips trembled, and his voice sunk to a mere whisper at the last words: "You remember what he said last night. 'Poor fellow! he was every inch a soldier.' "

Such was his epitaph.

I turned my head toward the scene of our late encounter; some dismantled guns and broken wagons alone marked the spot; while, far in the distance, the dust of the retreating columns showed the beaten enemy, as they hurried toward the frontiers of Spain.

Appendix C

CAVALRY TABLES OF ORGANIZATION

(SHANNON, *The Organization and Administration of the Union Army, 1861–1865*, II, 272f.)

UNION

THE regiment of cavalry consisted of three battalions, each battalion of two squadrons, and each squadron of two companies, each of which was organized as follows: Minimum—1 captain, 1 first lieutenant, 1 second lieutenant, 1 first sergeant, 1 company quartermaster sergeant, 4 sergeants, 8 corporals, 2 musicians, 2 farriers, 1 saddler, 1 wagoner, 58 privates; aggregate 79. The maximum included 72 privates; aggregate 95.

The battalion officers were the same as in the infantry, except that the battalion adjutant was not necessarily a lieutenant, and there were, as additional officers, 1 saddler-sergeant and 1 veterinary-sergeant. The minimum size was 325 and the maximum was 389 officers and men.

The regiment when it included three battalions totaled from 997 to 1,189 officers and men.* The regimental officers were 1 colonel, 1 lieutenant-colonel, 1 regimental adjutant (lieutenant), 1 regimental quartermaster and commissary (lieutenant), 2 chief buglers [trumpeters], 16 musicians (later omitted).

* [An infantry regiment up to strength mustered from 2,020 to 2,452.]

CONFEDERATE

A regiment originally consisted of two squadrons; a squadron of two troops of companies; a company of 80 enlisted men and 3 officers, a captain and two lieutenants. The senior troop commander led the squadron. The regimental staff was a colonel, lieutenant-colonel, and major.

The strength of a regiment, 650 effectives at the most, sank in 1862 to 500, in 1863 toward 350, a figure which it thereafter never exceeded. Some regiments had diminished to 100 by the end of the war.

From two to five regiments made up a brigade. There was no divisional organization for the cavalry.

Horse artillery batteries, usually four guns, were handled as brigade units.

Appendix D

ORGANIZATION OF THE UNION AND CONDERERATE FORCES AT THE BATTLE OF BRANDY STATION, JUNE 9, 1863.

UNION

(*Official Records*, Series I, Vol. XXVII, Part I, pp. 168-170, as embodied in Return of Casualties)

Cavalry Corps
Brig. Gen. Alfred Pleasonton
1st Division

Brig. Gen. John Buford, commanding right wing, consisting of 1st Cavalry Division, Cavalry Reserve Brigade, and brigade of infantry under Brig. Gen. Adelbert Ames.

1st Brigade. Col. Benjamin F. Davis

8th Illinois Cavalry
3rd Indiana Cavalry

8th New York Cavalry
Batteries B and L, 2nd Artillery

2nd Brigade. Col. Thomas C. Devin

6th New York Cavalry
9th New York Cavalry
17th Pennsylvania Cavalry
3rd West Virginia Cavalry

Reserve Brigade. Maj. Charles J. Whiting

6th Pennsylvania Cavalry
1st U.S. Cavalry
2nd U.S. Cavalry
5th U.S. Cavalry
6th U.S. Cavalry
Battery E, 4th Artillery

2nd Division. Col. Alfred N. Duffié
1st Brigade. Col. Louis P. di Cesnola

1st Massachusetts Cavalry
6th Ohio Cavalry
1st Rhode Island Cavalry

2nd Brigade. Col. J. Irvin Gregg

3rd Pennsylvania Cavalry
4th Pennsylvania Cavalry
16th Pennsylvania Cavalry
Battery M, 2nd Artillery

3rd Division. Brig. Gen. David McM. Gregg
1st Brigade. Col. Judson Kilpatrick

1st Maine Cavalry
2nd New York Cavalry
10th New York Cavalry
Orton's Company, District of Columbia Cavalry

2nd Brigade. Col. Percy Wyndham

1st Maryland Cavalry
1st New Jersey Cavalry

1st Pennsylvania Cavalry
6th New York Battery

Attached Troops
Brig. Gen. Adelbert Ames

2nd Massachusetts Infantry
33rd Massachusetts Infantry
86th New York Infantry
124th New York Infantry
3rd Wisconsin Infantry
Battery K, 1st Artillery

Brig. Gen. David A. Russell

2nd Wisconsin Infantry
7th Wisconsin Infantry
56th Pennsylvania Infantry

CONFEDERATE

(Official Records, Series I, Vol. XXVII, Part 2, pp. 712f)
Cavalry Corps. Maj. Gen. J. E. B. Stuart

Robertson's Brigade

4th North Carolina Cavalry
5th North Carolina Cavalry

Hampton's Brigade

1st North Carolina Cavalry
1st South Carolina Cavalry
2nd South Carolina Cavalry
Cobb's Legion
Jeff Davis Legion
Phillips Legion

Fitzhugh Lee's Brigade

1st Virginia Cavalry
2nd Virginia Cavalry
3rd Virginia Cavalry
4th Virginia Cavalry
5th Virginia Cavalry

W. H. F. Lee's Brigade

2nd North Carolina Cavalry
9th Virginia Cavalry
10th Virginia Cavalry
13th Virginia Cavalry
15th Virginia Cavalry

Jones's Brigade

6th Virginia Cavalry
7th Virginia Cavalry
11th Virginia Cavalry
12th Virginia Cavalry
35th Virginia Battalion

Stuart Horse Artillery

Breathed's Battery
Chew's Battery
Griffin's Battery
Hart's Battery
McGregor's Battery
Moorman's Battery

Appendix E

GENERAL ALFRED PLEASONTON'S REPORTS
Official Records, Ser. I, Vol. XVII, Pt. 1, 902-905.

HEADQUARTERS, CAVALRY CORPS
Beverly Ford, June 9, 1863, 6 A.M.

ENEMY has opened with artillery, and shows some force of cavalry. Had a sharp skirmish. Col. Davis, commanding Second Brigade, 1st Division, led his column across, and is badly wounded.

11 A.M.

General: All the enemy's forces are engaged with me. I am holding them until Gregg can come up. Gregg's guns are being heard in the enemy's rear.

12.30 P.M.

Gen. Gregg has joined me, and I will now attack the enemy vigorously with my whole force. Prisoners report that Stuart has 30,000 cavalry here. Both Lees, Jones, and Hampton are with him. We have had a sharp fight, and have lost heavily, as we had the whole force in front of one-half of my command. Colonel Davis, Eight New York, and Captain Canfield, Second [U.S.] Cavalry, are killed; Major Morris, Sixth Pennsylvania Cavalry, a prisoner, with a number of others. We have about 100 in hospital, wounded; Major Beveridge, Eighth Illinois, amongst number. Buford and Ames have driven their whole force out of their strongest positions. It would be well to send a good force of the Fifth Corps toward Brandy Station, if it can be spared.

8 P.M.

General: A short time after my last dispatch to you, General Gregg, with his infantry and cavalry, joined me about 2 miles from the river, to which point I had driven the enemy. He reported that he had encountered a much superior number of the enemy's cavalry and had a severe fight; also that a train of cars had been run up to Brandy Station filled with infantry, who opened on his men. I also received information from letters and official reports captured in the enemy's camp, as well as from prisoners, that the enemy had upward of 12,000 cavalry (which was double my own force cavalry) and twenty-five pieces of artillery. I also learned from contrabands and prisoners that a large force of infantry had been sent from Culpeper as well as Longstreet's command to Ellis' Ford. And having crippled the enemy by desperate fighting so that he could not follow me, I returned with my command to the north side of the Rappahannock. Gregg's command crossed at Rappahannock Bridge.

Tomorrow morning Stuart was to have started on a raid into Maryland, so captured papers state. You may rest satisfied he will not attempt it.

Buford's cavalry had a long and desperate encounter, hand to hand, with the enemy, in which he drove handsomely before him very superior forces. Over 200 prisoners were captured and one battle-flag.

The troops are in splendid spirits, and are entitled to the highest praise for their distinguished conduct.

June 10, 1863—5.30 A.M.

We had splendid fighting yesterday, and I think it will prevent Stuart from making his raid, which he was to have commenced this morning. Toward night, they opened 20-pounder Parrott guns at a long distance, showing that they were reinforced. They did not attempt to follow us with any vigor. My old division and the regulars have covered themselves with glory. We captured Stuart's camp, with his orders, letters, &. He was to move to Maryland with 12,000 cavalry and twenty-five guns, and he was camped at the ford we crossed, a perfect hornet's nest, but we drove them over 2 miles before Gregg came up, and, when I found out he had had as hard a time as ourselves, and no fresh troops to call on, I retired to the north bank of the Rappahannock. The enemy lost very heavily.

Buford's loss is 250 wounded, killed not yet known. At least a dozen officers among the latter. I don't know Gregg's losses yet. Gregg lost two guns before he joined me, but they were lost with honor; all his people were engaged, and his battery without support. The battery men fought their pieces until cut down at their side. One gun in the same battery burst—Sixth New York. We blew up a caisson for the enemy, and killed a number.

Tell the general I will send in a report today, as soon as I can collect the facts.

[Foregoing report to Brig. Gen. R. Ingalls, Chief Quartermaster, Army of the Potomac. Preceding reports to General Hooker.]

FINAL REPORT
O.R., op. cit., pp. 1044ff.

General: I have the honor to submit the following report on the operations of the expedition placed under my orders by your instruction of the 7th inst.:

On the 8th, two commands were formed as follows: The First Cavalry Division, the Reserve Brigade, and Brigadier-General Ames' command of infantry constituted the command, under the orders of Brigadier-General J. Buford, to cross the river at Beverly Ford. The other command, under the orders of Brigadier-General D. McM.

Gregg, was to cross the Rappahannock at Kelly's Ford, and was composed of the Second and Third Cavalry Divisions and the infantry command of Brigadier General D. A. Russell.

I myself remained with Buford's command until the junction of the two forces near Brandy Station, when I directed the movements of the whole.

The orders to each command were to cross the river at daylight on the 9th instant and push rapidly for Brandy Station. Buford's command at half past 4 o'clock in the morning crossed Beverly Ford in splendid style, attacked the enemy at once before he had time to form, and would have captured his guns but for the untimely loss of the brave and accomplished Colonel B. F. Davis, of the 8th New York Cavalry, who, while commanding a brigade, charged with the head of his column into the midst of the enemy, and was shot through the head.

In less than an hour I succeeded in forming my entire line, covering the field, and advanced on the enemy. His force was so superior to mine, at least three to one at every point, that I determined to hold him until I could hear from Gregg. After very heavy skirmishing and artillery firing for several hours, the distant boom of Gregg's guns was heard coming up on the left and rear of the enemy. I immediately ordered the whole line to advance, and the enemy gave way rapidly, the camp of the Stuart Horse Artillery with important papers, was captured, and Gregg's force seized Stuart's headquarters with all its documents. A junction was then formed with Gregg, and orders were issued to press the enemy at all points. This was done until it was discovered infantry was being brought up on the cars to Brandy Station very rapidly; as was also a heavy column on foot from Culpeper. We had also captured infantry soldiers. These facts determined me to withdraw to the north side of the Rappahannock. Orders were given to Gregg to retire by the ford at Rappahannock Bridge, while Buford should retire by way of Beverly Ford. Before, however, this movement commenced, a grand attack was made by our right, and the finest fighting of the war took place. Regiments of our cavalry would charge whole brigades of the enemy, would rally and charge again, never yielding, and always crushing the mass opposed to them. The enemy's cavalry would retreat, and their officers were seen to saber and shoot their men to keep them up to the fight. I rapidly reinforced this battle, and General Buford withdrew his command in beautiful style to this side, the enemy not daring to follow, but showing his chagrin and mortification by an angry and sharp cannonading.

The Third Division, under the immediate orders of General Gregg, inflicted a severe loss on the enemy near Brandy Station, and would have advanced more had Colonel Duffié, commanding the Second Division, brought up his command to his assistance in the time he should have done. This delay caused the loss of two guns of the 6th New York Battery, as Gregg had his whole force engaged with superior masses and the section could not be properly supported; but this mishap only reflected higher honor on Lieutenant Martin, who fought his guns to the last, had 21 men of his small party killed and wounded, with 32 horses, and then rendered his guns useless by spiking one and ramming a shot the wrong way into the other; but 30 rounds were left to those guns when taken, and all the fuses were destroyed by the gunners. I request this battery may be permitted to place the name of Beverly Ford on their guidon. I also ask the honor be accorded to the regiments of the Third Division, the First Division, and the Reserve Brigade of Cavalry.

Three colors and 279 prisoners, including a number of officers, were captured in this battle.

I have the honor to recommend Brigadier-Generals Buford and Gregg for promotion for the gallantry and ability with which they fought their respective commands. The records of these officers are also fully indorsed:

The following officers came especially under my notice: Colonel Devin, 6th New York, commanding First Division [Second Brigade]; Captain Harrison, 6th Cavalry, commanding the regiment; Captain Merritt, 2nd Cavalry, commanding the regiment; Captain Lord, 1st Cavalry, commanding the regiment; Major McClure, 3rd Indiana, commanding the regiment; Captain Farnsworth, 8th Illinois; Captain Waite, 8th Illinois.

Captains Dahlgren and Cadwalader, aides-de-camp of Major-General Hooker, were frequently under the hottest fire, and were untiring in their generous assistance in conveying my orders.

Captain Dahlgren was among the first to cross the river and charged with the first troops; he afterwards charged with the 6th Pennsylvania Cavalry when that regiment won the admiration of the entire command, and his horse was shot four times. His dashing bravery and cool intelligence are only equalled by his varied accomplishments.

First Lieutenant Custer, 5th Cavalry, aide-de-camp, charged with Colonel Davis, in the taking of Beverly Ford, and was conspicuous for gallantry throughout the fight.

First Lieutenant Thompson, First New Jersey Cavalry, aide-de-camp, is mentioned most favorably by General Gregg, with whose column he served.

Lieutenant-Colonel Alexander, chief of staff and adjutant-general, rendered valuable and important service in obtaining information of the enemy's movements and communicating with General Gregg.

Captain J. M. Robertson, Second Artillery, commanding Brigade of Horse Artillery, while serving on my staff, had two horses shot under him; his services in placing batteries, and serving the artillery were distinguished as were those of Captain Elder, Captain Graham, Lieutenants Vincent and Williams, of the horse batteries.

Lieutenant-Colonel Smith, of the Sixth Pennsylvania; Captain Newhall of the Sixth Pennsylvania; Captain Green, Second Cavalry; Major Crocker, Sixth New York Cavalry; First Lieutenant Walker, Fifth Cavalry; First Lieutenant Yates, Fourth Michigan Infantry; First Lieutenant Thompson, Sixth Pennsylvania Cavalry [probably Lieutenant George H. Thompson, First Rhode Island Cavalry— O.R.], and Captain Drummond, Fifth Cavalry, acted as aides-de-camp and in other capacities on the field, and were frequently under hot fire, and rendered valuable assistance.

Surgeon Pancoast, medical director, and Assistant Surgeon McGill, formed efficient and ample arrangements for the wounded, and by their operations facilitated the return of the troops.

Captain von Koerber, topographical engineer, took an accurate sketch of the entire field during the engagement.

To Brigadier-Generals Russell and Ames, with their respective commands, I am under many obligations for the efficient cooperation they gave at all times. The marked manner in which General Ames held and managed his troops under a galling fire of the enemy for several hours, is entitled to higher commendation than I can bestow.

A sketch of the battle-field [not found—O.R.] with the reports of brigade commanders and a nominal list of casualties are herewith transmitted.

I am, very respectfully, your obedient servant,

A. PLEASONTON
Brigadier-General, commanding.

Appendix F

GENERAL J. E. B. STUART'S REPORT
Official Records, Ser. I, Vol. XXVII, Pt. 2, 679-687.

HEADQUARTERS, CAVALRY DIVISION

June 13, 1863

GENERAL: I have the honor to submit the following report of the battle of Fleetwood, fought on the 9th inst.:

Soon after dawn on the morning of the 9th, sharp firing of small-arms was heard in the direction of Beverly Ford, indicating a crossing of the Rappahannock by the enemy. Brigadier-General Jones, whose pickets were at that ford, having heard the firing, notified me of it, and having first sent forward his grand guard, put the remainder of his command quickly in the saddle, and repaired to the support of his pickets. The Horse Artillery, encamped on the Beverly Ford road, was hastily hitched up and put in position, and orders were given to Brigadier-Generals Hampton and Robertson to move their brigades to the front, and to W. H. F. Lee, near Well-ford's, to move his brigade toward Beverly, drawing toward him Fitz. Lee's brigade, commanded by Colonel [Thomas T.] Munford, each having a section of [James] Breathed's battery.

Before the commands had reached Fleetwood heights, where I encamped the night before, I received notice from General Robertson's pickets, at Kelly's Ford, that the enemy was crossing infantry with some cavalry at that point, two regiments being already over. I therefore sent Colonel [John L.] Black's First South Carolina Cavalry, of Hampton's brigade, down that road, to hold the enemy in check till Robertson's brigade could relieve him.

Hampton's brigade was directed to a more central position between the two roads, on Jones' right, excepting the Second South Carolina Cavalry, Colonel [M. C.] Butler, which was held in reserve at Brandy.

While these dispositions were being made, Jones' brigade became hotly engaged with the enemy's infantry and cavalry forces, which were advancing through the extensive woodland on the Beverly Ford road, and extricated the Horse Artillery from its exposed position. Brigadier-General Jones commanded in this contest (in which Acting Brig. Gen. B. F. Davis, U.S. Army, was killed), the Horse Artillery taking position to command the road and the open space on either side, near Saint James' Church, being at the same time in plain view of Fleetwood.

Robertson's brigade having been sent toward Kelly's, I repaired in person to Jones' position, and found the enemy checked, and his advance apparently abandoned. The movement of W. H. F. Lee's brigade toward Beverly Ford contributed to check the advance of the enemy at this point, for, attacking him in flank, he seriously threatened his rear, while Hampton closed upon his left flank, deploying sharpshooters in the woods in his front.

Hearing from General Robertson that the enemy was still crossing at Kelly's, and that the cavalry that had crossed there (apparently two regiments) was moving in the direction of Stevensburg, Colonel Butler's First [Second] South Carolina Cavalry was ordered at once to the latter point, and Wickham's regiment, Fourth Virginia Cavalry, was sent to his support; also one piece of artillery, and the promise of more force, if he needed it. I had all the wagons of the division sent to the rear, toward Culpeper Court-House, including every vestige of my own camp. I also sent Asst. Engineer F. S. Robertson to Brandy, to attend in person to the posting of a dismounted battalion of Hampton's brigade down the road from Brandy Station toward Carrico's Mills, one of the approaches from Kelly's. I afterward ascertained that this battalion could not be found, and was consequently never posted. General Robertson reported the enemy in force of artillery and infantry in his front, and the cavalry bearing farther to his right. Brigadier-General Jones had sent me an infantry prisoner of Slocum's corps. These facts, as well as the strength and advantages of the position, determined me to make the real stand on the Fleetwood ridge. To this point I also ordered a section of artillery in reserve, and posted there my adjutant-general, Major [H. B.] McClellan, in observation, while I was absent on the left.

On a field geographically so extensive, and much of it wooded, presenting to the enemy so many avenues of approach, I deemed it highly injudicious to separate my command into detachments to guard all the approaches, as in such case the enemy could concentrate upon any one, and, overwhelming it, take the others in detail, especially as I was aware that the entire cavalry force of the enemy had crossed the river, with a large proportion of artillery, and supported by nine regiments of infantry on the road to Kelly's, and seven on the road to Beverly Ford. I conceived it to be my policy to keep my command concentrated, excepting sufficient to watch and delay the enemy as to his real move, and then strike him with my whole force.

Major McClellan reported to me that the column referred to appeared to be advancing upon the Fleetwood Hill, having turned to the right from the Stevensburg road. The artillery sent to that hill unfortunately had little ammunition. Ordering more artillery to that point, and directing General Jones to send two regiments without delay to hold the heights, I repaired in person to that point, leaving General Jones with the remainder of his brigade to occupy the enemy in his front.

The force moving on Fleetwood was at first reported to be two regiments, but, as I approached, I saw that the force was larger, and then sent orders to Hampton and Robertson to move up their brigades, and to Jones to follow, notifying General W. H. F. Lee to rejoin the command on the left.

Harman's and White's regiments (Jones' brigade) led the advance, and the former reached the hill about 50 yards in advance of the enemy, and just as the piece of artillery, which had up to that time checked the enemy's advance, having fired its last round, was retiring from the hill.

The contest for the hill was prolonged and spirited. Harman's regiment (Twelfth Virginia Cavalry) attacked the enemy, driving back his advance, but broke in confusion at the approach of the enemy's reserve, and, in doing so, deranged very much White's column, which was advancing to his support, and lessened materially the force of White's charge. That dashing officer, with the brave spirits he could hold together, broke the enemy's advance, and penetrated to his artillery, for which he was endeavoring to gain position on the hill, but the enemy was too strong for him. The more effectually to support White, the Sixth Virginia Cavalry (Major [C. E.] Flournoy commanding) was ordered by me to leave the house to the right, facing southward, and attack that portion of the enemy in flank which Harman and White engaged in front. This regiment, it appears, also reached the enemy's battery, but was unable to hold it.

The artillery was hurried up after White and Harman, and participated in their charge to such an extent that the cannoneers were for a time engaged hand to hand with the enemy. At this critical moment, the leading regiment of Hampton's brigade (Colonel [P. M. B.] Young's Georgia regiment) came up, and made a brilliant charge upon the flank of the enemy, supported by Black's First South Carolina Cavalry, thus checking his advance on the hill, while the First North Carolina Cavalry (Colonel Baker), supported by the Jeff. Davis Legion, Lieutenant-Colonel Waring (Hampton's brigade), sweeping around on Young's left, facing southward, made a series of charges most successful and brilliant.

Colonel Lomax, Eleventh Virginia Cavalry (Jones' brigade), charged directly over the crest, took the enemy's artillery (three pieces), capturing the cannoneers, and it was soon after turned upon the enemy. Colonel Lomax pushed thence directly to Brandy Station, a short distance to his front and right, and, dispersing the enemy at that point, after a sharp encounter pursued his fleeing forces down the road toward Kelly's till the fire of our artillery, directed upon the retreating column, made it necessary to desist. The dust was so great that it was impossible to distinguish friends from foes at that distance.

General Hampton had an opportunity, being directly on the enemy's flank, of cutting off a large portion of the force which attack our right flank, which he was directed to improve, but the fire of our artillery, it appears, stopped him also. Two of his regiments (the Cobb Legion and First South Carolina Cavalry) were ordered by me to reform in the flat near Fleetwood, as a support to our artillery.

Robertson's brigade, which, in withdrawing from the vicinity of Kelly's Ford, had some distance to march, reached the scene of action too late to participate in the fight.

My first care now was to open communication with Culpeper and Stevensburg, which Colonel Lomax was directed to do, and which was soon effected.

Until this time, I had heard nothing from Stevensburg since Colonel Butler first moved down from Brandy.

The enemy, with infantry and artillery, now debouched rapidly from the direction of Thompson's house and Saint James' Church (Jones' late position on our left), and threatened an immediate attack on the hill (Fleetwood), firing furiously.

This advance upon Fleetwood made it absolutely necessary to desist from our pursuit of the force retreating toward Kelly's, particularly as the infantry known to be on that road would very soon have terminated the pursuit.

Jones' brigade was posted behind Fleetwood, with artillery on the heights, and his sharpshooters were engaged with the enemy's infantry to the left.

Hampton's brigade was in position on the right as we now faced (northward).

Our artillery had scarcely a round of ammunition left, but great exertions were made to supply it.

Brig. Gen. W. H. F. Lee having joined our left, facing northward, on the same range of hills, was closely followed by Buford's division, composed principally of regulars, while the infantry skirmishers pushed through the woods to within 300 yards of our position. At this moment, General W. H. F. Lee engaged the enemy in a series of brilliant charges with his regiments, alternately routing the enemy, and, overpowered, falling back to reform. This continued till Munford's brigade, which, having been anxiously expected, arrived opposite this portion of the field, and was ordered in at once to the attack in flank. The enemy fell back, and Munford's sharpshooters pressed him all the way to Beverly Ford, on the left. Our whole line followed the enemy to the river, skirmishing with his rear, and our line of pickets was re-established that night. Our infantry skirmishers, advancing through the woods, did not engage the enemy.

About the time of General W. H. F. Lee's hot engagement on the left, I received intelligence of affairs at Stevensburg. The two regiments sent there failed to resist the enemy effectually, and one (the Fourth Virginia Cavalry) broke in utter confusion without firing a gun, in spite of every effort of the colonel to rally the men to the charge. This regiment usually fights well, and its stampede on this occasion is unaccountable. Colonel Wickham's report is herewith forwarded.

The First [Second] South Carolina Cavalry (Colonel Butler), which had the advance there, had also a portion of its column thrown into confusion, which extended through the whole of the Fourth Virginia. Owing to the casualties to officers of the First South Carolina Regiment, no report has yet been received of its operations. The movement of the enemy on Stevensburg ought to have been checked by the force sent there sufficiently long for re-enforcements to be sent.

Attention is called to the accompanying reports of subordinate commanders for a more detailed account of their operations in this battle, and the names of those specially distinguished.

Brigadier-Generals Hampton, W. H. F. Lee, and Jones were prompt in the execution of orders, and conformed readily to the emergencies arising.

Brigadier-General Robertson kept the enemy in check on the Kelly's Ford road, but did not conform to the movement of the enemy to the right, of which he was cognizant, so as to hold him in check or thwart him by a corresponding move of a portion of his command in the same direction. He was too far off for me to give orders to do so in time. His detailed report will, I hope, account for this.* General Robertson's command, though not engaged, was exposed to the enemy's artillery fire, and behaved well.

Colonel Munford's delay in coming to the field has not been satisfactorily accounted for, as the distance was not very great.

General Jones' brigade had the hardest fighting, all five regiments having been engaged twice. The Twelfth Virginia Cavalry broke unnecessarily after a successful charge, which confusion entailed, as usual, harder fighting and severe loss on itself as well as on the rest of the command.

Brig. Gen. W. H. F. Lee's brigade was handled in a handsome and highly satisfactory manner by that gallant officer, who received a severe wound through the leg in one of the last of the brilliant charges of his command on the heights. I regret very much the absence of his report, especially because his brigade being not so much under my own eye, I am unable to mention with particularity the gallantry of the officers and men of his brigade. Still more do I deplore the casualty which deprives us, for a short time only, it is hoped, of his valuable services. The command of his brigade thereafter devolved upon Col. J. R. Chambliss, jr., Thirteenth Virginia Cavalry.

* See Robertson's report of June 13, p. 734.

The conduct of the Horse Artillery, under that daring and efficient officer, Maj. R. F. Beckham, deserves the highest praise. Not one piece was ever in the hands of the enemy, though at times the cannoneers had to fight pistol and sword in hand in its defense. The accompanying report of Major Beckham shows one instance particularly deserving special mention: Lieutenants [C. E.] Ford and [William] Hoxton, of the Stuart Horse Artillery, charged the enemy with their detachments, and Private Sudley, of the same battery, knocked one of the enemy off his horse with the sponge-staff. The officers and men behaved with the greatest gallantry, and the mangled bodies of the enemy show the effectiveness of their fire. Two of the enemy's guns were turned upon him with decided effect; the other was disabled.

The enemy's loss is not known, and will, as far as possible, be carefully concealed by him. His dead on the field, together with the wounded and prisoners taken, exceed our entire loss, while he claims to have carried off his dead officers and all his wounded. A list of 192 of his wounded who reached one hospital in Alexandria, among whom were infantry as well as cavalry, is published in his papers, and in that list thirty-six regiments are represented, and it is not claimed that this hospital received all. Their dead, among whom were several field officers, were buried on different parts of the field before an opportunity was afforded to count them. A large number of arms, equipments, horses, 6 flags, and 3 pieces of his best ordnance (2 of which are serviceable) were captured. A list of captures is appended, as well as a statement of our killed, wounded, and missing, amounting to about 480 total.*

Among our gallant dead, the memory of whose deeds of heroism on the battle-field will be an heir-loom to posterity, I am grieved to record Col. Solomon Williams, Second North Carolina Cavalry—as fearless as he was efficient; the brave and chivalrous Lieut. Col. Frank Hampton, Second South Carolina, mortally wounded. The names of the other officers killed will be found appended.

The limits of this report will not admit of the names of those brave spirits who have fallen in the ranks, but their names are recorded on the muster-rolls of fame, and will live in the lasting remembrance of a grateful people.

* See Inclosures Nos. 7 to 11 to Stuart's report of August 20, 1863, pp. 718, 719. and Cooke's report, p. 720.

Lieutenant-Colonel [J. C.] Phillips, Thirteenth Virginia Cavalry (a gallant officer), and Maj. M. D. Ball, Eleventh Virginia Cavalry, are among the wounded.

Capt. Benjamin S. White, of the regular army, serving on my staff, behaved with the most distinguished gallantry, and was wounded painfully in the neck.

Colonel Lomax, Eleventh Virginia Cavalry, Colonel Young, Georgia Legion, and Lieutenant-Colonel White, Thirty-fifth Virginia Battalion, as coming under my own eye, handled their regiments admirably, and behaved with conspicuous daring; the last-mentioned, though painfully wounded, is still in command of his regiment, on active and important duty.

Col. A. W. Harman, Twelfth Virginia Cavalry, while bravely leading his regiment, was wounded in the neck, but retained command till night.

Col. M. C. Butler, Second South Carolina Cavalry, received a severe wound, causing the loss of his foot, which deprived his regiment and the country of his gallant and valuable services for a time.

Capt. W. D. Farley, of South Carolina, a volunteer aide on my staff, was mortally wounded by the same shell, and displayed even in death the same loftiness of bearing and fortitude which have characterized him through life. He had served without emolument, long, faithfully, and always with distinction. No nobler champion has fallen. May his spirit abide with us!

My own staff, on this, as on all other occasions, acquitted themselves handsomely.

Maj. Heros von Borcke, a gallant Prussian, who has fought bravely and served faithfully for one year, was everywhere, animating by his presence and prowess, and checking the wavering and broken.

Maj. H. B. McClellan, assistant adjutant-general, displayed the same zeal, gallantry, and efficiency which has on every battle-field, in the camp, or on the march, so distinguished him as to cause his selection for his present post.

Surg. Talcott Eliason; Maj. Andrew R. Venable, assistant adjutant-general; Capt. W. W. Blackford, engineers; Capt. John Eston Cooke, chief of ordnance; Capt. J. L. Clarke, volunteer aide; First Lieut. C. Dabney, aide-de-camp, and Maj. Norman R. Fitzhugh, division quartermaster, all in their respective spheres acquitted themselves in a highly creditable manner. Surgeon Eliason, though without a superior in his profession, would, from his conduct on the field, excel as a colonel of cavalry.

First Lieut. Robert H. Goldsborough, aide-de-camp, while bearing an important message to Colonel Wickham, was captured by the enemy.

Captain Blackford, engineers, has prepared a map of the country embraced in these operations.*

To members of my personal escort, composed of privates from the ranks, I am specially indebted, acting as they did in the capacity of bearers of dispatches, oral or written. They discharged their duty with a zeal, fidelity, and intelligence deserving high praise.

Private Foy, of General Robertson's escort, was the first who brought me reliable news of the enemy's movement toward Stevensburg.

Capt. W. B. Wooldridge, Fourth Virginia Cavalry, Lieut. J. L. Jones, Second Virginia Cavalry, and Lieut. R. B. Kennon, Provisional Army, Confederate States, members of general court-martial, Fitz. Lee's brigade, lately adjourned, while *en route* to join their commands, met near Brandy a party of the enemy. Collecting a few stragglers, they attacked and routed the party, which was more than double their number, capturing a lieutenant, 6 privates, and a guidon.

I am, general, most respectfully, your obedient servant,

J. E. B. STUART,
Major-General, Commanding.

Brig. Gen. R. H. Chilton,
Asst. Adjt. and Insp. Gen., Army of Northern Virginia.

Addenda.

Headquarters Army of Northern Virginia,
June 16, 1863.

Maj. Gen. J. E. B. Stuart,
Commanding Cavalry:

General: I have received and read, with much pleasure, your report of the recent engagement at Fleetwood.

The dispositions made by you to meet the strong attack of the enemy appear to have been judicious and well planned. The troops

---

* See p. 686.

were well and skillfully managed, and, with few exceptions, conducted themselves with marked gallantry.

The result of the action calls for our grateful thanks to Almighty God, and is honorable alike to the officers and men engaged.

Very respectfully, your obedient servant,

R. E. LEE,
General.

Appendix G

POEMS AND SONGS OF CIVIL WAR CAVALRY

"CAVALRY CROSSING A FORD"

WALT WHITMAN, *Drum-Taps*

A LINE in long array where they wind betwixt green islands,
They take a serpentine course, their arms flash in the sun,
    hark to the musical clank,
Behold the silvery river, in it the splashing horses loitering
    stop to drink,
Behold the brown-faced men, each group, each person, a picture,
    the negligent rest on the saddles,
Some emerge on the opposite bank, others are just entering
    the ford—while,
Scarlet and blue and snowy white,
The guidon flags flutter gayly in the wind.

"THE CAVALRY CHARGE"

FRANCIS A. DURIVAGE

With bray of the trumpet
And roll of the drum,
And keen ring of bugles,
The cavalry come.
Sharp clank the steel scabbards,
The bridle-chains ring,

And foam from red nostrils
The wild chargers fling.

Tramp! tramp! o'er the green sward
That quivers below,
Scarce held by the curb-bit
The fierce horses go!
And the grim-visaged colonel,
With ear-rending shout,
Peals forth to the squadrons,
The order—"Trot out."

One hand on the sabre,
And one on the rein,
The troopers move forward
In line on the plain,
As rings the word "Gallop!"
The steel scabbards clank,

And each rowel is pressed
To a horse's hot flank;
And swift is their rush
As the wild torrents flow,
When it pours from the crag
On the valley below.

"Charge!" thunders the leader
Like shaft from the bow
Each mad horse is hurled
On the wavering foe
A thousand bright sabres
Are gleaming in air;
A thousand dark horses
Are dashed on the square.

Resistless and reckless
Of aught may betide,
Like demons, not mortals,
The wild troopers ride.

Cut right! and cut left!
　For the parry who needs?
The bayonets shiver
　Like wind-shattered reeds.

Vain—vain the red volley
　That bursts from the square—
The random-shot bullets—
　Are wasted in air.
Triumphant, remorseless,
　Unerring as death,—
No sabre that's stainless
　Returns to its sheath.

The wounds that are dealt
　By that murderous steel
Will never yield case
　For the surgeons to heal.
Hurrah! they are broken—
　Hurrah! boys, they fly—
None linger save those
　Who but linger to die.

Rein up your hot horses
　And call in your men;
The trumpet sounds "Rally
　To color" again.
Some saddles are empty,
　Some comrades are slain,
And some noble horses
　Lie stark on the plain,
But war's a chance game, boys,
　And weeping is vain.

"THE DEATH OF PELHAM"

(From *Southern Bivouac,* March, 1884. Author unknown)

Up to the forefront, spoke never a breath,
Up to the battle, the cannon and death,

Up to the fierce guns over the ford,
Rode young John Pelham, his hat on his sword.
Out spoke bold Stuart, our cavalry lord:
"Back to your guns, lad;" never a word
Uttered the gunner as onward he spurred,
On with the cavalry; no business there;
Backward the wind blew his bright yellow hair,
Back blew the battle-smoke from the red fire,
Up rose the battle-dust higher and higher;
Out rang the saber notes, clear as a bell,
Heard above bursting of shrapnel and shell;
Out rang the order from Fitz Lee the brave—
"Charge the left battery!" God! 'tis his grave!
On by the crashing balls, hissing balls then—
Saber and pistols and horses and men
Over the hills went, over the dead,
Fitz Lee and cavalry, Pelham ahead!
Down by the sulphur smoke to the red plain,
On the left battery Pelham is slain.
Gently now comrades, take up the bier,
Bear it back quickly, the battle is near,
Rein down the charger, muffle the tread,
Weep, Light Artillery, Pelham is dead.

"THE CAVALRY CHARGE"
Edmund C. Stedman

Our good steeds snuff the evening air,
  Our pulses with their purpose tingle;
The foeman's fires are twinkling there;
  He leaps to hear our sabres jingle!
     Halt!
  Each carbine sent its whizzing ball:
  Now, cling! clang! Forward, all,
     Into the fight!

Dash on beneath the smoking dome:
  Through level lightnings gallop nearer!
One look to Heaven! No thoughts of home;

The guidons that we bear are dearer.
　　Charge!
Cling! Clang! Forward, all!
Heaven help those whose horses fall—
　　Cut left and right!

They flee before our fierce attack!
They fall! they spread in broken surges.
Now, comrades, bear our wounded back,
And leave the foeman to his dirges.
　　Wheel!
The bugles sound the swift recall:
Cling! clang! Backward, all!
　　Home, and good-night!

"CAVALRY SONG"

Elbridge Jefferson Cutler

The squadron is forming, the war-bugles play
To saddle, brave comrades, stout hearts for a fray!
Our Captain is mounted—strike spurs, and away!

No breeze shakes the blossoms or tosses the grain;
But the wind of our speed floats the galloper's mane,
As he feels the bold rider's firm hand on the rein.

Lo! Dim in the starlight their white tents appear!
Ride slowly! ride slowly! the onset is near!
More slowly! More slowly! the sentry may hear!

Now fall on the rebel—a tempest of flame!
Strike down the false banner whose triumph were shame!
Strike, strike for the true flag, for freedom and fame!

Hurrah! sheathe your swords! the carnage is done.
All red with our valor, we welcome the sun.
Up, up with the stars! we have won! we have won!

"DRAGOON'S SONG"
GEORGE H. BOKER

Clash, clash goes the sabre against my steed's side,
Kling, kling go the rowels as onward I ride;
And all my bright harness is living and speaks,
And under my horse-shoe the frosty ground creaks;
I wave my buff glove to the girl whom I love,
Then join my dark squadron, and forward I move.

The foe all secure, has laid down by his gun;
I'll open his eyelids before the bright sun;
I burst on his pickets—they scatter, they fly;
Too late they awaken—'tis only to die.
Now the torch to their camp; I'll make it a lamp,
As back to my quarters so slowly I tramp.

Kiss, kiss me my darling; your lover is here,
Nay, kiss off the smoke-stains; keep back that bright tear;
Keep back that bright tear till the day when I come,
To the low wailing fife and deep muffled drum,
With a bullet half through the bosom so true,
To die, as I ought for my country and you.

"JINE THE CAVALRY"

(Sung to the tune now usually known as "The Old Gray Mare."
Each stanza contains only one new line, the rest being repetitions
of all or part of that line as patterned in the first stanza.)

1. We are the boys that went around McClellian,
   Went around McClellian,
   Went around McClellian,
   We are the boys that went around McClellian,
   Bully boys, ho.
   Bully boys, hey—Bully boys, ho.
   Bully boys, hey—Bully boys, ho.

Chorus:
>   If you want to have a good time, jine the Cavalry,
>   Jine the Cavalry,
>   Jine the Cavalry,
>   Want to have a good time, jine the Cavalry,
>   Bully boys, hey.

2. We are the boys that crossed the Potomacum,
   Etc. . . .

Chorus:

3. And then we went into Pennsylvania,
   Etc. . . .

Chorus:

4. Then the big, fat Dutch gals hand around the bread-ium,
   Etc. . . .

Chorus:

5. Old Joe Hooker won't you come out o' the Wilderness,
   Etc. . . .

Chorus:

Appendix H

SABRE EXERCISE

(*Cavalry Tactics.* COLONEL PHILIP ST. GEORGE COOKE, I, 52-65.
Illustrations from
PATTEN, G. W., *Cavalry Drill and Sabre Exercises.*)

28.—For this lesson the squad is composed of from 6 to 8 men,
armed only with sabres; they are placed in one rank, 9 feet from
each other.

The object of the moulinet is to render the joints of the arm and wrist supple, and as it adds to the confidence of the men when isolated, by increasing their dexterity, they should first be exercised at it, as a preparation for the other motions.

Each lesson is therefore commenced and ended with moulinets, executed with a quickness proportioned to the progress of the troopers. The instructor pays particular attention that the men do not employ a degree of force in the sabre exercise, which not only is less necessary than skill and suppleness, but which is even prejudicial. He observes, also, that they do not lean to one side, in such a manner as to lose the seat, when mounted; he requires more especially, in the motions of the sabre to the rear, that the blade shall not fall too near the body, for fear of wounding the horse. In describing a circle, the flat of the blade should be to the side, and the edge to the front, and it should be so directed as not to touch either the horse's head, or his haunches, or the knees of the rider.

When the troopers execute all the motions with regularity, the instructor requires each cut to be given without decomposing it; the last syllable of a command is the signal for the quick execution of it. All the cuts are then terminated by a half-moulinet, which brings back to the position of GUARD.

Thrusts should always be used in preference, as they require less force, and their result is more prompt, sure, and decisive. They should be directed quickly *home* to the body of the adversary, the sabre being held with the full grasp, the thumb pressing against the guard in the direction of the blade.

The parries against the lance are the same as against the point.

29.—The instructor explains what is meant by *right and left side of the gripe;* by *tierce,* and by *quarte.*

The right side of the gripe is the side opposite to the guard.

The left side of the gripe is the side next to the guard.

Tierce is the position in which the edge of the blade is turned to the right, the nails downwards.

Quarte is the position in which the edge of the blade is turned to the left, the nails upwards.

To rest, the sabres being returned, the instructor conforms to what is prescribed, No. 2.

30.—The troopers being placed as prescribed, No. 28, the instructor commands:

Draw—Sabre.

2 *times.*

1. At the first part of the command, unhook the sabre with the left hand, and bring the hilt to the front; run the right wrist through the sword-knot; seize the gripe, draw the blade 6 inches out of the scabbard, pressing the scabbard against the thigh with the left hand, which seizes it at the upper ring.

Par 32

2. At the command, SABRE, draw the sabre quickly, raising the arm to its full extent, at an angle of about 45 degrees: the sabre in a straight line with the arm, make a slight pause, carry the blade to the right shoulder, the back of it against the hollow of the shoulder, the wrist resting against the hip, the little finger on the outside of the gripe.

Return—SABRE.

2 *times.*

31.—At the command, RETURN, carry the sabre vertically to the front, the thumb opposite to and 6 inches from the neck, the blade vertical, the edge to the left, the thumb extended on the right side of the gripe, the little finger by the side of the others.

2. At the command, SABRE, carry the wrist opposite to and 6 inches from the left shoulder; revolve the point of the blade to the rear, until it is nearly under the right hand, which, at the same time, is raised; the left hand, also at the same time, takes hold of the upper part of the scabbard; turn the eyes slightly to the left, return the blade, free the wrist from the sabre knot, drop the right hand by the side; turning with the left the hilt toward the body, and so round to the rear, hook up the sabre, and drop the left hand.

32.—The sabres being drawn, the instructor commands:

GUARD.

1 *time.*

At the command, GUARD, carry the right foot about 20 inches from the left, the heels on the same line; place the left hand closed, 6 inches from the body, and as high as the elbow, the fingers towards the body, the litte finger nearer than the thumb, (*position of the bridle hand;*) at the same time, carry the right hand about 10 inches in front of the right hip, the blade in an oblique position, the point a little raised, the edge upward, the back of the blade resting in the hollow of the left arm, as near the body as possible; the right hand without constraint, or feeling the weight of the sabre.

Left—MOULINET.

1 *time, 2 motions.*

33.—1. At the command, MOULINET, extend the right arm to the front to its full length, the hand in tierce and as high as the eyes; the point to the front, and a little higher than the hilt.

2. Commencing by lowering the blade, make rapidly a circle

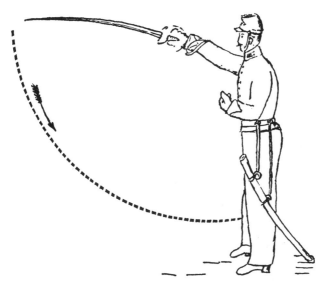

Left -Moulinet
Par 33

Right -Moulinet
Par 34

round the hand, to the left of, and as near as safe, to the horse, and to the elbow; returning to the first position, and then to guard.

Right—MOULINET.

1 time, 2 motions.

34.—1. At the command, MOULINET, extend the right arm to the front to its full length, the hand in quarte, and as high as the eyes, the point to the front, and a little higher than the hilt.

2. Commencing by lowering the blade, make rapidly a circle round the hand, to the right of the horse and body, returning to the first position, and then to guard.

35.—To execute the moulinet without stopping, if the instructor wishes to begin by the left, he commands:

Left and right—MOULINET.

1 time, 2 motions.

36.—If he wishes to begin by the right, he commands:

Right and left—MOULINET.

1 time, 2 motions.

At either of these commands, the troopers, commencing from the position of GUARD, execute alternately what is laid down in Nos. 33 and 34, without stopping at any motion.

Rear—MOULINET.

1 time, 2 motions.

37.—1. At the command, MOULINET, raise the arm to the right and rear to its full extent, the point of the sabre upwards, the edge to the right, the thumb extended on the back of the gripe, the body slightly turned to the right.

2. Describe a circle in rear, commencing by motion of the sabre towards the left, the arm being motionless to the wrist, return to the 1st position and then to guard.

When the troopers execute the moulinets well, the instructor

requires them to execute several in succession, until the command
GUARD.

In tierce—POINT.

1 time, 3 motions.

38.—1. At the command, POINT, raise the hand in tierce, as high as the right ear, and 7 inches from it, throw back the right shoulder, carrying the elbow to the rear, the point of the sabre to the right of the horses's head and neck, and a little below the horizontal, the edge upwards, the thumb on the back of the gripe.

2. Thrust forward, extending the arm to its full length, the edge of the sabre up.

3. Return to the position of guard.

In quarte—POINT.

1 time, 3 motions.

39.—1. At the command, POINT, lower the hand in quarte near the right hip, the thumb extended on the right side of the gripe, the point a little higher than the wrist, edge to the left.

2. Thrust to the right, front, extending the arm to its full length, the edge of the blade to the left.

3. Return to the position of guard.

Par 40

Left—POINT.

1 *time,* 3 *motions.*

40.—1. At the command, POINT, turn the head to the left, (half face to the left in the saddle,) raise the hand in tierce as high as the right ear, and 7 inches from it, the thumb on the back of the gripe, the edge of the blade upwards, the point directed to the left.

2. Thrust to the left, or left front, extending the arm to its full length, the edge up.

3. Return to the position of guard.

Right - Point
Par 41

Right—POINT.

1 *time*—3 *motions.*

41.—At the command, POINT, turn the head to the right, (half face to the right in the saddle,) carry the hand in quarte near the left breast, the edge upwards, the point directed **to the right.**

2. Thrust to the right, or right front, extending the arm to its full length, edge to the front.

3. Return to the position of guard.

Rear—POINT.

1 time, 3 motions.

42.—1. At the command, POINT, turn the head to the right and rear, (half face to the right in the saddle,) bring the hand in quarte in front of the right shoulder, the arm half extended, the blade horizontal, the point to the rear, the edge upwards.

2. Thrust to the rear, or right rear, extending the arm to its full length, edge to the right.

3. Return to the position of guard.

Against infantry left—POINT.

1 time, 3 motions.

43.—At the command, POINT, turn the head to the left, (half face to the left in the saddle,) raise the hand in tierce near the neck, the thumb on the back of the gripe, the point of the sabre directed at the height of the breast of a man on foot.

2. Thrust down in tierce.

3. Return to the position of guard.

Against infantry right—POINT.

1 time, 3 motions.

44. 1. At the command, POINT, turn the head and body toward the right, carry the hand in quarte near the right hip, the thumb on the right side of the gripe, the point of the sabre directed at the height of the breast of a man on foot.

2. Thrust in quarte.

3. Return to the position of guard.

Against infantry—FRONT POINT.

1 *time.*

45.—At the command, POINT, bear the weight on the right stirrup, bend well down to the right, extend the right arm well downwards, and, with the back of the sabre upwards, thrust forward, horizontally, and resume the guard.

Par 45

Front—CUT.

1 *time, 3 motions.*

46.—1. At the command, CUT, raise the sabre, the arm half extended, the hand a little higher than the head, the edge upwards, the point to the rear and higher than the hand.

2. Cut to the right of the horse's neck, extending the arm to its full length.

3. Return to the position of guard.

USED AGAINST CAVALRY AND INFANTRY.

Left—CUT.

1 *time,* 3 *motions.*

47.—1. At the command, CUT, turn the head to the left, (half face to the left in the saddle,) raise the sabre, the arm extended to the front and right, the hand in quarte, and as high as the head, the point higher than the hand.

2. Cut diagonally to the left, in quarte.

3. Return to the position of guard.

This is also used against infantry, bending well forward and down, and cutting at the necessary angle.

Right—CUT.

1 *time,* 3 *motions.*

48.—1. At the command, CUT, turn the head to the right, carry the hand near the left shoulder, the point of the sabre upwards, the edge to the left.

2. Extend the arm quickly to its full length, give a backhanded cut horizontally, in tierce.

3. Return to the position of guard.

This is used against infantry, leaning to the right, and cutting at the necessary angle.

Rear—CUT.

1 *time,* 3 *motions.*

49.—1. At the command, CUT, turn the head to the right, throwing back the right shoulder, (half face to the right in the saddle,) carry the hand near the left shoulder, the sabre perpendicular, the edge to the left.

2. Extend the arm quickly to its full length, and give a backhanded cut horizontally to the rear, in tierce.

3. Return to the position of guard.

Right, in tierce and quarte—CUT.

1 *time,* 4 *motions.*

50.—1. At the command, CUT, execute the 1st motion of *right cut,* No. 48.

2. Execute the 2d motion of *right cut,* No. 48.

3. Turn the hand in quarte, and cut horizontally to the left.

4. Return to the position of guard.

Left, in quarte and tierce—CUT.

1 *time,* 4 *motions.*

51.—1. At the command, CUT, execute the 1st motion of *left cut,* No. 47.

2. Execute the 2d motion of *left cut,* No. 47.

3. Turn the hand in tierce, and cut horizontally to the right.

4. Return to the position of guard.

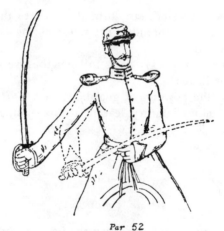

Par 52

Right—PARRY.

1 *time,* 2 *motions.*

52.—1. At the command, PARRY, grasp the sabre firmly, extend the arm to the right, the hand moving horizontally, the point at the same time describing a circular motion upwards, and with the edge to the right, parry as strongly as possible the blow aimed at the right side.

2. Return to the position of guard.

Par 53

Left—PARRY.

1 *time, 2 motions.*

53.—1. Raise the hand above, and about seven inches in front of the eyes, the elbow somewhat bent, edge to the left, point downwards and about a foot outside the horse's left shoulder, and parry as strongly as possible the blow aimed at the left side.

2. Return to the position of guard.

Head—PARRY.

1 *time, 2 motions.*

54.—1. At the command, PARRY, raise the sabre quickly above the head, holding it with the utmost firmness, the arm nearly extended, the edge upward, the point to the left, and about 6 inches higher than the hand.

The hand is carried more or less to the right, left, or rear, according to the position of the adversary.

2. Return to the position of guard.

Against Infantry Right - Parry
Par 55

*Against infantry right—*PARRY.

1 time, 3 motions.

55.—1. At the command, PARRY, turn the head to the right, (half facing to the right in the saddle,) raise the sabre, the arm extended to the right and rear, the point upwards, the thumb extended on the back of the gripe, the edge to the left.

2. Parry the bayonet with the back of the blade, by a rapid

circular motion of arm and blade, from rear to front, bringing the hand as high as the head, the point upwards, edge to the front.

3. Return to the position of guard.

*Against infantry left—*PARRY.

1 *time, 3 motions.*

56.—1. At the command, PARRY, turn the head to the left, (half face to the left in the saddle,) raise the sabre, the arm extended to the front and right, the point upwards, the thumb extended on the back of the gripe, the back of the blade to the front.

2. Parry the bayonet with the back of the blade, by a forcible circular motion of the arm and blade from front to rear, bringing the hand above the left shoulder, edge to the rear, the point upwards.

3. Return to the position of guard.

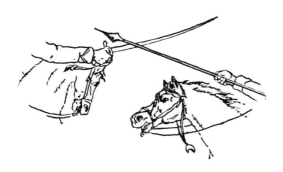

In tierce - Parry.
Par 57

PARRIES AGAINST THE LANCE, (OR SABRE.)

*In tierce—*PARRY.

1 *time, 2 motions.*

57.—1. At the command, PARRY, carry the forearm and blade quickly to the front and right, the elbow but little moved, edge to the right, thumb on the back of the gripe, the point being carried to the right front, at the height of the eyes.

2. Return to the position of guard.

In quarte—PARRY.

1 *time*, 2 *motions.*

58.—1. At the command, PARRY, carry the arm and blade quickly to the left front, edge to the left, the point as high as the eyes, the thumb on the back of the gripe.

2. Return to the position of guard.

59.—When the troopers begin to execute correctly the above cuts, thrusts, and parries, the instructor requires them to make the application of them by combined motions, such as follow:

In tierce—POINT AND FRONT CUT.

In quarte—POINT AND FRONT CUT.

Left—POINT AND CUT.

Right—POINT AND CUT.

Rear—POINT AND CUT.

Against infantry right—POINT AND CUT.

Against infantry left—POINT AND CUT.

Carry—SABRE.

As it is prescribed in No. 30, and carry the right foot to the side of the left.

GENERAL OBSERVATIONS AND DIRECTIONS.

60.—Great attention should at all times be paid to maintain the proper position and balance of the body; as by too great an exertion in delivering a cut or point a horseman may be thrown, or be so discomposed as to lose advantage of his skill, both for attack and defence; and he should have confidence in his parries, and not trust to his avoiding the attack of his opponent by turning or drawing back the body.

In delivering a forward point very little force is necessary when the horse is in quick motion, as the extension of the arm, with a good direction of the point, will be fully sufficient; nor should a cut, under such circumstances, be given too strong, as the impetus of the horse will give effective force. Even the drawing of the edge can frequently be applied with advantage, particularly when the point, by being given too soon, may not have taken effect; by a quick turn of the wrist the edge is drawn along the face of your opponent, or other exposed part. The forcing, also, of the edge can be resorted to when very near and closely pressed upon by an adversary by suddenly extending the arm and directing the edge across his face, or where an opening is given.

When sufficient space is allowed for choosing the point of attack you should endeavor to take advantage of it; if not, at all events to avoid its being made on your left rear, when a change of position alone can bring you upon an equality with your opponent; it may be done either by making a sudden halt, so as to allow him to pass, and then pressing upon his left rear, or by turning quickly to the left about, and thereby having your right opposed to his. Should you be prevented from doing this, and he still keeps upon your left, you must bear up as close as possible to him, otherwise your opposition will be ineffectual; for in his situation, by keeping at the proper distance from you, his cut will reach when yours will not, and consequently you will be reduced to the defence alone.

In meeting your opponent on the left front turn sharply to the left on your own ground, which brings you immediately with your sword arm free, and at liberty to act upon his left. And in meeting him upon the right front, press your horse quickly on, and by a sharp turn to the right gain his left rear, or if pursued endeavor to keep your adversary on the right rear. When attacked by more than one you will naturally endeavor to keep them both either to the right or left, but when they have been enabled to place themselves on both sides, press close upon the left opponent, and endeavor to keep the right one at a distance.

The attack or defence against the lance (it is the common weapon of the mounted Indians) depends much upon horsemanship, and the judgment of the rider. It is parried like the sword; and you must press in at your opportunity to close upon your antagonist. You must invariably endeavor to gain his *right rear* when he is least able to attack or defend; the left rear and *left*, weakest for the sabre, are the strongest positions for the lance; the same may be said of the bow and arrow; in pursuit always approach at the right rear.

When opposed to infantry, endeavor to meet an opponent on your right; in the parry the bayonet must be struck, and by the stronger part of your sabre; the cuts form a defence as well as attack upon infantry, but the point should be chiefly used in pursuit.

In the use of the sabre at speed, it is important that the horseman should aid the impetus of the cut, and secure his own seat by supporting the sway of the body with the opposite leg to that side on which he intends to cut or point; for instance, in the left cut he should support the body by a strong pressure of the inside of the right thigh and leg against the saddle and horse; in the right cuts support the body with the left leg, the lower down the grip can be taken the better, not touching the horse with the spur. It is particularly applicable and necessary in pursuit over rough and varied ground.

Cuts very often fail from the sabre turning enough to make the blow one with the flat; at best the wound is generally trifling compared to those made by thrusts.

The instructor should impress upon the recruits such occasional observations as become applicable. Opportunities should be taken in pauses of rests; the squad should not be kept very long in positions or movements.

Appendix I

THE CHARGE
(*Cavalry Tactics*. COLONEL PHILIP ST. GEORGE COOKE, II, 60-63)

HE charge is the decisive action of cavalry.

Cavalry, like each of the three great arms, depends on the others, the battle once begun awaits their action. Its opportunities pass in moments. Its successful commander must have a *cavalry eye;* once launched, its bravery is successful.

Infantry columns, battered by artillery, have failed in their attack upon a position. The cavalry charges the batteries and supports; the infantry hastens to make good the advance; the cavalry, disunited and attacked, or threatened by the enemy, rallies under cover of the other arms.

At the moment of the enemy's first success—he has perhaps broken the first line, and makes a disordered pursuit—the cavalry seizes the moment to overthrow his battalions.

An enemy expecting a charge should be deceived, if possible, by some demonstrations. If he attempts to change his order, then instantly begin the gallop.

If possible, at the moment of the charge, assail your enemy in flank;—or charge him in flank, when seriously engaged with your infantry in front.

Cavalry charges the enemy's cavalry to drive him from the field, to return against his battalions with more liberty.

Meeting an enemy by surprise, the cavalry should instantly charge his. The decision will give the advantage.

A line of cavalry should meet the rapid and disordered charge of another at the *trot*. The enemy's line, already broken, will recoil—be thrown off from its imposing order.

The pursuit of cavalry broken by a charge depends upon the relative circumstances of the armies, but specially upon the cavalry reserves. Every effort of impetuosity should be made to throw a defeated line upon a second, so as to disorder and involve it in defeat. It is well to push the defeated until they are thoroughly disorganized in flight; but this may be carried out by the flanker squadrons. It is generally important to rally promptly. This can be done with advantage while advancing. Then attack the enemy in rear or flank.

The commander of cavalry sends two well-mounted officers or non-commissioned officers to precede his advance and reconnoitre ground over which he is likely to charge, and of which he is ignorant; if the enemy is in sight, they will gallop straight toward him, and as near as they can without risk of being captured; they may discover features of ground of which advantage may be taken, or which may have been ruinous or destructive in a charge.

Cavalry never charges without a reserve.

The charge is made with the greatest velocity and regularity possible; in speed and order there must be mutual sacrifice; seek in the charge, with a judicious proportion, to attain the maximum of each.

Circumstances permitting, the line approaches within 200 paces of the enemy at the trot, then galloping with increasing speed, the charge is commanded at 50 or 60 yards.

Crowding and pressure, when the horse is exerting his powers, impede him, and make him uncontrollable; every jostle or rub diminishes his strength. Although rapidity in the approach to the enemy is generally important, very important too it is that the horses should not arrive exhausted, or even distressed or blown.

The centre of the squadron exactly follows the Captain; the troopers do their best to preserve their intervals and alignment by the centre; the flankers must not be in advance.

The formation for attack should seldom consist of more than a third of the cavalry; the second, or support, disposed in squadron columns 300 to 400 yards in the rear; the reserve equally in their rear in close column. If the enemy be deficient in cavalry, this third body is more dispensable; (it is here considered a distinct body from those whose movements are prescribed).

Under circumstances which require and admit of a more concentrated attack, the regiments charge in column of squadrons. . . .

The charge as foragers, from close order or by skirmishers, has the advantage of granting freedom of motion and will in the troops; and less loss of fire; and it prepares the way for a decisive shock of the charge in line; it is the usual charge against batteries, the gunners being more or less covered by their pieces and isolated; the pistol is used in it at will; the flanking squadrons will sometimes second the charge of the line by thus charging the enemy in the flank.

The regiment being order of battle, the Colonel wishing to charge, if sabres be not drawn, commands them to be drawn; he then commands:

1. *Attention to charge.*
2. *Forward.*
3. MARCH.

The regiment being in regular motion, he commands:
Trot—MARCH.

After passing over 150 paces at this gait (according to circumstances) he commands:
Gallop—MARCH.

After galloping about 150 paces, he directs the charge be sounded —it is repeated by all the trumpeters—he commands:
CHARGE.

In charging infantry, the troops shout; against cavalry silence is recommended. . . .

The enemy's infantry once struck, the charge is successful; but charges which fail utterly, approaching very near, they slacken the gait,—take time to turn about,—or turn in front of other infantry in line,—or pass by other faces of the square; thus adding two-fold to their exposure to fire;—suffering the disgrace of defeat,—doubling the individual chances of being shot down.

Notes and References

CHAPTER 1

1. Freeman, *R. E. Lee*, I, 449.
2. Freeman, *Lee's Lieutenants*, III, 6.
3. Sometimes called the Battle of Fleetwood Heights or of Beverly's Ford.
4. Grimsley, *Battles in Culpeper County, Virginia*, p. 2.
5. Squadron and troop, as designations of cavalry units, were in partial use at the time and are generally employed in the text, although battalion and company were also current and continued as cavalry terms through and for some years after the Civil War.

CHAPTER 2

6. Table IX, "Breeds of Horses Recognized by the U. S. Department of Agriculture," 1914.
7. "Uniformity in troops is all the beauty. In a regiment everything should be of a piece, every thing alike. The Officers' horses should always be the colour of the men's. 'Tis a greater disadvantage than people realize to have them otherwise." Colonel Hawley in *Journal of the Society for Army Historical Research*, XXVI (1948), 92.
8. Capt. Charles King in preface to Rodenbough, *The Army of the United States*.
9. McClellan's report on his European inspection trip, p. 122.
10. "Old horse cavalrymen and horse or horse-drawn artillerymen can recall that a new horse of a different color, entering the corral, the troop columns, of the traces of a battery, was due for a much longer probationary period of bites and kicks than that accorded a 'recruit' of the same familiar hue as the 'veterans.' A black from 'B' Battery would be given short shrift if he wandered away from his own kind into a group of grazing bays from 'A.' In earlier times, tying the trumpeter's gray well out on the end of the line not only provided the benefits of rountine orderliness, but it saved that battlefield marker many a nip and drubbing." Col. Harry C. Larter, Jr., "On horses of the U.S. Artillery, Early 1800's," *Journal of the Company of Military Collectors and Historians* (MCH), VI, No. 3 (Sept., 1954), 67.
11. This practice, still in use in the U. S. Army as late as 1851, had been modified so that the musicians of the Civil War period were easily distinguished from their comrades-in-arms by the simple device of additional rows of braid on the front of their jackets and tunics. It followed

the use of full plastrons of the branch color, continued until about 1855.

12. Blackford, *War Years with Jeb Stuart*, p. 29.

13. "During the first two years of the war the Confederate cavalry exercised a tremendous moral effect. Beginning with the cry of 'The Black Horse Cavalry,' at First Bull Run, so terrible to the panic-stricken Federal troops in their race to Washington and safety; Mosby's frequent dashes at poorly guarded Union trains and careless outposts; Stuart's picturesque and gallant promenade around McClellan's unguarded encampment on the Chickahominy, in 1862, the war record of the Southern horse notwithstanding its subsequent decline and the final disasters of 1864-65 will always illumine one of the brightest pages of cavalry history." Rodenbough in *Photographic History of the Civil War* (hereinafter *PH*), IV, 31f.

14. Thomason, *Jeb Stuart*, p. 72.

15. *Richmond Times*, Feb. 23, 1896, on the Black Horse Troop. "They wielded their sabres like the cuirassiers of old, and used their pistols with the truth and nerve of expert marksmen. They so familiarized themselves with the country in which they operated, that they kept the enemy constantly speculating on their movements by checkmating them at every point in the game of war, and achieved such prestige by their strange ubiquity and stratagem that the name of the little legion became a watchword for danger and a signal for action with the Union troops."

16. Their "firm front ... probably saved a large part of the main body from capture; but they never received the recognition that was deserved." Rhodes in *PH*, IV, 50.

17. Carl Schurz in his *Reminscences*, II, 231, relates that he made an offer to General Scott to raise a regiment of cavalry from German immigrants with previous service in that arm. Scott in refusal declared that the war would be over long before any cavalry could be made fit for active service; that the theater of war would be Virginia, "and the surface of Virginia was so cut up with fences and other obstructions as to make operations with large bodies of cavalry impractical. The regular dragoons he had were quite sufficient for all needs."

However, as early as May 1, 1861, Schurz succeeded in obtaining an authorization with strings on it from Secretary of War Simon Cameron. The Secretary's letter, addressed to the Governors of the Several States, ran: "I have authorized Colonel Carl Schurz to raise and organize a volunteer regiment of cavalry. For the purpose of rendering it as efficient as possible, he is instructed to enlist principally such men as have served in the arm before. The Government will provide the regiment with arms, but cannot provide the horses and equipments. For these necessaries we rely upon the patriotism of the States and the citizens, and for this purpose I take the liberty of requesting you to afford Colonel Schurz your aid in the execution of this plan." *PH*, IV, 52.

In view of the required provision of horses *and* equipment, it is small wonder that Schurz abandoned his cavalry scheme and accepted an infantry command.

18. Sheridan, *Personal Memoirs*, II, 355.

19. Downey, *The Guns at Gettysburg*.

20. Crowninshield, *A History of the First Regiment of Massachusetts Cavalry Volunteers*, p. 6.

21. Henderson, *Stonewall Jackson and the American Civil War*, I, 198.

22. Massachusetts Historical Society, *Proceedings*, V. 47, p. 22.

23. Davis, *Trooper's Manual* (1861), p. viii.

24. Eggleston, *A Rebel's Recollections*, pp. 32f.

25. *Ibid.*, p. 35.

26. Tobie, *History of the First Maine Cavalry*, pp. 3f.

27. Lever's novel, *Charles O'Malley, the Irish Dragoon*, first published in the United States in 1841, is mentioned in a number of regimental histories and other works. Widely read, its martial passages and illustrations served as cavalry recruiting pamphlets and posters. For an extract, such as fascinated would-be cavalrymen of the Civil War, see Appendix B.

28. Preston, *History of the Tenth Regiment of Cavalry, New York State Volunteers*.

CHAPTER 3

29. For stories of some of the famous chargers see *PH*, IV, 292-318.

30. "Staunch infantry, more dreaded by the savages who preferred to match their own fine horsemanship against riders in blue rather than launch a charge against the volleys of the steady foot." Downey, *Indian-Fighting Army*, p. 30.

31. Downey, *Sound of the Guns*, p. 205.

32. Blackford, *War Years with Jeb Stuart*.

33. Thomason, *Jeb Stuart*, p. 720.

34. In November, 1862, purchase of 1,000 horses in Texas was directed. "These small animals were of course unsuited for artillery draught purposes, but their purchase tended to relieve the situation in Virginia by leaving the heavier horses for the light batteries." Wise, *The Long Arm of Lee*, I, 332.

35. McClellan, *The Life and Campaigns of Major-General J. E. B. Stuart*, p. 257.

36. See Note 17.

37. Crowninshield in *Papers of the Military Historical Society of Massachusetts*, V, No. 13.

38. Charles F. Hammond bought Morgans at from $125 to $225 a head for Company H, 5th New York Cavalry, enrolled by his son John. Charles F. Hammond, "Morgan Horses in the Civil War," *Vermont Horse and Bridle Trail Bulletin*, II, 1ff.

39. *PH*, IV, 74.

40. House Reports, 32nd Congress, 2nd Session. Report No. 2, "Government Contracts."

41. Crowninshield, *A History of the First Regiment of Massachusetts Cavalry Volunteers*.

42. Adams, *A Cycle of Adams Letters*, II, 101.

43. Denison, *Sabres and Spurs*. Stable frocks, for base camp or garrison wear, were discarded in field service.

44. Tobie, *History of the First Maine Cavalry*, p. 14.

45. *Ibid.*, p. 15.

46. *Ibid.*, p. 16.

47. Glazier, *Three Years in the Federal Cavalry*, pp. 35f.

48. *Cavalry Tactics*, 1841 (republished in 1863).

49. Cooke, *Cavalry Tactics*, I.

50. Glanders at times all but immobilized the cavalry of both sides. Known since antiquity and long called "farcy," this highly infectious disease is manifested by running noses and nodules and sores inside the nostrils or elsewhere on the skin. It was transmitted by the close contact of war conditions and by drinking from a common trough or pail. The only known treatments were isolation or the destruction of the infected animal. Under favorable conditions a horse might recover; acute cases resulted in death within a few days.

Greased heel also flourished under war hardships when horses were forced to stand night after night in mud or snow. The skin around the pasterns and fetlocks grew hot and cracked. Warty growth appeared, legs swelled, and the animal was lamed. Rubbing with oil sometimes helped, but the chief preventive was keeping the feet clean and dry. Horse-wise cavalrymen took infinite pains to provide dry footing for their picketed mounts with such planks, bricks, or bits of tile as they could find. Information from Dr. L. A. MacLeod, veterinarian, Lebanon, N. H.

51. Many cavalrymen learned to sleep bolt upright in their saddles, maintaining balance for hours. If a rider began to sway, he might waken before he slid to the ground, or a comrade might catch him. Some, sound asleep, wandered off at a tangent, or were carried past the officer at the head of the column.

52. Captain de Condenbove, French Army, World War I. "The Artillery Horse's Prayer."

53. Massachusetts Historical Society *Papers*, XIII, 25.

54. *PH*, IV, 324.

55. Freeman, *R. E. Lee*, III, 252.

56. *A Cycle of Adams Letters*, II, pp. 3-6.

57. See Ramsdall, "Lee's Horse Supply" in *American Historical Review*, XXXV, 758-777; also Freeman, *R. E. Lee*, II, 417, 491f.

CHAPTER 4

58. "There are many recorded instances of bodies of horsemen charging saber in hand during that war, but the increased accuracy and rapidity of fire provided by the revolver soon began to affect tactics. There was an increasing tendency to empty the revolver before closing for combat with the saber, and some engagements were decided without the drawing of a blade." Peterson, *The American Sword*, p. 16.

59. See Philip Van Doren Stern, "Dr. Gatling and His Gun," *American Heritage*, October, 1957. The author, quoting a Union officer's speech, mentions use of the Geary machine gun against enemy cavalry at Middleburg, Virginia, March 29, 1862. "One of these guns was brought to bear on a squadron of cavalry at 800 yards, and it cut them to pieces terribly, forcing them to fly." This instance, however, was a rare one.

60. Tobie, *History of the First Maine Cavalry*, p. 17.

61. *MCH*, Vol. 7, No. 2 (1955).

62. When cavalry began to be equipped with breech-loading carbines and their brass cartridges, drafts for that arm increased from men who lacked teeth to bite off ends of paper cartridges, or who had had teeth pulled out to escape the call. *New York Tribune*, Aug. 14, 1863.

63. See Buckeridge, *Lincoln's Choice*.

64. Gluckman, *United States Muskets, Rifles and Carbines*, p. 438.

65. McClellan, *The Life and Campaigns of Major-General J. E. B. Stuart*, pp. 260f.

66. Buckeridge, *op. cit.*, pp. 43, 46f.

67. Dodgson, *Through the Looking-Glass*.

68. Scott, *The Story of a Cavalry Regiment*, pp. 26ff. Shannon, *The Organization and Administration of the Union Army*, pp. 232ff.

69. Rhodes in *PH*, IV, 64.

70. Scott, *op. cit.*, p. 29.

71. *Ibid.*, pp. xviif. "Even as late as the beginning of the last campaign of the war, a certain famous old division and corps general quarreled with Wilson, because that able cavalryman refused to break up one of his brigades to supply the usual escorts to brigadiers and outposts for infantry camps."

72. Tobie, *op. cit.* The 1st Maine Cavalry was a frequent victim of detachment calls.

73. *Official Records of the Rebellion* (hereinafter *OR*), Ser. 1, Vol. XVII, Pt. 1, p. 170. *Cf.* Bibliography, U.S. War Department.

CHAPTER 5

74. Townsend, *Rustics in Rebellion*.

75. "I have known him [Sweeney] to ride with his banjo, playing and singing, even on a march which might be changed at any moment into a battle; and Stuart's laugh on such occasions was sure to be heard as an accompaniment as far as the minstrel's voice could reach." Eggleston, *A Rebel's Recollections*, p. 128.

76. Gen. A. P. Hill said of the cavalry leader, "Keep him away—keep him away from my camp. Every time Jeb Stuart comes around, with Sweeney and his banjo, he makes all my division want to 'jine' the cavalry." Thomason, *Jeb Stuart*, p. 50.

77. Adams, *A Cycle of Adams Letters*, II.

78. Kearny, like Pleasonton a dragoon in the Mexican War, lost his left arm charging the gates of Mexico City. Thereafter he rode with reins

in his teeth, saber in right hand. His undoubted flair for cavalry and his distinguished service with foreign armies, as well as our own, made him a promising leader. Given command in the earlier years of the war when the Federal horse was neglected and misused, he might well have redeemed it. "General Phil Kearny was spoken of as a natural cavalry leader, but was killed while leading his infantry division at Chantilly. If he was as bold and resolute a commander as many think, it is a pity he could not have been placed over the cavalry, and a different story might have been told for 1861 and 1862," Crowninshield in *Papers of the Massachusetts Historical Society*, XIII, 28.

79. The improvement in the Union cavalry, following Hooker's reorganization, lost ground during the command of the Army of the Potomac by Meade who, it is generally conceded, failed to make proper use of his horsemen. The mounted arm therefore was forced to wait not only for Sheridan but for Grant, who gave his brilliant subordinate full scope.

80. Wellman, *Giant in Gray*, p. 115.

81. The other three were James H. Wilson of the Union Army and "Fighting Joe" Wheeler and Matthew Calbraith Butler of the Confederate.

82. After the war both Duffié and di Cesnola, becoming U.S. citizens, were rewarded for their services by consulships. Officiating at Cyprus, di Cesnola organized the excavations that founded the fine Metropolitan Museum of Art collection named in his honor.

83. A stanch and authoritative defender of Kilpatrick was a fellow cavalryman, Gen. James H. Wilson, who wrote in Kilpatrick's biography in Cullum: "The severest criticism ever made of Kilpatrick was that he did not take proper care of his horses, and the sufficient answer to this is that neither he nor anybody else could have done better under the system in vogue. At a later day, under Sheridan, the cavalry was used more in masses, and both men and horses were cared for in a manner unknown before. Kilpatrick himself, under Wilson in the West, although engaged in the exacting work of covering Sherman's flanks, front, and rear in the March to the Sea and through the Carolinas, took as good care of his men and horses as any other cavalry commander of the war could have done."

84. Toombs, *New Jersey Troops in the Gettysburg Campaign*, pp. 402ff.

85. Wise, *The Long Arm of Lee*, II, 578-597.

86. Downey, *The Guns at Gettysburg*, Foreword.

87. Gen. C. A. Baehr. Letter to the author.

88. At the Battle of Kelly's Ford, March 17, 1863. See Appendix G, "The Death of Pelham."

89. Swarthout, *They Came to Cordura*, p. 41.

90. *Cornhill Magazine*, London, December, 1862.

91. Merrill, *The Campaigns of the First Maine and First District of Columbia Cavalry*.

92. Hard, *History of the Eighth Cavalry Regiment, Illinois Volunteers*.

93. Crowninshield, *A History of the First Regiment of Massachusetts Cavalry Volunteers*, p. 113.

94. Denison, *Sabres and Spurs*, p. 27.
95. Pyne, *The History of the First New Jersey Cavalry.*
96. Preston, *History of the Tenth Regiment of Cavalry, New York State Volunteers*, p. 82.
97. Peck, *Reminiscences of a Confederate Soldier of Company C, 2nd Virginia Cavalry.*
98. Notable among contemporary chroniclers of the Confederate cavalry were H. B. McClellan, W. W. Blackford, and U. R. Brooks. The various biographies of J. E. B. Stuart of course devote much attention to the arm he led. Heros von Borcke, the Prussian officer on Stuart's staff, was closely concerned with Brandy Station in his *Memoirs* and in his small volume on the battle, *Die Grosse Reiterschlacht bei Brandy Station.* A thread of cavalry yellow runs through the works of Douglas Southall Freeman and one of artillery scarlet through Wise's.
99. Borcke, *Memoirs*, II, 273.

CHAPTER 6

100. *O.R.* lists engagements at Brandy Station on August 20, 1862, and the following in 1863: April 29, June 9, August 1, 4, and 9, September 8 and 13, October 11–12, and November 8.
101. Lieutenant Colonel Blackwood of Stuart's staff states in *War Years with Jeb Stuart*, p. 98: "At that time their cavalry could not stand before us at all, and it was not until the great battle on this same ground on the 9th of June, 1863, 'Fleetwood Fight,' that they offered us any determined resistance. From that time the difficulty of getting remounts acted distressingly upon the strength of our cavalry arm, not only in diminishing the numbers but in impairing the spirit of the men. Many of the men knew that when their horses were disabled they could not get others, and this injured their dash; they were willing to risk getting shot themselves but not willing to risk being sent into the infantry service if their horses were killed.... Up to this time the cavalry of the enemy had no more confidence in themselves than the country had in them, and whenever we got a chance at them, which was rarely, they came to grief."
102. This fight, not listed by *O.R.* among the Brandy Station engagements, is known as the Battle of Kelly's Ford.
103. Wise, *The Long Arm of Lee*, I, 432.
104. See Appendix G, "The Death of Pelham."
105. Stoneman's report, quoted in *B. & L.*, III, 153. The value of the initial stage of Stoneman's raid was estimated as follows by Pleasonton in an article in *B. & L.*, III, 172n. "This corps did great service by drawing off General Lee's cavalry, under General J. E. B. Stuart, to Brandy Station and Culpeper, thus depriving General Lee of their services; for General Hooker moved the three corps with him with such celerity that they passed between Stuart and Lee's army, and Stuart could not get through to communicate to Lee what was going on."

CHAPTER 7

106. "Taps," composed by General Daniel Butterfield as an identifying call for the units of his infantry brigade, was adopted by buglers of other commands as a night call. It was first used for a military funeral by Battery A, 2nd U.S. Artillery.

107. "Sheridan's bands were generally mounted on gray horses, and instead of being relegated to the usual duty of carrying off the wounded and assisting the surgeons, they were brought out to the front and made to play the liveliest tunes in their repertory, with great effect on the spirits of the men." *B. & L.*, IV, 711n.

Custer, one of Sheridan's commanders, carried on the tradition into the Indians wars when he used his 7th Cavalry band on the bitter cold day of the Battle of the Washita. " 'Play!' Custer shouted to his chilled bandsmen. *Garry Owen*, the 7th's battle song, blared forth. A bar or so and the instruments were jammed solid with frozen saliva, and only the drums rolled on. But to the Indians that brazen blast from the snow-covered hills, sounding 'like a deep-throated, terrible shout,' was terror-striking. And it carried the cheering 7th into battle behind its streaming standards and wind-whipped guidons." Downey, *Indian-Fighting Army*, p. 88.

108. This was the second cavalry band from Maine. The first had performed creditably. As soon as the newly-organized regiment received saddles, it began to practice on horseback. At the first dress parade the bandsmen " 'beat off' mounted, and did it wonderfully well for the time the horses had been under drill with music." In August, 1862, the band, which had cheered the regiment and won an enviable reputation for its fine music, was mustered out as a needless and costly luxury and went home, much to the regiment's sorrow. The second Maine band was formed for the 1st District of Columbia Cavalry, which contained many Maine men and often served alongside the 1st Maine. Its instrumentation consisted of two B-flat cornets, two E-flat cornets, three E-flat basses, three B-flat tenors, three E-flat altos, B-flat bass, cymbals, side- and bass drums. Tobie, *History of the First Maine Cavalry.*

109. See Appendix G for full text.

110. The tradition of Sweeney's banjo was carried on in the First World War. The author of this book, his brother, a cousin, and a friend, were members of the banjo quartet of the 12th Field Artillery, 2nd Division, which, though it never managed mounted performances, played in dugouts in the line. It was the custom of the regimental commander, Col. Manus McCloskey, on a quiet night to call up French generals on the field telephone to listen to a lively rendition of "The Darktown Strutters' Ball" or "Madelon." "McCloskey must have recruited his headquarters staff from Yale, for it included Fairfax Downey, his brother Faber, Stuart Landstreet, a fine lad who died shortly after the war, and James C. Lysle, all former members of the Yale Banjo Club. To the assembled talent I contributed Fielding S. Robinson, who played guitar and had brought one to the war with him. Pell Foster, an officer of one of the batteries, joined with a

violin. Nearly every evening we had music." Harbord, *The American Army in France*, p. 288.

111. Arthur Woodward in *Los Angeles County Museum Quarterly*, Vol. VII, No. 3 (Spring, 1949), credits Joel Sweeney with the invention of the skin head for the banjo (formerly it had been strung over a gourd) and with the addition of a fifth string.

112. Emmett, strongly loyal to the Union, expressed his resentment by rewriting the words to his song to blast the Secessionists. The new version bitterly referred to Dixie as "the land of traitors and alligators." His efforts were vain. The original remained the South's anthem until after Appomattox when Lincoln, asking a band in front of the White House to play it, declared that now it belonged to the nation.

113. Bruce Lancaster in *Night March* describes the arrival of a train load of ladies at Brandy Station for a Washington's Birthday ball on the eve of the Kilpatrick-Dahlgren raid on Richmond.

CHAPTER 8

114. "The problem before General Pleasonton was to ascertain whether the Confederate army or any considerable portion of it was moving upon the road between Fredericksburg and Culpeper, If such a maneuvre were in progress, he was to ascertain something as to its state of forwardness. Had one corps or more reached Culpeper? Was any force in motion to the west of that town, and if so, in what direction? He knew that Stuart's command was bivouacked somewhere in the vicinity of Brandy Station, and this knowledge would be of avail in determining the strength and composition of his reconnoitering columns." Davis, "Cavalry in the Gettysburg Campaign," *Cavalry Journal*, I, 328.

115. Thomason, *Jeb Stuart*, p. 397.

116. Freeman, *Lee's Lieutenants*, III, 1.

117. Neese, *Three Years in the Confederate Horse Artillery*, p. 167.

118. Freeman, *op. cit.*, p. 3.

119. "It was a genuine pleasure to see the skill and assurance with which the men managed their horses, the spirit with which they rode, and the genuinely fine breed of horses that passed before the spectators, although a sporadic mule was running along here and there among them. These animals are generally tabooed in the cavalry, as well as in the artillery, since they are gun shy." Scheibert, *Seven Months in the Rebel States during the North American War*, p. 87.

120. Neese, *op. cit.*, pp. 169-170, declared he cared little about his own dismissal but that "the mule looked a little bit surprised, and, I think, felt ashamed of himself and his waving ears, which cost him his prominent position in the grand cavalcade."

121. Stuart's friends on Davis's staff thought the letter amusing and sent him a copy, suggesting "that he cease his attentions to the ladies or make them more general." Stuart, receiving the letter on his march through Pennsylvania, was infuriated.

122. See Appendix D, Organization of the Confederate Forces at the Battle of Brandy Station.

CHAPTER 9

123. See Appendix D, Organization of the Union Forces at the Battle of Brandy Station.
124. See Appendix C.
125. After "Lord Dundreary," a character in *Our American Cousin* (1858), the play President Lincoln was attending when he was assassinated.
126. Paris, *History of the Civil War in America*, III, 462.
127. Thomason, *Jeb Stuart*, p. 397.
128. Gracey, *Annals of the Sixth Pennsylvania Cavalry*, p. 157.

CHAPTER 10

129. For full text see Appendix G.
130. Gracey, *Annals of the Sixth Pennsylvania Cavalry*, p. 158.
131. Opie, *A Rebel Cavalryman with Lee, Stuart, and Jackson*, pp. 148f. That night in camp Opie's company acclaimed him as "Charles O'Malley" and Murat. "O pshaw! boys," he replied, "my horse ran away with me."
132. For Pleasonton's reports see Appendix E.

CHAPTER 11

133. In its article of June 12, 1863, the *Richmond Examiner* did not name Stuart, but the target of its bitter accusations was unmistakable.

"The more the circumstances of the late affair at Brandy Station are considered, the less pleasant do they appear. If this was an isolated case, it might be excused under the convenient head of accident or chance. But this puffed up cavalry of the Army of Northern Virginia has been twice, if not three times, surprised since the battles of December, and such repeated accidents can be regarded as nothing but the necessary consequences of negligence and bad management. If the war was a tournament, invented and supported for the pleasure of a few vain and weak-headed officers, these disasters might be dismissed with compassion. But the country pays dearly for the blunders which encourage the enemy to overrun and devastate the land, with a cavalry which is daily learning to despise the mounted troops of the Confederacy. The surprise on this occasion was the most complete that has occurred. The Confederate cavalry was carelessly strewn over the country, with the Rappahannock only between it and an enemy who has already proven his enterprise to our cost. . . . In the end the enemy retired, or was driven, it is not yet clearly known which, across the river. Nor is it certainly known whether the fortunate result was achieved by the cavalry alone or with the assistance of Confederate infantry in the neighborhood. . . . Events of this description have been lately too frequent to admit of the supposition that they are the results of hazard. They are the effects of causes which will produce like effects while they are permitted to operate, and they require the earnest attention both of the chiefs of the Government and the heads of the Army. The enemy is evidently determined to employ his cavalry extensively, and has spared no pains or cost to perfect that arm. The only effective means of preventing the mischief it may do is to reorganize our own forces, enforce a stricter discipline among the men and insist on more earnestness among the officers in the discharge of their very important duty."

On the other hand Stuart's devoted partisan, the cavalry commander John S. Mosby, defends him at every point in *Stuart's Cavalry in the Gettysburg Campaign*. Even the posting of Beckham's artillery in its exposed position was, according to Mosby, "fortunate." "It is clear," the writer concludes, "that Pleasonton was more surprised than the Confederates were. He had not then gone more than a mile from the river; he stayed where he was nearly all day. It was the commanding ability of Stuart that 'from the nettle of danger plucked the flower safety,' and won the battle of Brandy." (p. 30). However, Blackford and other Confederates, present on the field, support the surprise charge.

134. McClellan, *Major-General J. E. B. Stuart*, pp. 266f.

135. Neese, *Three Years in the Confederate Horse Artillery*, p. 173.

136. Curiously the 6th Pennsylvania's disliked and early discarded lances reappeared as decorations around its Gettysburg monument which bears the name Lancers.

137. Quoted in McClellan, *op. cit.*, p. 268.

138. Gracey, *Annals of the Sixth Pennsylvania Cavalry*, pp. 160f.

139. Pleasonton, inspecting the 6th Pennsylvania the following day, commended it highly: "Those men did splendidly yesterday. I call them now the Seventh Regulars."

CHAPTER 12

140. *O.R.*, V. 27, Pt. 2, 737.

141. Myers, *The Comanches*, p. 183.

142. McClellan, *Major-General J. E. B. Stuart*, pp. 269f.

143. Hart in *The Philadelphia Weekly Times*, June 26, 1880.

144. McClellan, *op. cit.*, p. 270.

CHAPTER 13

145. Crowninshield, *History of the First Regiment of Massachusetts Cavalry Volunteers*, pp. 129f.

146. McClellan (p. 289) writes of the 4th Virginia: "There was not a finer body of men in the service. They had frequently proved their valor on other battle-fields, and on many subsequent occasions they confirmed their good reputation. But on this day a panic possessed them. They did not respond to the efforts of their officers...."

The description of a cavalry rout is from Pyne, *The History of the First New Jersey Cavalry*, p. 55 (Battle of Cross Keys, June 8, 1862).

147. Crowninshield, *op. cit.*, p. 133.

148. Brooks, *Butler and His Cavalry*, pp. 168f.

149. First Lieutenant William V. Kennedy, "The Cavalry Battle at Brandy Station." *Armor* (Jan.-Feb., 1956), p. 31. This article is an admirable and concise account of the battle.

CHAPTER 14

150. Borcke, *Memoirs*, II.

151. See Appendix E for successive reports by Pleasonton.

152. Moore, *The Civil War in Song and Story*, pp. 453ff, and Foster, *New Jersey in the Rebellion*.

153. *Ibid.*

154. Meyer, *Civil War Experiences under Bayard, Gregg, Kilpatrick, and Custer*, pp. 27ff.

155. Scheibert, *Sieben Monate*.

156. Neese, *Three Years in the Confederate Horse Artillery*, p. 177.

157. Pleasonton (see Report) blamed the loss of the New York guns on Duffié's delay.

158. See Stuart's Report, Appendix F.

CHAPTER 15

159. Preston, *History of the Tenth Regiment of Cavalry, New York State Volunteers*, p. 86.

160. *Ibid.*, pp. 87f.

161. Wilson's report, *O.R.*, V. 22, Pt. 1, 1026ff.

162. Merrill, *The Campaigns of the 1st Maine and 1st District of Columbia Cavalry*.

163. Tobie, *History of the First Maine Cavalry*, pp. 147ff.

164. Merrill, *op. cit.*

165. Freeman, *R. E. Lee*, III, 31. *O.R.* V. 27, Part 3, 876.

CHAPTER 16

166. Beale, *A Lieutenant of Cavalry in Lee's Army*, p. 96, the best account of this phase of the battle despite some minor errors.

167. *Ibid.*

168. Blackford, *War Years with Jeb Stuart*, pp. 215f.

169. *Ibid.*, p. 217.

170. *Mort à cheval, au galop.* Part of the citation of Brigadier de Dragons Gaston Bonnett, killed in a First World War cavalry charge, September 14, 1914. The phrase is the theme of a poem by Edmond Rostand in his volume, *Le Vol de la Marseillaise.*

171. Blackford, *op. cit.*, p. 217.

172. *O.R.*, V. 27, Pt. 1, 170; Pt. 2, 719. McClellan gives the casualties as: Confederate, 423; Union, 936, of whom 486 were prisoners of war.

173. See Pleasonton's reports, Appendix E.

174. "It would have been certainly a remarkable circumstance if so prudent a man as General Lee had formulated his intentions at so early a period in the campaign; it is still more remarkable that he should have entrusted them in writing to even a trusted subordinate." Davis, "The Operations of the Cavalry in the Gettysburg Campaign," *Cavalry Journal*, I, No. 3 (Nov., 1888), 320.

175. *B. & L.*, III, 265.

176. Freeman, *Lee's Lieutenants*, III, 18. Dr. Freeman observes that "... it hurt Stuart to think that the bluecoats could at any time hold him. He had fought his heaviest battle after thunderous, demonstrative reviews of more troops than ever had been under his command. Instead of a thrilling victory that every man in the army would have to acclaim, there was sarcastic talk of an exposed rear and of a surprise!"

177. *O.R.*, V. 27, Pt. 2, 719f. General Order No. 24, June 18, 1863.

178. *Ibid.*, p. 687.

179. Freeman, *op. cit.*, p. 18.

180. Freeman, *R. E. Lee*, III, 32, quoting Taylor mss.

181. "The Federal Commander, however, had accomplished his mission and reported to Hooker the information he had gained. Hooker estimated correctly that Lee was concentrating on the Confederate left and was planning to move around the Federal right. He (Hooker) planned to check it by throwing an overwhelming force against Fredericksburg and, if successful at that point, to move against Richmond.... The Federal authorities refused to approve Hooker's plan.... Lincoln's dispatch to Hooker on the day after Pleasonton's raid shows a grasp of matters quite unlike that of the year before. 'Your long dispatch of today is just received.... I think Lee's army, and not Richmond, is your true objective point.' " *Pageant of America*, VII, 109.

182. McClellan, *Major-General J. E. B. Stuart*, p. 294.

183. Thomason, *Jeb Stuart*, p. 409. The reference to Yellow Tavern is of course to the mortal wound General Stuart received in the battle.

CHAPTER 17

184. Freeman, *R. E. Lee*, III, 41. Criticism of Stuart was noted by the Union high command. "The Richmond papers of the 13th blame Stuart much for allowing himself to be surprised in his camp by Pleasonton, and call upon him to do something to retrieve his reputation." Telegram to Halleck, *O.R.*, V. 27, Pt. 1, 41.

185. For cavalry actions at Gettysburg see *B. & L.*, III, 393-406.

186. A good account of the October action is found in Beale, *A Lieutenant of Cavalry in Lee's Army*, pp. 128-132.

187. Sheridan's first cavalry assignment was as colonel of the 2nd Michigan, May 20, 1862.

188. Rhodes, *History of the Cavalry of the Army of the Potomac,* pp. 189f. The following would cause personnel to be listed on returns as not present for duty: (a) Wounded or sick in hospitals. (b) On leave or furlough, in some cases to recover from wounds or sickness. (c) Engaged in transferring horses to and from Remount Depots and units in the field. (d) Escort duty for other supply matters, wagon trains, etc. (e) Screening missions, pickets, courier service, vedettes. (f) Temporary attachment to various commands.

189. *Ibid.,* p. 172. "Side by side with the charge of the German cavalry at Mars-la-Tour, we can place the effective charge of the Eighth Pennsylvania Cavalry under Huey, at Chancellorsville. For the charge of the English Light Brigade at Balaklava, we can name that of the lamented Farnsworth upon the Confederate right flank at Gettysburg. With the charge of the French cuirassiers at Sedan, we can class the devoted charge of the First and Fifth United States Cavalry at Gaines' Mill, or that of the Sixth United States and Sixth Pennsylvania upon the Confederate artillery at Brandy Station."

190. Hackley, *The Little Fork Rangers.*

Bibliography

ADAMS, CHARLES FRANCIS, JR. *A Cycle of Adams Letters,* vols. 1 and 2. Boston and New York: Houghton Mifflin & Co., 1920.

ALEXANDER, GENERAL E. P. *Military Memoirs of a Confederate.* New York: Charles Scribner's Sons, 1907.

AMERICAN HISTORICAL ASSOCIATION. *Annual Reports.* Washington: 1885–1954.

Annals of the War, Written by Leading Participants, North and South. Originally published in the *Philadelphia Weekly Times.* Philadelphia: Times Publishing Co., 1879.

Armor. Jan.-Feb., 1956. First Lieutenant William V. Kennedy, "The Cavalry Battle at Brandy Station."

Battles and Leaders of the Civil War. Robert Underwood Johnson, ed. 4 vols. New York: The Century Co., 1884–87.

BAYLOR, GEORGE. *Bull Run to Bull Run.* Richmond: B. F. Johnson Publishing Co., 1900.

BEALE, G. W. *A Lieutenant of Cavalry in Lee's Army.* Boston: Gorham Press, 1918.

BEALE, R. L. T. *History of the Ninth Virginia Cavalry.* Richmond: 1897.

BELCHER, HENRY. *The First American Civil War.* 2 vols. London: The Macmillan Co., 1911.

BILL, LEDYARD, comp. *Pen-Pictures of the War.* New York: 1864.

BIRKHIMER, WILLIAM E. *Historical Sketch of the Organization, Administration, Matériel, and Tactics of the Artillery, United States Army.* Washington: 1884.

BLACKFORD, LIEUTENANT COLONEL WILLIAM WILLIS. *War Years with Jeb Stuart.* New York: Charles Scribner's Sons, 1945.

———. *Letters from Lee's Army.* New York: Charles Scribner's Sons, 1947.

BORCKE, HEROS VON. *Memoirs of the Confederate War for Independence.* 2 vols. New York: Peter Smith, 1938.

BORCKE, HEROS VON. *Die Grosse Reiterschlacht bei Brandy Station* (with Justus Scheibert). Berlin: 1893. Ms. translation by Dr. Robert L. Crispin, Allegheny College.

BROOKS, U. R. *Stories of the Confederacy.* Columbia, South Carolina: The State Co., 1912.

———. *Butler and His Cavalry in the War of Secession, 1861–65.* Columbia, South Carolina: The State Co., 1909.

BUCKERIDGE, J. O. *Lincoln's Choice.* Harrisburg, Pennsylvania: Stackpole Co., 1956.

CASLER, JOHN O. *Four Years in the Stonewall Brigade.* Guthrie, Oklahoma: State Capital Printing Co., 1893.

CARTER, COLONEL WILLIAM H. *Horses, Saddles and Bridles.* Baltimore: The Lord Baltimore Press, 1902.

CATTON, BRUCE. *Mr. Lincoln's Army.* Garden City, New York: Doubleday & Company, Inc., 1951.

———. *Glory Road.* New York: Doubleday & Company, Inc. 1952.

———. *A Stillness at Appomattox.* New York: Doubleday & Company, Inc., 1953.

———. *This Hallowed Ground.* New York: Doubleday & Company, Inc., 1956.

CHILD, B. H. *From Fredericksburg to Gettysburg.* Providence: 1895.

Civil War Papers Read before the Commandery of the State of Massachusetts, Military Order of the Loyal Legion of the United States. Boston: Printed for the Commandery, 1900.

CLARK, WALTER, ed. *Histories of the Several Regiments and Battalions from North Carolina in the Great War, 1861–65.* 5 vols. Raleigh, North Carolina: E. M. Uzzell, 1901.

COMMAGER, HENRY STEELE, ed. *The Blue and the Gray,* 2 vols. Indianapolis: Bobbs-Merrill Company, 1950.

Confederate Veteran, The. 40 vols. Nashville, Tennessee: 1893–1932.

COOKE, JOHN ESTEN. *Wearing of the Gray.* New York: E. B. Treat and Company, 1867.

———. *Mohun, or the Last Days of Lee and His Paladins.* New York: 1869.

COOKE, PHILIP ST. GEORGE. *Cavalry Tactics.* 2 vols. Philadelphia: J. B. Lippincott & Co., 1862.

COULTER, E. MERTON. *Travels in the Confederate States: a Bibliography.* Norman: University of Oklahoma Press, 1948.

CROTTY, D. G. *Four Years Campaigning in the Army of the Potomac.* Grand Rapids, Michigan: 1874.

CROWNINSHIELD, BENJAMIN W. *A History of the First Regiment of Massachusetts Cavalry Volunteers.* Boston and New York: Houghton Mifflin & Co., 1891.

CULLUM, GEORGE W. *Biographical Register of the Officers and Graduates of the U.S. Military Academy.* 7 vols. Boston: 1891–1930.

DAVIS, BURKE. *Jeb Stuart, the Last Cavalier.* New York: Rinehart & Co., 1957.

DAVIS, GEORGE B. "Operations of the Cavalry in the Gettysburg Campaign." *Cavalry Journal*, I, No. 3 (November, 1888), 325-348.

DAVIS, JAMES L. *The Trooper's Manual.* Richmond: Charles H. Wynne, 1861.

DENISON, REVEREND FREDERIC. *Sabres and Spurs: the First Regiment Rhode Island Cavalry in the Civil War, 1861–65.* Central Falls, Rhode Island: E. L. Freeman & Co., 1876.

DODGSON, CHARLES LUTWIDGE (Lewis Carroll). *Through the Looking-Glass.* New York: The Macmillan Co., 1875.

DOWNEY, FAIRFAX. *Sound of the Guns.* New York: David McKay Company, Inc., 1956.

————. *The Guns at Gettysburg.* New York: David McKay Company, Inc., 1958.

————. *Indian-Fighting Army.* New York: Charles Scribner's Sons, 1941. New York: Bantam Books, 1957.

DYER, FREDERICK H. *A Compendium of the War of the Rebellion.* Des Moines, Iowa: The Dyer Publishing Co., 1908.

EGGLESTON, GEORGE CARY. *A Rebel's Recollections.* New York: Hurd & Houghton, 1875.

EVANS, GENERAL CLEMENT A. ed. *Confederate Military History.* 12 vols. Atlanta, Georgia: Confederate Publishing Co., 1899.

Field Artillery Journal. Washington: 1911–45.

FORBES, EDWIN. *Life Studies of the Great Army.* New York: 1899.

FOSTER, JOHN Y. *New Jersey and the Rebellion.* Newark, New Jersey: Martin R. Dennis Co., 1868.

FOX, WILLIAM F. *Regimental Losses in the American Civil War.* Albany: 1889.

FREEMAN, DOUGLAS SOUTHALL. *Lee's Lieutenants, a Study in Command.* 3 vols. New York: Charles Scribner's Sons, 1942-44.

FREEMAN, DOUGLAS SOUTHALL. *R. E. Lee, A Biography*. 4 vols. New York: Charles Scribner's Sons, 1934–35.

GANOE, WILLIAM ADDLEMAN. *The History of the United States Army*. New York: D. Appleton-Century Co., Inc., 1942.

GILMOR, COLONEL HARRY. *Four Years in the Saddle*. New York: Harper & Brothers, 1866.

GLAZIER, CAPTAIN WILLARD. *Three Years in the Federal Cavalry*. New York: R. H. Ferguson & Co., 1874.

GLUCKMAN, COLONEL ARCADI. *United States Muskets, Rifles and Carbines*. Harrisburg, Pennsylvania: Stackpole Co., 1948.

GRACEY, SAMUEL L. *Annals of the Sixth Pennsylvania Cavalry*. Philadelphia: E. H. Butler Co., 1868.

GRIMSLEY, DANIEL A. *Battles in Culpeper County, Virginia, 1861–1865*. Culpeper, Virginia: 1900.

HACKLEY, WOODFORD B. *The Little Fork Rangers, a Sketch of Company "D," Fourth Virginia Cavalry*. Richmond: Dietz Printing Co., 1927.

HARD, ABNER. *History of the Eighth Cavalry Regiment, Illinois Volunteers*. Aurora, Illinois: 1868.

HASKIN, BREVET MAJOR W. L. *History of the First Regiment of Artillery*. Portland, Maine: 1879.

HEDRICK, MARY A., *Incidents of the Civil War*. Lowell, Massachusetts: Vox Populi Press. 1888.

HEITMAN, FRANCIS B., *Historical Register and Dictionary of the United States Army*. 2 vols. Washington, 1900.

HENDERSON, LIEUTENANT COLONEL G. F. R. *Stonewall Jackson and the American Civil War*. 2 vols. New York: Longmans, Green & Co., 1898.

HENRY, ROBERT SELPH *"First with the Most,"* Forest, Indianapolis: The Bobbs-Merrill Co., 1944.

———. *The Story of the Confederacy*. Forest, Indianapolis: The Bobbs-Merrill Co., 1931.

HERR, GENERAL J. K., and WALLACE, EDWARD S. *The Story of the U.S. Cavalry*. Boston: Little, Brown and Co., 1953.

History of the Third Pennsylvania Cavalry. Philadelphia: Franklin Printing Co., 1905.

JONES, REVEREND J. WILLIAM. *Army of Northern Virginia*. Richmond: J. W. Randolph and English, 1880.

226 BIBLIOGRAPHY

Journal of the Military Service Institution of the United States. Vols. 1-61. New York: 1880–1917.

KENNEDY, LIEUTENANT WILLIAM V. "The Cavalry Battle at Brandy Station." *Armor,* Jan.-Feb., 1956.

KIDD, J. H. *Personal Recollections of a Cavalryman with Custer's Michigan Cavalry Brigade in the Civil War.* Ionia, Michigan: Sentinel Printing Co., 1908.

LEE, ROBERT E., JR. *Recollections and Letters of General Robert E. Lee.* New York: 1924.

LEVER, CHARLES JAMES. *Charles O'Malley, the Irish Dragoon.* Philadelphia: Carey and Hart, 1841.

LEWIS, BERKELEY R. *Small Arms and Ammunition in the United States Service.* Washington: Smithsonian Institution, 1956.

LEWIS, CAPTAIN CHARLES EDWARD. *War Sketches. No. 1 With the First Dragoons of Virginia.* London: Simmons and Botten, (n.d.)

LONN, ELLA. *Foreigners in the Union Army & Navy.* Baton Rouge: Louisiana State Press, 1951.

———. *Foreigners in the Confederacy.* Chapel Hill, North Carolina: University of North Carolina Press, 1940.

LLOYD, WILLIAM PENN. *History of the First Regiment, Pennsylvania Reserve Cavalry.* Philadelphia: King & Baird, 1864.

LUVAAS, JAY. "A Prussian Observer with Lee." *Military Affairs,* V. XXI, No. 3, Fall, 1957.

McCARTHY, CARLTON. *Detailed Minutiae of a Soldier's Life in the Army of Northern Virginia.* Richmond: Carlton McCarthy & Co., 1882.

McCLELLAN, GEORGE B. *McClellan's Own Story.* New York: Charles L. Webster & Co., 1887.

McCLELLAN, H. B. *The Life and Campaigns of Major General J. E. B. Stuart.* Boston and New York: Houghton Mifflin & Co., 1885.

McDONALD, CAPTAIN WILLIAM N. *A History of the Laurel Brigade.* Baltimore: 1907.

McKINNEY, E. P. *Life in Tent and Field, 1861–1865.* Boston: The Gorham Press, 1922.

MASSACHUSETTS HISTORICAL SOCIETY. *Proceedings.*

MERCER, PHILIP. *The Life of the Gallant Pelham.* Macon, Georgia: The J. W. Burke Co., 1929.

MERRILL, SAMUEL H. *The Campaigns of the First Maine & First District of Columbia Cavalry.* Portland: Bailey & Noyes, 1866.

MEYER, HENRY C. *Civil War Experiences under Bayard, Gregg, Kilpatrick, Custer.* New York: Raulston & Newberry, 1911.

Military Affairs. V. 21, No. 3, Fall, 1957. Jay Luvaas, "A Prussian Observer with Lee."

MILITARY COLLECTORS AND HISTORIANS. *Journal.* Files.

MILITARY HISTORICAL SOCIETY OF MASSACHUSETTS. *Papers.* Boston: 1906 & 1913.

MILLIS, WALTER. *Arms and Men.* New York: G. P. Putnam's Sons, 1956.

MITCHELL, LIEUTENANT COLONEL JOSEPH B. *Decisive Battles of the Civil War.* New York: G. P. Putnam's Sons, 1955.

MOORE, EDWARD A. *The Story of a Cannoneer under Stonewall Jackson.* Lynchburg, Virginia: J. P. Bell Co., 1910.

MOORE, FRANK, ed. *The Civil War in Song and Story.* New York: P. F. Collier, 1892.

MOORE, JAMES. *Kilpatrick and Our Cavalry.* New York: W. J. Widdleston, 1865.

MOSBY, JOHN S. *Stuart's Cavalry in the Gettysburg Campaign.* New York: Moffat, Yard & Co., 1908.

MYERS, FRANK M. *The Comanches.* Baltimore: 1871.

NEESE, GEORGE M. *Three Years in the Confederate Horse Artillery.* New York and Washington: Neale Publishing Co., 1911.

NORTON, HENRY. *Deeds of Daring or the History of the Eighth New York Volunteer Cavalry.* Norwich, New York: Chenango Telegraph Printing House, 1889.

OPIE, JOHN N. *A Rebel Cavalryman with Lee, Stuart, and Jackson.* Chicago: W. B. Conkey Co., 1899.

PARIS, LOUIS PHILIPPE ALBERT D'ORLÉANS, COMTE DE. *History of the Civil War in America.* 4 vols. Philadelphia: Porter and Coates, 1875–1888.

PATTEN, GEORGE WASHINGTON. *Cavalry Drill and Sabre Exercises.* Richmond: West and Johanston, 1862.

Photographic History of the Civil War. Francis Trevelyan Miller, ed. 10 vols. New York: 1911.

PECK, R. H. *Reminiscences of a Confederate Soldier of Company C, 2nd Virginia Cavalry.* Fincastle, Virginia: 1913.

PETERSON, HAROLD L. *The American Sword, 1775–1945*. New Hope, Pennsylvania: Robert Halter, 1954.

PICKERILL, W. N. *History of the Third Indiana Cavalry*. Indianapolis: 1906.

POAGUE, WILLIAM THOMAS. *Gunner with Stonewall Jackson*, Tennessee: McCowat-Mercer Press, 1957.

PRESTON, NOBLE D. *History of the Tenth Regiment of Cavalry, New York State Volunteers*. New York: D. Appleton Co., 1892.

PYNE, HENRY R. *The History of the First New Jersey Cavalry*. Trenton: J. A. Beecher, 1871.

RAMSDELL, CHARLES M. "General Robert E. Lee's Horse Supply, 1862–1865." *American Historical Review*, v. 35 (1930), 758-777.

RHODES, CHARLES D. *History of the Cavalry of the Army of the Potomac*. Kansas City, Missouri: Hudson-Kimberly Printing Co., 1900.

RODENBOUGH, THEOPHILUS F., and HASKINS, WILLIAM L., eds., *The Army of the United States, Historical Sketches of Staff and Line*. New York: Maynard, Merrill & Co., 1896.

SCHAFF, MORRIS. *The Spirit of Old West Point*. Boston and New York: Houghton Mifflin & Co., 1907.

SCHEIBERT, MAJOR JUSTUS. *Sieben Monate in den Rebellen Staaten wahrend des Nordamerikanischen Krieges*. Stettin, Germany: 1868.

SCHURZ, CARL. *The Reminiscences of Carl Schurz*. 3 vols. New York: The McClure Co., 1907–1908.

SCOTT, WILLIAM FORSE. *The Story of a Cavalry Regiment*. New York: G. P. Putnam's Sons, 1893.

SHANNON, FRED ALBERT. *The Organization and Administration of the Union Army, 1861–1865*. 2 vols. Glendale, California: Arthur H. Clark Co., 1928.

SHERIDAN, PHILIP H. *Personal Memoirs of P. H. Sheridan*. New York: Charles L. Webster & Co., 1888.

SOUTHERN HISTORICAL SOCIETY. *Papers*, vols. 1-50. Richmond: 1914–1953.

SPAULDING, COLONEL OLIVER LYMAN, JR. *The United States Army in War and Peace*. New York: G. P. Putnam's Sons, 1937.

STEELE, MAJOR MATTHEW FORNEY. *American Campaigns*. 2 vols. Washington: War Department Document No. 324, 1943.

STINE, J. H. *History of the Army of the Potomac*. Philadelphia: 1892.

SWARTHOUT, GLENDON. *They Came to Cordura*. New York: Random House, 1958.

SWINTON, WILLIAM. *Campaigns of the Army of the Potomac*. New York: Charles B. Richardson, 1866.

THOMASON, JOHN W. *Jeb Stuart*. New York: Charles Scribner's Sons, 1934.

TIDBALL, GENERAL JOHN C. *Remarks upon the Organization, Command, and Employment of Field Artillery during War; Based on Experiences of the Civil War, 1861–5*. Typescript MS in Library, Artillery & Guided Missile Center, Fort Sill, Oklahoma: c. 1907.

TOBIE, EDWARD PARSONS. *History of the First Maine Cavalry*. Boston: Emery and Hughes, 1887.

TOOMBS, SAMUEL. *New Jersey Troops in the Gettysburg Campaign*. Orange, New Jersey: Evening Mail Publishing House, 1888.

TOWNSEND, GEORGE ALFRED. *Rustics in Rebellion: A Yankee Reporter on the Road to Richmond, 1861–1865*. Chapel Hill, North Carolina: University of North Carolina Press, 1950.

U.S. DEPARTMENT OF THE ARMY. U.S. MILITARY ACADEMY. *Summaries of Selected Military Campaigns*. West Point: 1953.

U.S. DEPARTMENT OF THE ARMY. THE INFANTRY SCHOOL. *Selected Readings in American Military History*. 3 vols. Fort Benning, Georgia: 1953.

U.S. WAR DEPARTMENT. *Bibliography of State Participation in the Civil War, 1861–1866*. Washington: Government Printing Office, 1913.

U.S. WAR DEPARTMENT. *Cavalry Tactics*. Washington: Government Printing Office, 1863 (first published 1841).

U.S. WAR DEPARTMENT. *U.S. Military Commission to Europe, 1855–1856. Report of Captain George B. McClellan*. Washington: 1857.

U.S. WAR DEPARTMENT. *The War of the Rebellion: Official Records*. 130 vols. Washington: 1880–1901.

UPTON, EMORY. *The Military Policy of the United States*. Washington: 1917.

VAN DE WATER, FREDERIC. *Glory-Hunter, a Life of General Custer*. Indianapolis: The Bobbs-Merrill Co., 1934.

WAGNER, CAPTAIN ARTHUR L., ed. *Cavalry Studies from Two Great Wars*. "The Operations of the Cavalry in the Gettysburg Campaign" by Lieutenant Colonel George B. Davis. Kansas City, Missouri: Hudson-Kimberly Publishing Co., 1896.

WELLMAN, MANLY WADE. *Giant in Gray, a Biography of Wade Hampton of South Carolina*. New York: Charles Scribner's Sons, 1949.

WHITMAN, WILLIAM E. S., and TRUE, CHARLES H. *Maine in the War for the Union*. Lewiston, Maine: Nelson Dingley, Jr., and Co., 1865.

WILEY, BELL IRWIN. *The Life of Johnny Reb*. Indianapolis: Bobbs-Merrill Company, 1943.

———. *The Life of Billy Yank*. Indianapolis: Bobbs-Merrill Company, 1951.

WISE, JENNINGS CROPPER. *The Long Arm of Lee*. 2 vols. Lynchburg, Virginia: 1915.

WOOD, WILLIAM, and GABRIEL, RALPH HENRY. *In Defense of Liberty*. *Pageant of America*, v. 7. New Haven: Yale University Press, 1928.

Index

MILITARY ORGANIZATIONS

The following units, engaged at Brandy Station, are noted as they appear in the text. A complete list of all units on the field will be found in Appendix D.

See also names of commanders in main body of index, where units not at Brandy Station are listed.

Index

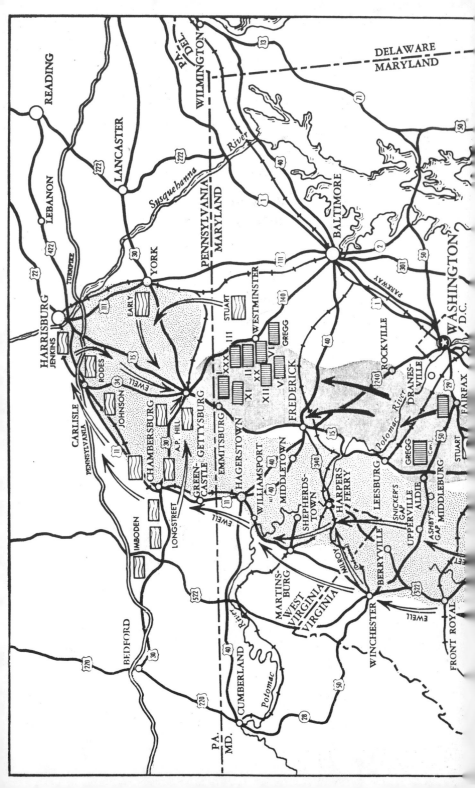